FRIENDS ON THE PATH

OTHER BOOKS BY THICH NHAT HANH

Be Still and Know: Reflections from Living Buddha, Living Christ

Being Peace

The Blooming of a Lotus: Guided Meditation Exercises
for Healing and Transformation

Breathe! You Are Alive: Sutra on the Full Awareness of Breathing

Call Me by My True Names: The Collected Poems of Thich Nhat Hanh

Cultivating the Mind of Love: The Practice of Looking Deeply
in the Mahayana Buddhist Tradition

The Diamond That Cuts through Illusion: Commentaries
on the Prajñaparamita Diamond Sutra

For a Future to Be Possible: Commentaries on the Five Mindfulness Trainings

Fragrant Palm Leaves: Journals 1962–1966

The Heart of the Buddha's Teaching: Transforming Suffering
into Peace, Joy, and Liberation

The Heart of Understanding: Commentaries on the Prajñaparamita Heart Sutra

Interbeing: Fourteen Guidelines for Engaged Buddhism

A Joyful Path: Community, Transformation, and Peace

Living Buddha, Living Christ

The Long Road Turns to Joy: A Guide to Walking Meditation

The Miracle of Mindfulness: A Manual on Meditation

Old Path White Clouds: Walking in the Footsteps of the Buddha

Our Appointment with Life: Discourse on Living Happily in the Present Moment

The Path of Emancipation: Talks from a 21-Day Mindfulness Retreat

Peace Is Every Step: The Path of Mindfulness in Everyday Life

A Pebble for Your Pocket

Plum Village Chanting and Recitation Book

Present Moment Wonderful Moment: Mindfulness Verses for Daily Living

Stepping into Freedom: An Introduction to Buddhist Monastic Training

The Sun My Heart: From Mindfulness to Insight Contemplation

Sutra on the Eight Realizations of the Great Beings

Teachings on Love

Thundering Silence: Sutra on Knowing the Better Way to Catch a Snake

Touching Peace: Practicing the Art of Mindful Living

Transformation & Healing: Sutra on the Four Establishments of Mindfulness

Transformation at the Base: Fifty Verses on the Nature of Consciousness

Under the Rose Apple Tree

Zen Keys: A Guide to Zen Practice

FRIENDS ON THE PATH

Living Spiritual Communities

~

Thich Nhat Hanh

Compiled by Jack Lawlor

Parallax Press
Berkeley, California

Parallax Press
P.O. Box 7355
Berkeley, California 94707
www.parallax.org

Parallax Press is the publishing division of Unified Buddhist Church, Inc.

Compiled by Jack Lawlor.
Cover and text design by Gopa & Ted2.
Author photgraph by Nang Sao.

Library of Congress Cataloging-in-Publication Data

Friends on the path : living spiritual communities / compiled by Jack
Lawlor ; with contributions from Thich Nhat Hanh and others.
      p. cm.
   ISBN 1-888375-21-3
  1. Buddhist sanghas. 2. Monasticism and religious orders, Buddhist.
3. Buddhism—Social aspects. I. Lawlor, Jack, 1951- II. Nhat Hanh,
Thich.
    BQ6082 .F75 2002
    294.3'65—dc21
                                    2002008819

1 2 3 4 5 6 7 8 9 10 / 10 09 08 07 06 05 04 03 02

Contents

Introduction

BY JACK LAWLOR

THERE IS A PATH along the western boundary of the Upper Hamlet in Plum Village. Because it runs along a ridge, one can enjoy very beautiful sunsets that cast long shadows into the bucolic valley below. It is all part of the gently undulating landscape of the Bordeaux region in southwestern France.

Everyone who passes the trailhead is attracted to take the journey. The limbs of a long line of mature trees on either side of the dirt trail meet together as if in prayer to form a chapel-like arch overhead. As one approaches, a simple wooden sign welcomes you from the side of a tree. It offers a very important — but often forgotten — suggestion from the Buddha: "Go as a Sangha."

In essence, this sign is inviting us to enjoy the path together as companions and "spiritual friends" (in the Sanskrit language, *kalyanamitra*). A Sangha is a group of people who practice mindfulness together, inspired by the historic Buddha, his teachings (the Dharma), and the presence of other mindfulness practitioners (the Sangha itself). Mindfulness is the fluid, gentle awareness and clear perception that arise within us naturally, with grace and ease, when we engage in simple meditative exercises based on conscious breathing. Venerable Thich Nhat Hanh (also known simply as "Thây") has described conscious breathing as the "miracle of mindfulness" that mends the dispersion between what the body is doing, on the one hand, and what the mind is doing, on the other. It enables us to dwell fully in the present and to enjoy the people we're with. Those who learn to practice mindfulness experience *shamatha*, the stopping of habit energy; *appamada*, freedom from agitation and madness; and *prajña*, insight and understanding into what is actually going on, so that *karuna*, compassion, may arise. It's a simple, refreshing way to live. And nearly everyone finds that it's easiest to do in the company of friends.

The Buddha spent most of his life in the company of a Sangha, and for 2,500 years the Sangha has been considered one of the Three Jewels—together with the Buddha and Dharma. Whenever a Sangha convenes, it does so in the spirit of "friends on the path."

Although for twenty-five centuries Buddhists have been taught to have faith in the Sangha, Thich Nhat Hanh has brought this teaching to life by demonstrating how taking refuge in the Sangha as friends on the path is a *practice*, not just a matter of faith or a declaration of loyalty. If the Buddha took care to find nourishment in this practice, we might explore the benefits of doing the same. Based on the teachings of Thich Nhat Hanh and experiences of mindfulness practitioners from around the world, this is what *Friends on the Path* invites us to do.

Part One, "Living Spiritual Communities," contains Thây's most recent teachings on Sangha. These insightful and inspirational pieces demonstrate the importance of Sangha in the world today. They also show how our practice deepens and grows when we learn from each other as spiritual friends rather than alone in the company of books and tapes.

During the 1980s, Thây traveled throughout the world urging students of meditation that, based upon the practice of conscious breathing, "we must practice in a way that removes the barrier between practice [in the meditation hall] and non-practice." Inspired by this message of engaged Buddhism, practitioners have done just that. In the past fifteen years, over 350 nonresidential lay Sanghas have emerged in over twenty countries throughout the world, together with several lay residential communities and three monastic centers. From their experiences there is a lot to share about how kalyanamitra can give birth to a healthy Sangha in our own local communities, and how we can nourish our Sanghas so that they mature into something alive, flexible, inclusive, tolerant, supportive, and vibrant.

The insights in this book are not offered from an academic or theoretical point of view about what has been or might become part of the Buddhist tradition. In every case—whether describing monastic practice, lay residential or nonresidential practice, or nonsectarian mindfulness practice centers—the contributions are offered by seasoned spiritual friends who are reporting on what they have learned from their experience. There is much that we can learn from the collective wisdom of the group.

In Part Two, "Gathering Good Friends," I offer an overview of lay Sangha practice. This section describes what it feels like to extend the joy and equanimity experienced during residential retreats right into the heart of your hometown and into your daily life by building a living spiritual community. After describing how local Sanghas enjoy a typical evening together, the overview explores frequently asked questions about the various skillful ways first to organize a lay Sangha and then to nourish and sustain it with a complementary spectrum of mindfulness practices—all with a light touch, and all in the spirit of friendship and caring.

Part Three, "Residential Practice," includes contributions from monastics (including Sister Annabel Laity, Abbess of Green Mountain Dharma Center) and lay Dharma teachers who practice within residential communities. Part Four, "Sangha-Building," includes insightful essays on starting a Sangha or Mindfulness Practice Center. Part Five, "Sangha Practice," looks deeply at residential and nonresidential Sangha practice. Part Six takes a look at "Practicing with Young People." Part Seven, "Engaged Practice," touches on the mindfulness practice of loving kindness and non-fear as spiritual friends in Sanghas encounter and meet the challenges of illness and death; practicing inclusiveness and embracing diversity; and building Sanghas in prisons.

Part Eight, "A Taste of Community Life," provides a sampling of Sangha life from contributors around the world. The Buddha spent his forty-five-year teaching career interacting with the many tribes and small kingdoms in northern India and listening to people from every level of society during his daily almsrounds with the monastic Sangha. The practices we now refer to as "Buddhism" are the result of this interaction, which continues throughout the world to this day, with Buddhism encountering and interpenetrating the West and the West interpenetrating Buddhism. The offerings on Sangha-building in Part Four illustrate this vibrant spiritual growth and diversification.

What do these articles suggest about the ability of spiritual friends to practice together in our own times? As you might suspect, Buddhism and mindfulness practice in the West have changed immensely in the last thirty years. Beginning in 1975, my wife, Laurie, and I have practiced consistently with organized Zen meditation groups in both the Japanese and Vietnamese traditions. Since then, books on Buddhism and mindfulness practice have moved from being misplaced alongside the occult and astrology books in bookstores and libraries to the "mainstream" displays. This has brought with it both advantages and disadvantages. On the one hand, mindfulness practice now has the potential to influence and transform certain habit energies in our society (such as materialism, militarism, and intolerance) with insight, equanimity, and compassion that are the fruits of sustained and wholehearted practice. On the other hand, some of the more challenging aspects of the Buddha's teachings — such as deep listening and insight, taking responsibility to change destructive personal habit patterns in order to transform suffering at its root, and the ability to live compassionately as a true friend of others — stand the risk of becoming diluted.

At a level more enduring than what is taking place in popular culture, what is most encouraging to me is the way that Western convert Sanghas have evolved in the past quarter century. In the immediate aftermath of the sixties, these Sanghas were almost exclusively devoted to formal sitting meditation and attended by single, college-educated people. Sangha members would convene in the meditation hall, sit, perhaps listen to a Dharma talk about sitting or *koan* practice, and go home without discussing the Buddha's teachings or how they applied to their daily lives. You could belong to many such groups for years and know little about the person sitting on the cushion next to you. Not surprisingly, it appeared to me that the average "time on the cushion" for a Zen enthusiast in many such groups in those days was about two years.

Today, Sanghas offer a much wider array of skillful means to address the real issues in people's lives, and they do so in a manner that gently and gradually cultivates more diverse groups of people and the formation of genuine spiritual friendships. In healthy Sanghas, formal sitting and walking meditation is still practiced on a consistent basis, but today Sanghas provide complements to these traditional meditation practices, such as Dharma discussions that offer opportunities to study the teachings of the historic Buddha and other Buddhist texts in a practice-orientated manner. Through these Dharma discussions and practices such as tea ceremonies (see Appendix) and recitation of *gathas* (which are short poems that invite us to return to the practice of conscious breathing as we engage in our everyday activities), people are encouraged to bring an engaged form of mindfulness, based on the practice of conscious breathing, into their relationships with others. This enables them to practice mindfulness once they return home to their families and workplaces.

In short, contemporary Sanghas now instruct their participants to bring mindfulness into their daily lives, and the results are encouraging. Perhaps it is not surprising that many people now tend to remain in a Sangha for more than just a few years. Some local Sanghas, such as ours in the Chicago area, have grown by word of mouth from only a handful of people to eighty or a hundred practitioners, many of whom have practiced together for over a decade. It is also not surprising that Sanghas offering an engaged form of Buddhist mindfulness practice based on multiple skillful means attract more diverse groups of people: families with children, ethnic and racial minorities, people from all walks of life and economic circumstances, Democrats and Republicans. What is most encouraging is the growing number of participants from so-called Generations X and Y who are seeking to live in a genuine, spiritual manner and heal the wounds of the past through their daily practice of mindfulness. Many college and high school students and recent graduates are also learning that the best way to take good care of the future without anxiety or fear is to live mindfully and wholeheartedly in the present. However, although there is this kind of diversification and integration in local Sanghas, there is much more progress needed in this area, especially with respect to the inclusion of minorities and people from a wider spectrum of ethnic and economic backgrounds.

All of this is a living, organic process that requires commitment, patience, persistence, good humor, and trust. From time to time, people advocate centralized, "top down" models of how Sanghas should grow or be organized, often borrowed from other religious traditions, from a practice center located thousands of miles away, from the distant past, or even from a political ideology. The organic growth of Sanghas we are now witnessing has defied anyone's predictions or conceptualizations. This is perhaps a good indication that Sanghas are being attentive to the people they are engaged with, as when the Buddha was teaching. The practices we now refer to as "Buddhism" are the outcome of a ceaseless, gradual interaction as they spread organically from culture to culture, addressing in a patient, compassionate, flexible manner the needs of those who are suffering. In the Buddhist experience, flexibility is not equated with weakness, but rather strength. After all, when you practice mindfulness with spiritual friends in a Buddhist-inspired Sangha, you are joining what scholars refer to as one of the longest-enduring groups in human history—over 2,500 years!

This volume explores what it means to "go as a Sangha," as spiritual friends down the path of a contemplative way of life, wonderfully and mindfully together. It is our hope that the teachings and descriptions of the ups and downs of Sangha life included in this book will be of benefit to all of us who practice mindfulness. The work being done by Sanghas from around the world that is being presented here is a modest but essential first step; such a compilation is never as complete and diverse as one hopes. You are wholeheartedly invited to read this book with your Sangha eyes, to write us with your thoughts and suggestions for the next edition, and to join hands with us as friends on the path of mindfulness practice.

PART ONE
Living Spiritual Communities

~

Spirituality in the Twenty-First Century 1

BY THICH NHAT HANH

IT HAS BEEN SAID that the twenty-first century will be a century of spirituality, and I think it must be a century of spirituality if we are to survive. There has been so much violence, so much suffering, so much despair, confusion, and fear. So it must be a century of spirituality, or no century at all.

Spirituality is something we can cultivate. To be spiritual means to be solid, calm, and peaceful, and to be able to look deeply inside and around us. It means having the capacity to handle our afflictions—our anger, craving, despair, and discrimination. It is being able to see the nature of interbeing between people, nations, races, and all forms of life. Spirituality is not a luxury anymore; we need to be spiritual in order to overcome the difficulties of our time.

Alone we are vulnerable, but with brothers and sisters to work with, we can support each other. We cannot go to the ocean as a drop of water—we would evaporate before reaching our destination. But if we become a river, if we go as a Sangha, we are sure to arrive at the ocean. Taking refuge in a Sangha will allow the Sangha to carry us, to transport us, and we will suffer less.

A true Sangha is a community that practices the teaching of liberation and becomes free; a true Sangha practices the teaching of understanding and becomes more understanding; a true Sangha practices compassion and becomes more compassionate. Climbing the hill of the twenty-first century can be very joyful if we climb as a Sangha. If we support each other, we become much stronger, and we can more easily resist the temptation of despair.

Despair is a great temptation of our century. Whether you are a political leader, a businessperson, a social worker, a teacher, or a parent, everyone needs to be reminded that the blue sky is still there for us. We should not allow ourselves to be overwhelmed by despair. That is why we need a Sangha; a Sangha can help us from sinking into despair. Sangha-building is the most important practice—the most important action—of our century. How can the twenty-first century be a century of spirituality if we do not take up the work of Sangha-building?

Jesus Christ did not have many years to build his Sangha, but he spent a lot of time with his disciples and he taught them well. He taught them how to walk, how to enter a village, how to treat the people in the village, how to sit, how to eat, how to say goodbye, much in the same way that the Buddha taught his monks and nuns.

The Sangha must be empowered by some kind of aspiration or vow. The disciples of Jesus were motivated by the desire to serve. There is something good, something beautiful in wanting to serve. It is very much like the mind of love, *bodhicitta*. Jesus was trying to help that mind of love to grow in the persons of his twelve disciples. Unfortunately, Jesus did not have as much time as the Buddha to educate his disciples and build his Sangha. The Buddha had forty-five years to build his Sangha, and the Buddha was assisted by many people like Shariputra, Maha Maudgalyayana, Kashyapa, and others.

In the last year of his life, the Buddha had the opportunity to meet the king of Koshala, Prasanajit. Prasanajit told Buddha, "Every time I see the noble Sangha I have faith, trust, and respect for the Lord Buddha." Looking at the *bhikshus* and seeing the way they practiced, the king of Koshala was inspired with confidence, love, and trust. Looking at the Sangha he saw the Buddha. If a Sangha practices well, it becomes a true Sangha and has the Dharma and the Buddha within it.

Like Jesus, the Buddha also encountered many difficulties. There were several attempts on his life, and there were those who tried to discredit his practice. Imagine, though, the day when Jesus had supper with his disciples for the last time, the Last Supper.

Jesus was aware that something was going to happen to him, and he broke bread and shared it with his disciples. Then he poured wine and shared that with his disciples. And he said to his disciples: "Enjoy this bread, my dear ones, this is my flesh, my body. Enjoy this wine, my dear friends, this is my blood." This was his way of telling his loved ones that he was in them, and that he had complete trust in them. It was a way to tell the disciples: "Dear friends, I want you to have all my wisdom, all my compassion. I entrust myself to you, like a tree entrusts itself entirely to the soil." The Last Supper is when Jesus entrusted himself to his disciples in the Sangha.

In the dining hall of the Upper Hamlet in Plum Village, there is a sign with a sentence written in French: "This piece of bread is the body of the cosmos." We don't say that "this piece of bread is the body of Jesus Christ," we say, "the body of the cosmos." It is very much the same, but it speaks more to the people of our times. Looking into a piece of bread, you can see the whole cosmos — the sky, earth, clouds, and sunshine — everything can be recognized in a piece of bread. It is very spiritual and very scientific at the same time. When you eat a piece of bread with mindfulness you are in touch with the whole cosmos. The cosmos is nourishing you, the cosmos is entrusting itself entirely to you, and you are entrusting yourself entirely to the cosmos.

So looking into the heart of Jesus, we see the desire, the expectation, the willingness to entrust himself to his Sangha. He wants to take refuge in the Sangha; he wants to build a beautiful Sangha to continue him.

We suffered tremendously during the twentieth century. Individualism prevailed. Families were broken up, society was deeply divided. That is why if the twenty-first century is to be a spiritual century, it should be built by the spirit of togetherness, where we do things together, we do everything together. When you live in a community, you learn how to see the Sangha body, the *Sanghakaya*, as your own body.

When the king of Koshala looked at the Buddha's Sangha, he saw the Buddha. Now we should be able to do the same when we look at the *Buddha-sangha*, we should see elements of the Buddha: the elements of loving kindness, compassion, understanding, and nondiscrimination. Then looking at the Sangha, people will have trust; they won't lose themselves in despair.

Whether we live in Amsterdam, London, Munich, or New York, it is our role to build a Sangha. We need each other to practice solidity, freedom, and compassion, and with our practice we can remind people in our society that there is always hope, the blue sky is always there, the Kingdom of Heaven is always at hand. We should walk and breathe in such a way that the Kingdom of Heaven, the Pure Land of the Buddha, is available in every step, in every breath. This is what we should do.

Do not say that the teaching of Buddha is too difficult. No, it is not. In fact, the teaching is simple. Every one of us, whether young or less young, can practice this simple teaching: "I have arrived, I am home." And when we are able to apply that to our daily life, we will not run anymore. Then every minute of our life can help generate the energy of solidity, peace, and compassion.

If we want to be safe, we have to build safety. What do we build to be safe? Not a fortress, not bombs or airplanes. The United States of America is very powerful in terms of armies and weapons, but the people living in America do not feel safe. Many people are thinking of safety in terms of weapons and armies, but even with a powerful army and a stock of weapons, there are moments when the American people feel very frightened, very vulnerable. So there must be some other kind of practice we can take refuge in, another way to be safe. We can learn how to build safety with our in-breath and our out-breath, with our steps, with the way we act or react, with a smile or a word, with our effort to restore communication.

You cannot feel safe with the person who lives with you if you cannot communicate with him or her. You cannot feel safe when the other person does not look at you with sympathy, when you are not capable of looking at him or her with compassion. Safety can be built with your way of looking, your way of smiling, with your way of walking. It can build confidence. Show the other person that you are truly not harmful, that he is safe in your presence, in the way you think, the way you breathe, smile, and walk. Everything you do is peaceful. So by expressing your peace, your compassion, the other person feels very safe. And when the other person feels safe, you are safe. Safety is not an individual matter.

A country cannot be safe if it doesn't do something to help other countries feel safe, too. We cannot just think of our own safety — because safety is not an individual matter. We have to think of the safety of other groups of people, of other nations, too. If the United States wants to have safety, then they have to take care of the safety of the people of other nations. If Great Britain wants safety, then people there have to think of the safety of other groups of people. The problem of terrorism should not be the concern of one nation, or a few nations. It should be the concern of all nations, namely, it should be the concern of the Sangha of all nations.

Any one of us can be victims of violence or terrorism. Nobody can say, "I am safe, I am special, my country is safe." Therefore we have to do something for safety to become a reality. We have seen clearly that violence and weapons are not the means for safety. Now we have to use other means to build safety. Maybe the first thing for us to do is to tell the other person, "Dear friend, I know that you want to live in safety. I do too. Why don't we work together in order to ensure safety for both of us?" This is a very simple thing to do, but why can't people do it? Communication is the key to all of this. We claim that this is an era of communication, where there are so many sophisticated means to communicate, and yet it is very difficult for individuals, for groups of people, or for nations to communicate with each other. We stop speaking to each other, and instead of using language, we use guns and explosives. This is the case in the Middle East.

We have to learn how to communicate again. We need to learn how to show the other party that we are harmless, that they don't have to be afraid of us. When we are able to show that we are not harmful, the other person will trust us and collaborate with us.

In Asian countries, when we meet each other, we bow with our hands in the lotus flower position; in the West when people meet each other, they offer their hands. The practice of shaking hands originated in olden times, when people were afraid of each other. Every time they would meet each other, they would show their hands so it was clear they weren't carrying any weapon. "Dear friend, I have no weapons. See, touch for yourself." That is the origin of the handshaking practice. Now we have to do the same kind of thing. "Dear friends, I am not harmful. You can touch me, there is no weapon hidden here."

We need some simple kind of practice like that in the beginning to build trust. And with trust, dialogue will be possible and we can help each other build safety for everyone. We all need safety. Not only the African people need safety, the people of the United States need safety, the British people need safety, the French people need safety, all of us need safety. If we don't do something, we will arrive at a point where we cannot talk to each other anymore, and we will have to use the language of guns. That is despair itself.

During the visit of our friends from Palestine and Israel to Plum Village this summer, I asked them whether they would accept an international peacekeeping force in the area to stop the violence and to work out solutions for both sides, the Israelis and the Palestinians. Our Israeli friends from this particular group said they cannot trust anyone at this time; they have a lot of suspicion. They do not trust the United Nations or the international peacekeeping force. Fear and suspicion go together.

The conflict between Palestinians and Israelis is the pain not only of these two groups of people, but of the whole of humanity, humanity as a Sangha. So if the UN were to become a true Sangha and play the role of embracing that painful spot of the Earth, the very heart of the pain, and the people in that area allowed themselves to be embraced by the Sangha body, then they would listen to the wisdom of the Sangha of all nations. They would accept the proposals and the practices that the Sangha of all nations prescribed for them. But there is a resistance. Many do not have faith in the Sangha of all nations.

The tension between India and Pakistan is another painful spot on the body of the Earth. But if both nations surrender to the Sangha body and listen to the advice and prescriptions of the Sangha body, then the crisis will be transformed very quickly. So, there is an urgent need that the United Nations become a real Sangha of nations.

How can we make the United Nations into a real Sangha of nations as it was intended when we don't really trust our Sangha body? Some nations are trying to make the United Nations into an instrument to serve their own national interests — this is what the United States and many other superpowers are doing. Our Sangha body should be a real Sangha body, and this should be discussed in a plenary session of the United Nations.

When there is trouble within any individual state, then the whole Sangha comes and helps. If there is a member of the Sangha who has difficulties, then the whole Sangha has to take care of this member, because it is a part of the body. If there is a conflict between two members of the Sangha, it is not their problem alone, it is a problem for the whole Sangha. It is a lot easier to solve problems in the Sangha because we have a Sangha body and Sangha eyes. Sangha eyes are always clearer than eyes of an individual, so the individual members of the Sangha have to surrender to the Sangha and learn how to make use of the Sangha eyes in order to look at the whole situation.

National interests go against the spirit of Sangha. In a real Sangha, you cannot operate on your ego; you have to accept the Sangha body as your body. You have to learn how to use the Sangha eyes as your eyes, and you have to learn how to profit from the wisdom of the Sangha. The collective wisdom and insight of a real Sangha are much more reliable than your own wisdom or insight.

So if the United Nations is to become a true Sangha body, then the conflict between the Israelis and the Palestinians should be taken care of by the Sangha eyes of the United Nations. We cannot allow things to continue the way they are. Every day bombs explode, every day people die. The United Nations Sangha body could go there right now and take care of this problem.

People don't believe in the United Nations as a true Sangha because the United Nations has not yet become one. But we can very well start from there. It is better than not having the United Nations at all. If the United Nations became a real Sangha body, the Security Council would become a true instrument and it would be able to help settle conflict and tension everywhere in the world. The entire United Nations Sangha body could come together with Pakistan and India and tell them that they are friends, they are brothers and sisters, and ask them to please hold hands with each other and serve the Sangha body. Instead of fighting with each other, they should be encouraged to become allies and serve the common cause, the cause of peace and stability in the world. It is possible that Pakistan and India, motivated by the desire to help, would become friends instead of being enemies. The same thing is true with Palestine and Israel.

That is Sangha-building in the twenty-first century. If you are a journalist, if you are a writer, if you are a professor, if you are a parent, it is time for you to speak out and make known what you want, what the world needs, and promise that you will help. Those of you who have experience in your practice and are already Sangha-builders, speak out in order to build a Sangha in your department, in your city hall, your village, your city, your parliament, and then finally we can propose that the United Nations should become a true Sangha of nations.

Sangha-building has to be done at every level—local, national, and international. Sangha is our hope. Our national assemblies and senates should become our Sanghas, where loving speech and deep listening are practiced. The United Nations General Assembly should also be a Sangha, where people learn to listen to each other as brothers and sisters. We should stop acting in the name of our so-called national interests.

If the twenty-first century is to become a century of spirituality at all, it depends on our capacity of Sangha-building. We need each other, we need to come together to pool our wisdom, our insight, and our compassion to build a lasting peace in the world. We should give up our personal and national interests, and think of the Earth as our true home, a home for all of us. To bring the spiritual dimension to your daily life, to your social, political, and economic life—that is your practice.

It is very clear that Jesus had that intention. It is very clear that the Buddha had this intention, too. And for those of us who come from the background of Christianity and Buddhism, we should be aware that our spiritual ancestors had that intention. We should be able to display the light of wisdom and come together in order to create hope, and to prevent society and the younger generation from sinking into despair.

(From transcriptions of talks given by Thich Nhat Hanh
in Plum Village, December 2001)

Go As a Sangha 2

BY THICH NHAT HANH

PERSONALLY, I want the twenty-first century to be called the "century of love," because we desperately need love, the kind of love that will not produce suffering. Unless we have enough loving kindness and compassion, we will not be able to survive as a planet. Our problems in the twenty-first century are not the same as the problems the Buddha and his friends and disciples encountered during their lifetimes. Today meditation has to be practiced collectively—as a family, a city, a nation, and a community of nations.

There is a Buddha that is supposed to be born to us named Maitreya or Loving Kindness, the Buddha of Love—Mr. Love, Ms. Love. A Sangha that practices loving kindness and compassion is the Buddha that we need for the twenty-first century. Each of us is a cell in the body of the Buddha of Love. Each cell has its own role to play, and we cannot afford to miss one of our cells. We have to stay together. We have the power to bring Sanghakaya, the Sangha body, and Maitreya Buddha into existence just by sitting together and practicing deeply.

So the next Buddha may not take the form of an individual. In the twenty-first century the Sangha may be the body of the Buddha. We have the power to bring the next Buddha into existence in this century. If we sit together and practice looking deeply, we can bring the Sanghakaya and the Buddha into existence. All of us have the duty to bring that Buddha into being, not only for our sake, but for the sake of our children and the planet Earth. This is not wishful thinking, this is a real determination.

What Is a Sangha?

A Sangha is a community of friends practicing the Dharma together in order to bring about and to maintain awareness. The essence of a Sangha is awareness, understanding, acceptance, harmony, and love. When you do not see these in a community, it is not a true Sangha, and you should have the courage to say so. But when you find these elements are present in a community, you know that you have the happiness and fortune of being in a real Sangha.

In Matthew 5:13 in the New Testament of the Christian Bible, we find this statement: "Ye are the salt of the earth; but if the salt hath lost its savor, wherewith shall it be salted? It is thenceforth good for nothing but to be cast out and to be trodden underfoot of men." In this passage, Jesus describes his followers as salt. Food needs salt in order to be tasty. Life needs understanding, compassion, and harmony in order to be livable. This is the most important contribution to life that the followers of Jesus can bring to the world. It means that the Kingdom of Heaven has to be realized here, not somewhere else, and that Christians need to practice in a way that they are the salt of life and a true community of Christians.

Salt is also an important image in the Buddhist canon, and this Christian teaching is equivalent to the Buddha's teaching about Sangha. The Buddha said that the water in the four oceans has only one taste, the taste of salt, just as his teaching has only one taste, the taste of liberation. Therefore the elements of Sangha are the taste of life, the taste of liberation, and we have to practice in order to become the salt. When we say, "I take refuge in the Sangha," it is not a statement, it is a practice.

In the Buddhist scriptures it is said that there are four communities: monks, nuns, laymen, and laywomen. But I also include elements that are not human in the Sangha. The trees, water, air, birds, and so on, can all be members of our Sangha. A beautiful walking path may be part of our Sangha. A good cushion can be also. We can make many things into supportive elements of our Sangha. This idea is not entirely new; it can be found throughout the sutras[1] and in the *Abhidharma*,[2] too. A pebble, a leaf, and a dahlia are mentioned in the *Saddharmapundarika Sutra* in this respect. It is said in the *Pure Land Sutra* that if you are mindful, then when the wind blows through the trees, you will hear the teaching of the Four Establishments of Mindfulness,[3] the Eightfold Path,[4] and so on. The whole cosmos is preaching the Buddhadharma and practicing the Buddhadharma. If you are attentive, you will get in touch with that Sangha.

SANGHA AS OUR ROOTS

I don't think the Buddha wanted us to abandon our society, our culture, or our roots in order to practice. The practice of Buddhism should help people go back to their families. It should help people reenter society in order to rediscover and accept the good things that are there in their culture and to rebuild those that are not.

Our modern society creates so many young people without roots. They are uprooted from their families and their society; they wander around, not quite human beings, because they do not have roots. Quite a number of them come from broken families and feel rejected by society. They live on the margins, looking for a home, for something to belong to. They are like trees without roots. For these people, it's very difficult to practice. A tree without roots cannot absorb anything; it cannot survive. Even if they practice intensively for ten years, it's very hard for them to be transformed if they remain an island, if they cannot establish a link with other people.

A community of practice, a Sangha, can provide a second chance to a young person who comes from a broken family or is alienated from his or her society. If the community of practice is organized as a family with a friendly, warm atmosphere, young people can succeed in their practice.

Suffering (*dukkha*) is one of the biggest problems of our times. First we have to recognize this suffering and acknowledge it. Then we need to look deeply into its nature in order to find a way out. If we look into the present situation in ourselves and our society, we can see much suffering. We need to call it by its true names—loneliness, the feeling of being cut off, alienation, division, the disintegration of the family, the disintegration of society. Our civilization, our culture has been characterized by individualism. The individual wants to be free from the society, from the family. The individual does not think he or she needs to take refuge in the family or in the society and thinks that he or she can be happy without a Sangha. That is why we do not have solidity, we do not have harmony, we do not have the communication that we so need.

The practice is, therefore, to grow some roots. The Sangha is not a place to hide in order to avoid your responsibilities. The Sangha is a place to practice for the transformation and the healing of self and society. When you are strong, you can be there in order to help society. If your society is in trouble, if your family is broken, if your church is no longer capable of providing you with spiritual life, then you work to take refuge in the Sangha so that you can restore your strength, your understanding, your compassion, your confidence. And then in turn you can use that strength, understanding, and compassion to rebuild your family and society, to renew your church, to restore communication and harmony. This can only be done as a community—not as an individual, but as a Sangha.

In order for us to develop some roots, we need the kind of environment that can help us become rooted. A Sangha is not a community of practice in which each person is an island, unable to communicate with each other—this is not a true Sangha. No healing or transformation will result from such a Sangha. A true Sangha should be like a family in which there is a spirit of brotherhood and sisterhood.

There is a lot of suffering, yes, and we have to embrace all this suffering. But to get strong, we also need to touch the positive elements, and when we are strong, we can embrace the suffering in us and all around us. If we see a group of people living mindfully, capable of smiling, of loving, we gain confidence in our future. When we practice mindful breathing, smiling, resting, walking, and working, then we become a positive element in society, and we will inspire confidence all around us. This is the way to avoid letting despair overwhelm us. It is also the way to help the younger generation so they do not lose hope. It is very important that we live our daily life in such a way that demonstrates that a future is possible.

WE NEED A SANGHA

In my tradition we learn that as individuals we cannot do much. That is why taking refuge in the Sangha, taking refuge in the community, is a very strong and important practice. When I say, "I take refuge in the Sangha," it does not mean that I want to express my devotion. No. It's not a question of devotion; it's a question of practice. Without being in a Sangha, without being supported by a group of friends who are motivated by the same ideal and practice, we cannot go far.

If we do not have a supportive Sangha, we may not be getting the kind of support we need for our practice, that we need to nourish our bodhicitta (the strong desire to cultivate love and understanding in ourselves). Sometimes we call it "beginner's mind." The mind of a beginner is always very beautiful, very strong. In a good and healthy Sangha, there is encouragement for our beginner's mind, for our bodhicitta. So the Sangha is the soil, and we are the seed. No matter how beautiful, how vigorous our seed is, if the soil does not provide us with vitality, our seed will die.

One of the brothers from Plum Village, Brother Phap Dung, went to Vietnam some years ago with a few members of the Sangha. It was a very important experience for him. He had been in the West since he was a small child. Then when he went to northern Vietnam, he got in touch with some of the most ancient elements in Vietnamese culture and with the mountains and the rivers of northern Vietnam. He wrote to me and said: "Our land of Vietnam is so beautiful, it is as beautiful as a dream. I don't dare take heavy steps on this earth of Vietnam." By this he meant that he had right mindfulness when he walked. His right mindfulness was due to the practice and support he had in the Sangha before he went to Vietnam. That is beginner's mind, the mind you have in the beginning when you undertake the practice. It's very beautiful and very precious, but that beginner's mind can be broken, can be destroyed, can be lost if it is not nourished or supported by a Sangha.

Although he had his little Sangha near him in Vietnam, the environment was very distracting, and he saw that if he stayed too long without the larger Sangha, he would be swept away by that environment, by his forgetfulness—not only his own forgetfulness, but the forgetfulness of everybody around him. This is because right mindfulness for someone who has only just started the practice is still weak, and the forgetfulness of the people around us is very great and capable of dragging us away in the direction of the five cravings.[5] Because most people around us are being drowned in the five cravings, it is this environment that drags us away and stops us from practicing right mindfulness.

To practice right mindfulness we need the right environment, and that environment is our Sangha. Without a Sangha we are very weak. In a society where everyone is rushing, everyone is being carried away by their habit energies, practice is very difficult. That is why the Sangha is our salvation. The Sangha where everyone is practicing mindful walking, mindful speaking, mindful eating seems to be the only chance for us to succeed in ending the vicious cycle.

And what is the Sangha? The Sangha is a community of people who agree with each other that if we do not practice right mindfulness, we will lose all the beautiful things in our soul and all around us. People in the Sangha standing near us, practicing with us, support us so that we are not pulled away from the present moment. Whenever we find ourselves in a difficult situation, two or three friends in the Sangha who are there for us, understanding and helping us, will get us through it. Even in our silent practice we help each other.

In my tradition they say that when a tiger leaves the mountain and goes to the lowland, it will be caught by humans and killed. When a practitioner leaves his or her Sangha, he or she will abandon her practice after a few months. In order to continue our practice of transformation and healing, we need a Sangha. With a Sangha it's much easier to practice, and that is why I always take refuge in my Sangha.

How a Sangha Helps Us

The presence of a Sangha is a wonderful opportunity to allow the collective energy of the Sangha to penetrate into our body and consciousness. We profit a lot from that collective energy. We can entrust ourselves to the Sangha because the Sangha is practicing, and the collective energy of mindfulness is strong. Although we can rely on the energy of mindfulness that is generated by our personal practice, sometimes it is not enough. But if you know how to use that energy of mindfulness in order to receive the collective energy of the Sangha, you will have a powerful source of energy for your transformation and healing.

Your body, your consciousness, and your environment are like a garden. There may be a few trees and bushes that are dying, and you may feel overwhelmed by anguish and suffering at the sight of that. You may be unaware that there are still many trees in your garden that are solid, vigorous, and beautiful. When members of your Sangha come into your garden, they can help you see that you still have a lot of beautiful trees and that you can enjoy the things that have not gone wrong within your landscape. That is the role that the Sangha can play. Many people in the Sangha are capable of enjoying a beautiful sunset or a cup of tea. They dwell firmly in the present moment, not allowing worries or regrets to spoil the present moment. Sitting close to these people, walking close to these people, you can profit from their energy and restore your balance. When their energy of mindfulness is combined with yours, you will be able to touch beauty and happiness.

Nothing is more important than your peace and happiness in the here and now. One day you will lie like a dead body and no longer be able to touch the beauty of a flower. Make good use of your time; practice touching the positive aspects of life in you and around you.

Don't lock yourself behind your door and fight alone. If you think that by yourself you cannot go back to embrace strong feelings, you can ask one, two, or three friends to sit next to you and to help you with their support. They can give you mindfulness energy so that you can go back home with strength. They can say, "My brother, I know that the pain in you is very deep, and I am here for you."

Taking refuge in the Sangha is a very important practice. Abandoned, alone, you get lost, you get carried away. So taking refuge in the Sangha is a very deep practice, especially for those of us who feel vulnerable, shaky, agitated, and unstable. That is why you come to a practice center, to take refuge in the Sangha. You allow the Sangha to transport you like a boat so that you can cross the ocean of sorrow.

When we throw a rock into a river the rock will sink. But if we have a boat, the boat can carry hundreds of pounds of rocks, and it will not sink. The same thing is true with our sorrow and pain. If we have a boat, we can carry our pain and sorrow, and we will not sink into the river of suffering. And what is that boat? That boat is, first of all, the energy of mindfulness that you generate by your practice. That boat is also the Sangha—the community of practice consisting of brothers and sisters in the Dharma.

We don't have to bring just joy when we come to the Sangha; we can also bring our suffering with us. But we have to walk on the path of joy with our suffering, we have to share joy with our brothers and sisters. Then we will be in touch with the seeds of happiness in ourselves, and the suffering will grow weaker and be transformed. Allow yourself to be supported, to be held by the Sangha. When you allow yourself to be in a Sangha the way a drop of water allows itself to be in a river, the energy of the Sangha can penetrate into you, and transformation and healing will become possible.

PRACTICE IS EASIER WITH A SANGHA

The only way to support the Buddha, to support our Sangha, to support the Earth, to support our children and future generations, is to really be here for them. "Darling, I am here for you" is a statement of love. You need to be here. If you are not here, how can you love? That is why the practice of meditation is the practice of being here for the ones we love.

To be present sounds like an easy thing to do. For many of us, it is easy because we have made it a habit. We are in the habit of dwelling in the present moment, of touching the morning sunshine deeply, of drinking our morning tea deeply, of sitting and being present with the person we love. But for some of us it may not be so easy, because we have not cultivated the habit of being in the here and the now. We are always running, and it is hard for us to stop and be here in the present moment, to encounter life. For those of us who have not learned to be present, we need to be supported in that kind of learning. It's not difficult when you are supported by the Sangha. Then you will be able to learn the art of stopping.

The Sangha is a wonderful home. Every time you go back to the Sangha, you feel that you can breathe more easily, you can walk more mindfully, you can better enjoy the blue sky, the white clouds, and the cypress tree in your yard. Why? Because the Sangha members practice going home many times a day—through walking, breathing, cooking, and doing their daily activities mindfully. Everyone in the Sangha is practicing in the same way, walking mindfully, sitting mindfully, eating mindfully, smiling, enjoying each moment of life.

When I practice walking I make mindful and beautiful steps. I do that not only for myself but also for all of my friends who are here; because everyone who sees me taking a step like that has confidence and is reminded to do the same. And when they make a step in the present moment, smiling and making peace with themselves, they inspire all of us. You breathe for me, I walk for you, we do things together, and this is practicing as a Sangha. You don't need to make much effort, and you enjoy doing it a lot. When you have a good Sangha, your practice is easy, because you feel that you are supported by the Sangha.

When we sit together as a Sangha, we enjoy the collective energy of mindfulness, and each of us allows the mindful energy of the Sangha to penetrate us. Even if you don't do anything, if you just stop thinking and allow yourself to absorb the collective energy of the Sangha, it's very healing. Don't struggle, don't try to do something, just allow yourself to be with the Sangha. Allow yourself to rest, and the energy of the Sangha will help you, will carry and support you. The Sangha is there to make the training easy. When we are surrounded by brothers and sisters doing exactly the same thing, it is easy to flow in the stream of the Sangha.

As individuals we have problems, and we also have problems in our families, our societies, and our nations. Meditation in the twenty-first century should become a collective practice; without a Sangha we cannot achieve much. When we begin to focus our attention on the suffering on a larger scale, we begin to connect with and to relate to other people, who are also ourselves, and the little problems that we have within our individual circle will vanish. In this way our loneliness or our feeling of being cut off will no longer be there, and we will be able to do things together.

If we work on our problems alone, it becomes more difficult. When you have a strong emotion come up, you may feel that you cannot stand it. You may have a breakdown or want to die. But if you have someone, a good friend sitting with you, you feel much better. You feel supported, and you have more strength in order to deal with your strong emotion. If you are taking something into your body that is toxic and realize it will make you sick, even with this insight you may not be able to change your habit. But if you are surrounded by people who do not have the same problem, it becomes easier to change. That is why it is very important to practice in the context of a Sangha.

It is fortunate when we have a friend who is strong in the practice, a Dharma brother or sister. Without a Sangha, without co-practitioners, the practice will be difficult. You can always ask your brothers and sisters to practice looking deeply with you every time you need support. Because you feel supported there, the Sangha is the most appropriate setting and environment for the practice of looking deeply. If you have a Sangha of two, three, maybe even fifty people who are practicing correctly — getting joy, peace, and happiness from the practice — then you are the luckiest person on Earth.

So practice in the setting of the Sangha is much easier. We don't have to practice so intensely. Our practice becomes the practice of "non-practice." That means a lot. We don't have to force ourselves to practice. We can give up all the struggle and allow ourselves to be, to rest. For this, however, we need a little bit of training, and the Sangha is there to make the training easy. Being aware that we are in a Sangha where people are happy with being mindful, where people are living deeply the moments of their days, that is enough. I always feel happy in the presence of a happy Sangha. If you put yourself in such an environment, then transformation will happen without much effort. This is my experience.

I TAKE REFUGE IN THE SANGHA

The reason we take refuge in anything is because we need protection. But very often we take refuge in people or things that are not at all solid. We may feel that we are not strong enough to be on our own, so we are tempted to look for someone to take refuge in. We are inclined to think that if we have someone who is strong and can be our refuge, then our life will be easier. We need to be very careful, because if we take refuge in a person who has no stability at all, then the little bit of solidity we have ourselves will be entirely lost. Many people have done that, and they have lost the little solidity and freedom they once had.

When a situation is dangerous, you need to escape, you need to take refuge in a place that is safe, that is solid. Earth is something we can take refuge in because it is solid. We can build houses on earth, but we cannot build on sand. The Sangha is the same. Mindfulness, concentration, and insight have built up Sanghas and individuals that are solid, so when you take refuge in the Sangha, you take refuge in the most solid elements.

When you are angry, if you know how to go back to your mindful breathing and take refuge in your mindfulness, you become strong. You can dwell peacefully in that moment and you are capable of dealing with the situation in a much more lucid way. You know that within you there are the elements of mindfulness, concentration, and insight. Those seeds are always there. If you have a friend, a teacher, a Sangha that can help you to touch those seeds and help them to grow, then you have the best kind of protection.

This is the role Sangha plays in supporting, protecting, and nourishing us. In the Sangha there is stability and joy. The Sangha is devoted to the practice of mindfulness, concentration, and insight, and while everyone in the Sangha profits from his or her own mindfulness, they can also take refuge in the collective energy of mindfulness, concentration, and insight of the Sangha. That is why there is a sense of solidity and security in the Sangha. We are not afraid because the Sangha is there to protect us.

It is like the flocks of wild geese that travel together from the north to the south in huge numbers. If one bird goes off on its own, it will be easily caught, but if they stay together, they are much safer. Near Plum Village there are hunters who use a bird cry to lure the geese down. If a wild goose leaves the flock and comes down alone, he will easily be shot by the hunters.

It's the same with the Sangha. If we think we can live alone, apart from the Sangha, we don't know our own strength or our own weakness. Thanks to the Sangha we do not enter paths of darkness and suffering. Even when the Sangha doesn't seem to be doing anything at all, it in fact is doing a lot, because in the Sangha there is protection.

Without the Sangha we easily fall into the traps of the five cravings. Once in those traps, we will be burnt by the flames of the afflictions and suffering. Keeping the mindfulness trainings and taking refuge in the Sangha's protection is a very good way to avoid being caught in the traps of the five cravings. We keep the mindfulness trainings so that they protect us. The rest of the Sangha will also be keeping the same mindfulness trainings and helping us.

Some people have told me that they have never felt secure before coming to a retreat. Then after sitting, eating, and walking mindfully with the Sangha, for the first time they get a feeling of security. Even small creatures living nearby feel safer, because we are mindful and do our best not to harm them. That feeling of security can lead to joy. We can practice like this:

> Breathing in, I see that I am part of a Sangha, and I am being protected by
>   my Sangha.
> Breathing out, I feel joy.

The Dharma can protect you — Dharma not in the sense of a Dharma talk or a book — but Dharma as the practice embodied by people like yourself. When you practice mindful breathing, mindful walking, mindful listening to the bell, you bring into yourself the elements of peace and stability, and you are protected during that time. You begin to radiate the energy of stability and peace all around you. This will help to protect your children and your loved ones. Although you may not give a Dharma talk with your words, you are giving a Dharma talk with your body, with your in-breath, with your out-breath, with your life. That is the living Dharma. We need that very much, just as we need the living Sangha.

PRACTICING IN THE SANGHA

If you are a beginner in the practice, you should not worry about what is the correct thing to do. When surrounded by many people, we might be caught by the idea, "I don't know what is the right thing to do." That idea may make us very uncomfortable. We may think, "I feel embarrassed that I'm not doing the right thing. There are people who are bowing, and I am not bowing. People are walking slowly, and I am walking a little bit too fast." So the idea that we may not be doing the right thing can embarrass us.

I would like to tell you what is really the right thing. The right thing is to do whatever you are doing in mindfulness. Mindfulness is keeping one's consciousness alive to the present reality. To bow may not be the right thing to do if you don't bow in mindfulness. If you don't bow but are mindful, not bowing is the right thing. Even if people are walking slowly and you run, you are doing the right thing if you run mindfully. The wrong thing is whatever you do without mindfulness. If we understand this, we will not be embarrassed anymore. Everything we do is right provided we do it in mindfulness. To bow or not to bow, that is not the question. The question is whether to bow in mindfulness or not, or not to bow in mindfulness or not.

If you take a step and you feel peaceful and happy, you know that is the correct practice. You are the only one who knows whether you are doing it correctly or not. No one else can judge. When you practice breathing in and out, if you feel peaceful, if you enjoy your in-breath and out-breath, you know you are doing it correctly. You are the best one to know. Have confidence in yourself. Wherever you find yourself, if you feel you are at ease and peaceful, that you are not under pressure, then you know you are doing it right.

The function of the bell in a Sangha is to bring us back to ourselves. When we hear the bell we come back to ourselves and breathe, and at that point we improve the quality of the Sangha energy. We know that our brother and our sister, wherever they are, will be stopping, breathing, and coming back to themselves. They will be generating the energy of right mindfulness, the Sangha energy. When we look at each other, we feel confident, because everyone is practicing together in the same way and contributing to the quality of the Sangha. So we are friends on the path of practice.

The Sangha is made out of the work of individuals, so we have the duty to help create the energy of the Sangha. Our presence, when it is a mindful presence, contributes to that energy. When we are absent during the activities of the Sangha, we are not contributing to Sangha energy. If we don't go to a sitting meditation, we are not feeding our Sangha. We are also letting ourselves go hungry, because we are not benefiting from the Sangha. We don't profit from the Sangha, and the Sangha doesn't profit from us.

Don't think that we sit for ourselves. You don't sit for yourself alone, you sit for the whole Sangha—not only the Sangha, but also for the people in your city, because when one person in the city is less angry, is smiling more, the whole city profits. If we practice looking deeply, our understanding of interbeing will grow, and we will see that every smile, every step, every breath is for everybody. It is for our country, for the future, for our ancestors.

The best thing we can do is to transform ourselves into a positive element of the Sangha. If members of the Sangha see us practicing well, they will have confidence and do better. If there are two, three, four, five, six, seven of you like that in the Sangha, I'm sure the Sangha will be a happy Sangha and will be the refuge of many people in the world.

THE SANGHA ISN'T PERFECT

Our transformation and healing depend on the quality of the Sangha. If there are enough people smiling and happy in the Sangha, the Sangha has more power to heal and transform. So you have to invest in your Sangha. Every member of the Sangha has his or her weaknesses and strengths, and you have to recognize them in order to make good use of the positive elements for the sake of the whole Sangha. You also have to recognize the negative elements so that you and the whole Sangha can help embrace them. You don't leave that negative element to the person alone, because he may not be able to hold and transform it by himself.

You don't need a perfect Sangha—a family or a community doesn't have to be perfect in order to be helpful. In fact, the Sangha at the time of the Buddha was not perfect. But it was enough for people to take refuge in, because in the Sangha there were people who had enough compassion, solidity, and insight to embrace others who did not have as much compassion, solidity, and insight. I also have some difficulties with my Sangha, but I'm very happy because everyone tries to practice in my Sangha.

If we lived in a Sangha where everyone was perfect, everyone was a bodhisattva or a Buddha, that would be very difficult for us. Weakness in the other person is very important, and weakness within yourself is also very important. Anger is in us, jealousy is in us, arrogance is in us. These kinds of things are very human. It is thanks to the presence of weakness in you and weakness in a brother or a sister that you learn how to practice. To practice is to have an opportunity to transform. So it is through our short-comings that we learn to practice.

There are some people who think of leaving the Sangha when they encounter difficulties with other Sangha members. They cannot bear little injustices inflicted on them because their hearts are small. To help your heart grow bigger and bigger, understanding and love are necessary. Your heart can grow as big as the cosmos; the growth of your heart is infinite. If your heart is like a big river, you can receive any amount of dirt. It will not affect you, and you can transform the dirt very easily.

The Buddha used this image. If you put a little dirt in a pitcher of water, then that water has to be thrown away. People cannot drink it. But if you put the same amount of dirt into a huge river, people can continue to drink from the river, because the river is so immense. Overnight that dirt will be transformed within the heart of the river. So if your heart is as big as a river, you can receive any amount of injustice and still live with happiness. You can transform overnight the injustices inflicted on you. If you still suffer, your heart is still not large enough. That is the teaching of forbearance and inclusiveness in Buddhism. You don't practice to suppress your suffering; you practice in order for your heart to expand as big as a river.

One time the Buddha said to his disciples: "There are people among us who do not have the same capacity as we do. They do not have the capacity to act rightly or to speak rightly. But if we look deeply, we see in their hearts that there are good seeds, and therefore we have to treat those people in such a way that those good seeds will not be lost."[6] Among us there are people who we may think do not have the capacity to practice as well as we do. But we should know that those people also have good seeds, and we have to cultivate those good seeds in such a way that these good seeds have a chance to be watered and to sprout.

The Buddha saw all his disciples as his children, and I think of mine in the same way. Any disciple of mine is my child that I have given birth to. In my heart I feel at ease, I feel light and happy, even though that child may still have a problem. You can use that method, too. If there is a person in the Sangha who troubles you, don't give up hope. Remember, "My teacher has given birth to that child. How can I practice in order to see that person as my sister? Then my heart will feel more at ease and I will be able to accept her. That person is still my sister, whether I want her to be or not." That feeling and those words can help dissolve the irritation that you are having with that person.

If we have harmony in the Sangha, we can give confidence to many people. We don't need to be perfect. I myself am not perfect, and you don't need to be perfect either. But if in your own way you can express your harmony in the Sangha, this is your gift.

THE SANGHA AS OUR MIRROR

Let us look at the *Anumana Sutra* (*Majjhima Nikaya*, Sutta No. 15 and *Madhyama Agama*, Sutra No. 89). Its title is *A Bhikshu's Request*. We are very fortunate to have two versions of this sutra coming from two different schools. Ninety percent of the text is the same in both versions, and the differences are not significant. That means that we have at least ninety percent of the original words of the speaker, Maha Maudgalyayana (Pali: Maha Mogallana), who was one of the most senior disciples of the Buddha. Because this sutra was an important text for Sangha-building, the text was frequently recited.

A good way to translate *anumana* in this context is "measuring and reflecting," so in English we can call this the *Sutra on Measuring and Reflecting*. "Measuring" means comparing ourselves with our friends in the practice. Seeing the other, we see ourselves reflected, and we learn what we need to do.

In the Sangha of the Buddha, there were a number of very mature practitioners. Perhaps the greatest of these were the two friends Shariputra and Maha Maudgalyayana. They were very adept at Sangha-building. Maha Maudgalyayana is best known for his loyalty to his parents and to Shariputra. Perhaps less emphasized, but no less important, was his ability to know his younger brothers and to teach them very practical ways of living together as a Sangha.

The beginning of the sutra describes the bhikshu's request. Maha Maudgalyayana says: "My friends, there may be a monk who requests other monks to talk to him." We may wonder why a monk would make such a request. It is because he feels isolated and no one wants to talk to him. "If he is difficult to speak to, if he has qualities that make him difficult to speak to, then his fellow practitioners will not speak to him, instruct him, or have trust in him."

Then Maha Maudgalyayana gives the reasons why others may not want to talk to or advise a monk. He also asks everyone to look at himself and see whether he has those traits that will make other practitioners not want to talk to him.

The first reason Maha Maudgalyayana gives for someone not being easy to talk to is "wrong wishes" *(papika icchana)*. "Wrong" means "not straight, crooked." It is true that our infatuations and desires can destroy us and our future. But there can be wholesome wishes. The wish to practice in order to help others without thought of fame, profit, or sex, that is not a wrong wish—especially when it's to help a monk that is stubborn, with the attitude "too bad, I'm going to do it anyway."

When we allow ourselves to be controlled by our wrong desires, this is expressed in our words and our attitude. At first our friends in the practice may try to help us, but they may give up. If so, we may lose our Sangha, because if our Sangha does not approach us we may abandon our Sangha. If we have some wrong desire that we are attached to, that can be the reason for our friends not wanting to speak to us, not wanting to teach us. We are caught in that wrong desire and don't have the chance to be taught by the Sangha, for the Sangha to shine the light of their understanding on that. We have to look deeply when someone is caught in their wrong desire. Nobody wants to talk to that person anymore—they don't want to give advice to that person, they don't want to help that person. It's not that they don't want to, but they can't, because that person doesn't listen to what they are told. And that person suffers. So that person cannot be loved by his friends in the practice, and he loses a golden opportunity to transform.

When somebody is caught in wrong desire and not respected or loved by the rest of the practitioners, everyone in the Sangha should ask themselves: Am I also caught in some sort of wrong desire? If I am, I will not be loved by my Sangha, I will not be helped by my Sangha, and I will be in a state of isolation.

There are other reasons people may not want to talk to us, as given in the Pali version. The second reason is: "He exalts himself and disparages others." When someone disparages everyone in their Sangha and says that no one is worthy to be their elder brother or sister, such an attitude isolates him and makes it difficult for Dharma friends to speak to that person.

In the community there may be some people who are not able to do what other people tell them. They only know how to think that they are worthy of praise, and they blame others. Nobody will want to talk to such people, remind or advise them, teach them, or look after them. If we are caught in a state of thinking that we already know everything, we lose the opportunity to enjoy the presence of the Sanghakaya.

If you live in a Sanghakaya, you have to ask yourself: Am I caught in the attitude of thinking I know everything? When somebody is caught in that attitude they cannot be reminded or taught, they cannot be loved and respected. And if I am caught in that state of mind, I will not be advised by the Sangha because of my difficult nature.

The third reason is: "He is wrathful and overpowered by wrath." We are ordinary people and not saints, so anger will arise in us from time to time. But a practitioner who has anger knows how to look after that anger. We have a right to be angry, but we also have a duty to look after that anger and transform it. When we can do that we will not be overpowered by our anger. Only when we do not practice are we overpowered by anger. When we grow red in the face and our eyes and words express anger, our friends find it difficult to approach us and help us.

Sometimes we do not even know that we are angry. We make angry gestures, but we do not know it. We speak in a threatening way, but we do not know it. We may even think we are easygoing and amiable. We need to ask someone else to be a mirror for us. "Let me know when my face turns red and I am difficult to bear." It is a difficult practice when we do not have a mirror in which to see ourselves. It is fortunate to have brothers and sisters to remind us when we are unpleasant to be with.

The fourth reason is: "He is wrathful and because of his wrath bears a grudge." When we are angry and do not recognize we are angry, the anger remains in our unconscious and becomes an internal knot, which we call a grudge. It is like when we have a cold. If we have a massage or some medication as soon as we catch a cold it will not worsen and become difficult to cure. When we do not treat our anger as soon as it arises, it goes deep into our being and our gestures and words express it, so that our Sangha does not want to be near us. We should use our Sangha as a mirror in which to see ourselves, because if we do not know how to transform our anger, it will destroy us.

The fifth reason is: "He is wrathful and because of his wrath is moody and easily takes offense." It is all right to take offense from time to time, but if we are moody twenty-four hours a day, people will withdraw from us.

The sixth reason is: "He is wrathful and utters words bordering on wrath." Here the moodiness is expressed in words rather than looks or actions. When we speak with emotion our words have vibrations that the listener will recognize immediately. Sadness, fear, and despair are all expressed by the tone of our voice. The other person hears that tone, but because of our lack of mindfulness, we do not. Three or four words spoken in anger are enough to lose a brother or sister and make him or her not want to talk to us anymore. The price of these words is therefore very high.

The seventh reason is: "Reproved, he blurts out reproof against the reprover." It may be that the reproof is clumsily worded or the result of wrong perception, but it is because we are so attached to our self-image that we lash out. The other person wants to help us, but we cannot listen or accept his or her help. We say, "You're blaming me!" and we proceed to blame the other. We say, "You are not a good friend," and we lose him. When we say the one who corrects us is not a friend, we lose a wonderful opportunity to transform our weak points.

Some time ago someone asked an elder sister, "Why does everyone here hate me and avoid me?" The elder sister replied, "It is not that everyone here hates you. You yourself have put up walls around you so that people cannot approach you." These were kindly words of advice, and I would not have replied any differently. But the younger sister shouted out, "So you're blaming me!" No one was blaming her but just trying to help. From that time on the elder sister no longer dared to advise her. She would greet her politely but would not say anything else. Because the younger sister responded like that to several other members in the Sangha, she lost her Sangha and could no longer bear to stay with us. The Sangha is our refuge. It is the thing we need most in this life but some of us still throw it away. Intellectually we see how much we need it, but we are too weak in our practice to be able to realize our need.

The eighth reason is: "He disparages the reprover for the reproof." He tries to say he has been wrongly corrected; he lacks understanding of the one who corrects him.

The ninth reason is: "Reproved, he turns on the reprover for the reproof." This means that the monk turns on the one who is correcting him and says, "That is not a fault of mine, it is a fault of yours. I am not angry, you are the one who is angry. I am not difficult, you are the one who is difficult."

The tenth reason is: "Reproved, he shelves the question by asking the reproved another question. He answers off the point and shows temper, ill-will, and sulks." If the monk refuses to talk to the point and avoids the issue, the friend advising or correcting him will grow weary and decide not to bother anymore.

The eleventh reason is: "Reproved, he does not succeed in explaining his movements to the reprover." He fails to explain why he has acted in a certain way or spoken in a certain way when given the opportunity to do so. He does not talk to the point.

The twelfth reason is: "He is harsh and spiteful."

The thirteenth reason is: "He is envious and grudging."

The fourteenth reason is: "He is treacherous and deceitful."

The fifteenth reason is: "He is stubborn and proud." You might say: "I have looked deeply, and what I am doing is correct. I am being true to myself, so I don't care if members of the Sangha think I should not behave in such a way. Even if the Sangha says that I should not do something, I do as I like." In that case you do not believe in the insight of the Sangha.

In principle we have to request the Sangha to help us to see our short-comings. But if the Sangha tells us: "No, don't do it like that," and we say, "I don't care, what I see is very important and correct," then what is the use of being with the Sangha?

The sixteenth reason is: "He is attached to the temporal, grasping it tightly, not letting go of it easily." Although a practitioner, he is attached to things of the world and does not know how to let go. He is told that a certain behavior is not fitting for a practitioner, but he cannot give up that behavior. He is attached to worldly things so that he lacks the quality of liberation and freedom.

These are the sixteen reasons that isolate a practitioner from the Sangha, that make him unapproachable, unteachable, and untrustworthy. After this Maudgalyayana speaks of the sixteen reasons that make a practitioner approachable, teachable, and trustworthy. Those qualities are the absence of the sixteen formerly mentioned traits. "And what, your Reverences, are the qualities that make him easy to speak to? A monk does not come to be of wrong desires or in the thrall of desires. He does not come to disparage others and exalt himself, he is not wrathful and overpowered by wrath," etc.

Maha Maudgalyayana goes on to tell the monks that they should look at others and come to an inference about themselves through this. "Monks, you should infer from the self of others what is true for yourself in the following way: 'That person has wrong wants and is in the thrall of those wrong wants. He is displeasing and disagreeable to me. Similarly, if I have wrong wants and am in the thrall of those wrong wants, I will be displeasing and disagreeable to others.'"

When a monk knows this he should make up his mind not to have wrong wants and be in the thrall of wrong wants. The same is true for the other fifteen qualities. This is very practical advice from the Venerable Maha Maudgalyayana. When we see someone is caught in wrong desires and is difficult to approach, we should look at ourselves to see whether people can approach us. If not, it may be because we are like that.

Maha Maudgalyayana teaches further that we should reflect on our own person: "'Do I have wrong wants and am I in their thrall?' If, while the monk is reflecting, he knows, 'I do have wrong desires and I am in their thrall,' he should strive to abandon that unskillful state. If, while reflecting, he knows: 'I do not have any wrong desires and am not in their thrall,' then with delight he abandons them altogether and trains day and night in that skillful state," and so on for the other fifteen qualities.

Maha Maudgalyayana concludes: "It is like a man in the prime of life who is pondering on his own reflection in a mirror that is quite clear. If he sees dust or a blemish, he tries to remove it. If he does not see dust or a blemish, he is pleased."

This sutra is long because the sixteen qualities are repeated four times in different contexts: (1) What makes a monk unapproachable? (2) What makes a monk approachable? (3) What should we infer about the consequences of our own behavior from seeing how others' behavior affects us? (4) How should we reflect on ourselves in order to transform?

TRUE TRANSMISSION

There is a lot of Dharma talk in the air and there is a lot of air in the Dharma talk. There is a sutra named after Yasoja, a monk who was the leader of a Sangha of about five hundred monks.[7] One day Yasoja led all five hundred monks to the Jeta Grove where the Buddha was living, hoping that they could join the three-month retreat with the Buddha. They arrived about ten days before the retreat began. They were in a very jovial mood, anticipating their meeting with the Buddha and all the other monks. There was a lot of talking. From his hut the Buddha heard the commotion and asked Ananda, "What is that noise? It sounds like fishermen landing a catch of fish." Ananda told him that the Venerable Yasoja had come with his five hundred monks and they were greeting and talking with the resident monks.

The Buddha told Ananda to ask the monks to come to him. When the monks came, they touched the earth before the Buddha and sat down. The Buddha immediately told them that they could not stay. "You are too noisy. I dismiss you." So all five hundred monks touched the earth and left the monastery at the Jeta Grove. They walked for many days to Vajji, which was on the east side of Koshala. When they arrived on the bank of the river

Vagamudi, they rested. There they began to build small huts for the rainy season retreat.

At the opening ceremony of the retreat, the Venerable Yasoja said, "The Buddha sent us away out of compassion. He wants us to know that he is expecting us to practice deeply and successfully. His chasing us away is an expression of his deep love." All the monks were able to see that. They agreed that they should practice very seriously during the rainy season retreat in order to show the Buddha that they were worthy disciples.

The monks practiced very ardently, deeply, and solidly, and after only three months of retreat the majority of them realized the Three Enlightenments: (1) remembering all their past lives; (2) seeing the lives of all beings and knowing how they have come here and where they will go after dying; and (3) ending the basic afflictions of craving, anger, and ignorance in themselves.[8]

One day after the rainy season retreat the Buddha told Ananda, "When I look into the direction of the east, I notice an energy of light and goodness. And when I concentrate deeply, I see that the five hundred monks that I sent away have achieved something quite deep."

Ananda said, "That is true, Lord, that is what I have heard. After having been sent out of the Jeta Grove they went to the Vajji territory and began serious practice, and have realized the Three Realizations."

The Buddha said, "That's good. Why don't we invite them to come for a visit?"

When the five hundred monks heard about the invitation of the Buddha they were very glad to come and visit him. After many days of traveling, they arrived at about seven o'clock in the evening. They saw the Buddha sitting quietly. They were told that the Buddha was in a state of concentration called "imperturbability." This state is one in which a person is not perturbed by anything; he dwells freely and very solidly, and nothing can shake him — including fame, craving, hatred, or even hope.

When the monks realized that the Buddha was in the state of *samadhi* called imperturbability they decided to sit like him. So they sat down on the ground in the Jeta Grove like the Buddha — very beautifully, very deeply, very solidly, all of them penetrating the state of imperturbability. They sat for a long time.

When the first watch of the night had finished, the Venerable Ananda came and knelt next to the Buddha and said, "Lord, it is already very late in the night, so why don't you address the monks?" The Buddha did not say anything; he continued to sit.

When at two o'clock in the morning the second watch of the night had gone by, Ananda came and once again knelt down next to the Buddha and said, "Lord, the night has gone very far. It is now the end of the second watch, please address the five hundred monks." The Buddha did not reply and continued to sit, and all the monks continued to sit also.

Finally, the third watch of the night was over and morning began to appear on the horizon. Ananda came for the third time and knelt near the Buddha, and said, "Great teacher, now night is over, so why don't you address the monks?"

The Buddha opened his eyes. He looked at Ananda and said, "Ananda, you did not know what was going on. If you did, you would not have come three times to me like this. I was sitting in samadhi with the monks. We were not disturbed by anything at all. There was nothing more that we could have done. There was no need for anything else, no need for communication, for greetings, for conversation. It is the most beautiful thing that can happen between teacher and students—to just sit like that, each one dwelling deeply in a state of peace, solidity, and freedom."

I found this sutra very beautiful. The communication depicted between teacher and disciples is perfect.

What should a student expect from a teacher? He should expect nothing less than freedom from a teacher. A teacher should be a free person— free from craving, fear, and despair. Do not expect small things, such as having a cup of tea with the teacher or receiving praise from him or her. Expect much more than that from a teacher. If your teacher does not have any solidity or freedom, then you should not accept him or her as your teacher because you will get nothing in return.

What should a Dharma teacher or a big brother or sister in the Dharma expect from students? You also should not expect small things. You should not expect him to bring you a cup of tea, a good meal, a cake, or words of praise. These things are nothing at all. You should expect from your student transformation, healing, and freedom. When teachers and their students are like that they are in a perfect state of communication. They don't have to say anything to each other. They don't have to do much, they just sit with each other like that in a state of solidity and imperturbability, and that is what is most beautiful in a teacher-student relationship. That is why I have found the sutra very, very beautiful.

When a student practices well, he can see the teacher in himself, in herself. And when the teacher practices well as a teacher, he can see himself, herself in the students. And they should not expect less than that. If you see a teacher as someone who is always outside of you, you have not profited much from your teacher. If you are unable to see that your teacher is in you, your practice has not gone well at all. The same is true of a teacher. If you look at your students, and you don't see yourself in your students, your teaching has not gone very far.

When I look into a disciple, whether a monastic or a layperson, I would like to see me in him or her. This is because my teaching has only one aim: to transmit my insight, my freedom, and my joy to my disciples. If I look at him and I see these elements in him, I'm very glad. I feel that I have done well in transmitting the best that is in me. Looking at her way of walking, smiling, breathing, and of moving about, I can see my teaching as being fruitful or not. And that is what is called "transmission."

Transmission isn't some organized ceremony with a lot of incense and chanting. Transmission is something that happens every day in a very simple way. If the teacher-student relationship is good, then that transmission is realized in every moment of our daily life. You don't feel far away from your teacher. You feel that he or she is always with you, because the teacher outside has become the teacher inside. You know how to look with the eyes of your teacher, you know how to walk with the feet of your teacher, and your teacher is never far away from you.

This is not something abstract; it is something that we can see for ourselves. When you look at a monk or a nun or lay disciple and you see Thây in him, you know that he is a real disciple of Thây. If you don't see that, then you might say that this is a newly-arrived person, he doesn't have any Thây within him, and this is seen very clearly. If in their way of walking, smiling, and thinking there are elements of freedom, joy, and compassion, then we know that Thây has penetrated and they are a true continuation of their teacher. When you look at the students, you can tell whether the teacher-student relationship is good. If it is good, transmission will be taking place in every moment of their daily life.

The Buddha and his monks did not have a lot of belongings, they did not have bank accounts, they did not own buildings or houses. Each monk had only three robes, a begging bowl, and a water filter. This is what they carried with them when they moved from place to place. The monks and nuns of our time try their best to follow this example. If you want to become a monk or a nun you should know that a monastic does not have a personal bank account or a personal car. Even the robes we wear do not belong to us; they belong to the Sangha. But if you need a robe, the Sangha will provide one for you. That does not mean that the robe becomes *your* robe, it still remains a robe of the Sangha.

Even your body is not your personal property. When you become a monk or a nun, your body doesn't belong to you as personal property. You have to take care of your body because it is part of the Sangha body. And all the other monks and nuns have to help take care of your body, and you have to allow them to take care of you. They can intervene if they see that the way you eat and drink are harmful to you. You don't own anything at all, including your body, and yet happiness is possible, freedom is possible. In fact, it makes happiness and freedom easier than if you own many things. Usually if we don't own anything we are very afraid, we feel insecure. But that is not the experience of a monastic. What guarantees well-being is not having possessions, but the giving away of all possessions.

You have to donate everything you have before you can be accepted as an ordained novice. You are advised not to donate it to the temple where you are going but to some other organization, not the temple you accept as your home. I remember when Sister Thuc Nghiem (Sister Susan) and other sisters, like Sister Eleni, became nuns. They took everything from their pockets and gave it to me — ten dollars, twenty-five cents, the keys to their cars — they gave everything to me. And I stored these things as souvenirs.

One day I asked all the monks and nuns to list their daily joys. They could use one page, two pages, or more. Many of them filled up more than two pages. And I remember what Sister Susan wrote: "My happiness is that I do not have any money anymore, not even one cent." Before she became a nun she handled very big sums of money, but it did not give her peace or happiness. After giving everything away and becoming penniless she was liberated, she gained a lot of freedom, and that is the foundation of happiness.

Many people believe that practicing as a monk or nun is the most difficult way to practice. But that's not the case. To practice as a monk or a nun is the easiest way to practice. When you have entrusted yourself entirely to the Sangha, you don't have to worry about anything at all—food, shelter, medicine, transportation—everything is provided. When everyone around you is practicing walking mindfully, enjoying every step, it would be unnatural for you not to do the same. So you are naturally transported by the boat of the Sangha. And even if you don't want to go, you go anyway; it carries you in the direction of peace and freedom anyway.

You have left behind your family, your father, your mother, your friends, and your job in order to become a monk or nun. Your purpose is to attain freedom, because you know that true happiness is not possible without freedom. That is why you aspire deeply to be free—free from afflictions. The purpose of the practice is to become free in order for the Kingdom of God to be available to you in the here and the now, to get free in order for true life to be possible to you in the here and the now, for the Pure Land of the Buddha to be available to you in the here and the now.

The reason we practice is not in order to become Dharma teachers or Sangha leaders. To become a teacher or a Sangha leader, what does it mean? It does not mean anything at all. What is the use of becoming the head of a temple if you continue to suffer deeply? The purpose of practice is to become free. And with freedom, happiness is possible. And when you have freedom and happiness you can help so many people because you have something to share, something to offer to them. It is not your ideas or the accumulated knowledge from your Buddhist studies that you share. This can be learned in the universities, and even professors of Buddhist Studies may suffer very deeply, because their study of Buddhism has not helped them at all. So although Buddhist Studies may be helpful it is not the purpose of practice. What you need is freedom.

We used to think that happiness was the accumulation of many things, such as knowledge, a position in society, fame, etc.—these are the things that people look for in society. And even those who get them are not truly happy. Our way is different, it is the way of freedom. Is it possible to be free? When we look at our Dharma brother, Dharma sister, or teacher and see how much freedom and happiness he or she has, we want to sit close to them and live close to them because we know we can profit from their happiness and their freedom. The happiness found in them is based on their freedom and not on things like fame, position, or power. What you can get from a Sangha is the opportunity to sit, walk, smile, and breathe with a Sangha with the aim of arriving, freedom, and stopping.

A few years ago we started the movement of Mindfulness Practice Centers. Mindfulness Practice Centers are places to practice in a nonsectarian, non-religious way. Everyone can come and feel comfortable, whether they are Christians, Jews, or communists. Mindfulness Practice Centers are a new Dharma door open to our society. This is very much in the direction Buddhism must go to cross the border of religion and engage in all sectors of society. This is a new awareness.

The Order of Interbeing[9] is also a new Dharma door that introduces spirituality into society. It is made up of both monastics and lay practitioners—lay men and women who work in mainstream society and who can bring their spiritual practice to many sectors of society. They first receive the Five Mindfulness Trainings[10] (see Appendix I) and then spend a meaningful period of time as aspirants who learn to practice mindfulness in the company of a Sangha. Once ordained, they agree to observe at least sixty Days of Mindfulness (or days of retreat) each year, even as they remain engaged in the world and in their Sangha-building activities. Lay members of the Order of Interbeing are also encouraged to set up Mindfulness Practice Centers everywhere they are, in order to offer Buddhism as a spiritual practice without any partisan spirit.

The meaning of wearing a brown jacket is not to say that you are an ordained member of the Order of Interbeing. That's nothing. That's like having a student identity card in a famous university and not studying. What is the purpose of having the identity card if you don't make use of the library or go to lectures? When we receive the Fourteen Mindfulness Trainings[11] (see Appendix I) and have ordination, we get a brown jacket, and that is our identity card. This allows us to profit from the Sangha, the teaching, and the practice. We are able to make good use of Dharma centers, monasteries, teachers, and Dharma brothers and sisters who practice in order to advance on our path of freedom. And as we have freedom in us we begin to make other people around us happy.

BUILDING A SANGHA

We know that practicing without a Sangha is difficult. That is why we try our best to set up Sanghas where we live. To be an Order of Interbeing member is wonderful. To be a Dharma teacher is wonderful. Wonderful, not because we have the title of OI membership or the title of Dharma teacher, but in that we have a chance to practice. As an OI member you must now begin to support a practice group or to organize one if none exists in your area. It does not mean anything to be an OI member if you do not do this in your area.

In a group from five to twenty people or more you can practice regularly. There are four levels of practice: local, regional, national, and international. Weekly practice in the local Sanghas include: Dharma discussion, tea meditation, walking meditation, Days of Mindfulness, and short retreats. From time to time local Sanghas invite other Sanghas to participate in a regional activity. This provides an opportunity to combine the talents and the experiences of OI members and Sangha-builders at the regional level, each contributing what they can and everyone learning from the regional activities. We come together to organize an event with our root Sangha at the national level. These events can be organized at a Dharma center, a monastery like Deer Park, Green Mountain Dharma Center, or Plum Village. And finally activities are organized at the international level, where practitioners from Europe and America share the practice and learn from each other's experiences.

The Sangha is there to support you in your practice. So building the Sangha means building yourself. If the Sangha is there, you will practice with the Sangha. So this is the benefit for a Sangha-builder—she has an opportunity to practice.

Being a Dharma teacher is also a good opportunity. As a Dharma teacher you cannot *not* practice. As you teach you have to practice in order for your teaching to have content. How can you open your mouth and give the teaching if you don't practice? So, teaching is an opportunity. Even if you are not an excellent teacher yet, being a Dharma teacher helps very much. Because when you begin to share the Dharma with others, you have to do what you are telling others to do, otherwise it would look funny. As a Sangha-builder or a Dharma teacher you are given the opportunity to practice, and every member of the Sangha can create favorable conditions for you. Good practitioners and those not so good in the practice can inspire you to help them.

So, if we know what it really means to be a Sangha-builder, an OI member, or a Dharma teacher, it is a very good thing. To receive the mindfulness trainings transmission and a brown jacket and decide not to build a Sangha would be like getting a student ID card at a university and not using the library or going to class, but telling people that you are a student of a famous university. It would be very funny. So Sangha-building is what we do. It is the practice.

Sangha-building means to identify the different elements of the Sangha and invite each element to join the practice. You are like a gardener who takes care of every member of the Sangha. There are members who are very easy to be with and to deal with, and there are members who are very difficult to be with and to deal with. And yet as a Sangha-builder you have to help everyone.

There are members of the Sangha whose presence you can enjoy deeply and some with whom you have to be very patient. Please don't believe that every monastic or layperson in Plum Village is equally easy for me. That's not the case. There are monastics that are very easy to be with and to help, but there are monastics that are very difficult. As a teacher you may have to spend more time and energy with those who are more difficult. You may be tempted to reject these practitioners, but that is to surrender. You cannot grow into a good practitioner or a good Dharma teacher if you want only the easy things.

In the Sangha there must be difficult people. These difficult people are a good thing for you—they will test your capacity of Sangha-building and practicing. One day when that person says something that is not very nice to you, you'll be able to smile and it won't make you suffer at all. Your compassion will have been born and you will be capable of embracing him or her within your compassion and your understanding. Then you will know that your practice has grown. You should be delighted that such an act does not make you angry or sad anymore, that you have enough compassion and understanding to embrace it. That is why you should not be tempted to eliminate the elements that you think are difficult in your Sangha. Sangha-building requires a lot of love and compassion, and if you know how to handle difficult moments you will grow as a Sangha-builder and as a Dharma teacher.

I am speaking to you out of my experience. I now have a lot more patience and compassion, and because I have more patience and compassion, my happiness has grown much greater. You suffer because your understanding and compassion are not yet large enough to embrace difficult people, but with the practice you will grow, your heart will grow, your understanding and compassion will grow, and you won't suffer anymore. And thanks to the Sangha practicing together, thanks to your model of practice, those people will transform. That is a great success, much greater than in the case of people who are easy to get along with.

In the *Sutra of Happiness* the Buddha said that to have regular contact with a Sangha is true happiness. To be able to practice the Dharma, to have the opportunity to learn the Dharma and to participate in Dharma discussions, is the greatest happiness. Together as a Sangha we can continue the work of the Buddha. We can achieve the things that the Buddha has not achieved, because there are many Dharma doors to be opened. There are teachings yet to be offered. To play the role of the continuation of the Buddha is the task of Sangha. Sangha is the continuation, the community that carries within its heart the Buddha and the Dharma. A true Sangha — one where there is mindfulness, awareness, understanding, and love — that Sangha is the Buddha in flesh and bones.

PART TWO

Gathering Good Friends

~

Sharing the Path:
An Overview of Lay Sangha Practice 3

BY JACK LAWLOR

INTRODUCTION

WHEN WE ATTEND a mindfulness retreat, we come into direct contact with something wonderful in ourselves — the capacity to be calm, insightful, and loving. Practicing conscious breathing, sitting meditation, and walking meditation with the support of other people can do this for us. When we return home, however, there are many distractions that await us, and it is difficult to find time for sitting and walking meditation, or simply looking mindfully at the blue sky. How is it possible, we wonder, to continue to practice in our daily lives as deeply as we did at the retreat? Yet we try, because we know that these simple mindfulness practices enable us to be truly present, understanding, and loving with one another, and they also help us stay engaged with others as our spiritual friends, participating together in the joys and sorrows of the world.

Without the support of others, we become discouraged. We might have the opportunity to sign up for additional retreats, and even find them to be immensely helpful. Yet there is always that "gap" between retreats, where we find ourselves caught in our habit energies and compulsions that consume our time and energy and cause so much stress and misunderstanding.

During these "gaps," we might decide to take refuge in the many fine books that have been published about Buddhism and mindfulness practices. Yet we may find that it is also hard to integrate the wisdom of these books into our daily lives without the benefit of someone to talk to. We might find that when life surprises us with challenges, we cannot remember what we have read, or even where to find the book we once found helpful.

How, we may wonder, did the Buddha succeed with his mindfulness practice? After all, his aspiration was the same as ours: to transform the suffering within himself and to find ways to help others do the same.

We sometimes view the Buddha as a kind of exemplary but solitary figure, like a magnificent oak living all by itself atop a hill or in the midst of a field. We may have had the opportunity to visit such a tree, to admire the strength of its trunk, the deeply grooved character of its bark, the tenacity of its roots, and the inventiveness of its limbs and leaves as they seek out the sunlight. What we tend to overlook is that the oak is a highly dependent member of a community. We know that if the sunlight and rain were to disappear, the oak would not be there. We may be a little less conscious that the oak depends not only on sunlight and rain, but also on other living beings—on the worms and insects that work the soil, and on other trees and vegetation whose leaves, windblown trunks, and branches also rejuvenate the ground.

Shakyamuni Buddha is a towering figure, much like the oak. But, like the oak, the Buddha lived as a member of a community. When we investigate the life story of the Buddha, we find that he lived in the context of community through the vast majority of his life both before and after his enlightenment. He learned much about sincerity and responsibility from his father, the king, despite his disagreements with him. He learned much about compassion from his stepmother and his wife. When practicing austerities for six years after leaving home, he visited the leading religious figures and communities of ancient India and practiced with a small group of spiritual friends.

One of the strongest impressions we may have after reading about the life of the Buddha is how deep, and how broad, his relationships were with every level of society throughout his entire lifetime. A biography of the Buddha reads like a Tolstoy novel, for it involves royalty, wealthy merchants, warriors, farmers, young dandies, prostitutes, the poor, outcasts, family people attempting to live religious lives, the widowed, parents distraught at the loss of a child, religious seekers of all kinds, criminals, and those—both in secular life and in religious communities—lusting after fame, power, and wealth.

When we observe the Buddha in the context of his life, we find that he was always looking and listening intently, always trying to learn from others in his community. His was an engaged mindfulness practice. He did not reject or isolate himself from society in any way. In fact, after his enlightenment, the Buddha formed a spiritual community known as a Sangha—comprised of monks, nuns, laywomen, and laymen—which continues to this day, over 2,500 years later. Each day the Sangha visited the homes of people from every level of society to seek alms and to offer instruction in mindfulness. The result of this engaged interaction between society and the Buddha's spiritual community is what we now refer to as Buddhism. Buddhism drew from non-Buddhist elements to form the religious community that still lives among us.

You are invited to join this community. If you feel that there is a "gap" in your mindfulness practice, it may be due to lack of community. You are not alone in this. As Thich Nhat Hanh has pointed out, much of the emphasis within Buddhist studies in the West in recent centuries has been on understanding the life and role of the Buddha and the body of his teachings, known as the Dharma. The Buddha and the Dharma are two of the Three Refuges, or Three Precious Gems, in Buddhism. But the Third Refuge, the Third Precious Gem, is the Sangha, and as Thây points out, the importance of Sangha has been only recently recognized in the West. He advised his students in recent Dharma talks that "you cannot afford not to have a Sangha body" and that Sangha-building "is the noblest task of our century."

In what spirit do we seek to fill this "gap" in Western mindfulness practice? How do we establish a relationship with a spiritual community, a Sangha? Do we sign up somewhere, fill out a computerized registration card, send in our check, and wait for a magazine to arrive or for someone to knock on our door? No. The process must be more personal, more engaging, and more genuine than that. Perhaps the best way to approach a Sangha first involves an openness to what it has to offer, an admission that we seek the company of others in our spiritual life. We have to be willing to let go a bit of our desire to be anonymous and private. And then, we need simply to seek out spiritual friends, and be sure to be a spiritual friend *in return* throughout the process. Be a kalyanamitra (spiritual friend) to yourself and to others. Thây has said, "Forming a Sangha is not difficult if we have support of friends on the path."

But what does a kalyanamitra do? A good spiritual friend is a fellow wayfarer willing to share the time and energy necessary to train in mindfulness—enjoying sitting and walking meditation, reciting the mindfulness trainings and practicing healthy ways of living, joining in Dharma discussion, and much, much more together. Spiritual friends cultivate mindfulness in order to look deeply into sensations in their body, their feelings, and their emotions before judging and reacting. Dwelling in mindfulness, they make themselves available to others—not only in good, fun times, but when challenges arise as well. They see what is best in others—their bodhicitta, or aspiration to practice mindfulness not only for their own well-being but to simultaneously help others transform suffering—and try to encourage its development. They refrain from watering negative seeds that encourage weaknesses in others.

The importance of the basics of mindfulness practice cannot be overlooked. In the *Samyutta Nikaya*, the Buddha is asked how we might become good companions to our parents, our family members, our friends, our coworkers, and members of our spiritual communities. The Buddha replied, "Becoming mindful benefits oneself and others. Mindfulness is the way to become a friend of others."

The Buddha spoke quite often on the subject of spiritual friendship. He urges us to associate with reliable friends in this verse found in the *Digha Nikaya:*

A friend who always lends a hand.
A friend in sorrow and joy.
A friend who offers good counsel.
A friend who sympathizes too—

These are four kinds of good true friends,
And one who is wise, having understood this,
Will always cherish and serve such friends
Just as a mother tends her only child.[12]

As indicated above, the Buddha cultivated spiritual friendships in the context of a spiritual community throughout his entire adult life, even before his enlightenment. We often see the Buddha depicted all by himself in this prodigious moment in religious history, or perhaps alone beneath the historic Bo tree. It would be more accurate to artistically depict the Buddha surrounded by all those who contributed to his enlightenment. This group would include his father, his stepmother, his wife, and the five spiritual friends who accompanied him during much of this period.

So if we can't just fill out a registration form to join a community, where do we begin? Or how do we form a community if none exists in our locality? And how do we become a genuine kalyanamitra once we find or create a community? These are important questions. To answer them, we might first ask what it would feel like to be part of a Sangha.

An Evening with a Lay Sangha

Let's say you're a layperson who has attended retreats with Thây and has had difficult weeks at work upon returning home. You have not incorporated many of the mindfulness practices you learned about during the retreat into your daily life as you had planned, because upon return there have been too many surprises and things have been intense. You've felt tired and a little bit frustrated. You wanted to practice meditation at home each evening, but there were too many distractions. The one evening you did have a chance to sit down on your meditation cushion, you felt very sleepy.

Sunday night is approaching, and you're aware that a local Sangha will be gathering across town in just a few hours. While a part of you wants to rest and watch television, your deepest desire is to share mindfulness practices with others and feel the same support you enjoyed at the retreat. Somewhat to your surprise, you find yourself in your car on your way to Sangha practice.

Each evening, somewhere, someplace, a group of friends gather in a largely empty room. Warm greetings are exchanged while meditation cushions are carefully placed in a circle or rectangle. Candles are lit in various locations, and the overhead lights are dimmed. A small altar containing a flower, a gently smiling Buddha figure, and a meditation bell is set up near the center of the now-inviting space.

One friend slowly raises the small meditation bell to eye level, gazes upon it, and invites the bell to sound. As she taps the bell softly, it responds in slow, undulating waves that envelop the room. Although the bell is small, its resonance lingers. Soft-spoken conversations come to an end and everyone walks toward a meditation cushion. One person volunteers to light the altar candle, bowing as he does so. The evening's randomly selected volunteer "bell master" then invites the bell to sound once again, and everyone bows to one another from the waist, palms held together, as a sign of respect. The bell master invites the bell yet again, and the friends take their seats, facing outward toward the perimeter walls.

For the next hour the group of men and women practice together in alternating twenty-minute rounds of sitting and walking meditation. Most sit on cushions in half-lotus position. A few sit on meditation benches or folding chairs. Their backs are held straight, their eyes cast downward toward the floor. Each is smiling gently, breathing not only from the upper chest but deeply into the lower lungs. With only one or two such cleansing breaths and a smile, they begin to feel at home, fully present, calm and at ease. Each person merges their attention with the breath, some experiencing its full length as the chest rises and falls, while others follow the breath through the movement of the diaphragm muscle between the lungs and the stomach. Each person is gradually settling into the present moment, transforming stress and agitation, bringing body, mind, and breath into oneness, into harmony.

Although it may seem to the casual observer that these people are asleep, or in a trance, they are actually extraordinarily awake. The practice of following the breath intently as it rises and falls leads to an unusual degree of concentration and relaxation. The incessant "chatter" of the mind—bits and pieces of conversations, fragmented ideas, remnants of previous sense impressions, sensations in various parts of the body, and emotional reactions—are all observed rather than repressed. The practitioners acknowledge their presence, breathe in and out through them, and watch them transform and dissipate. Perhaps for the first time that day an awareness exists, a recognition of the feelings that arise and color our thinking, which in turn spurs our actions and our dealings with others. As feelings and thoughts arise, the meditators smile and continuously recognize them for what they are without judging or reacting. After observing their rise and fall, the practitioners simply return to the breath.

After twenty minutes, the bell master invites the bell once again and each person prepares for walking meditation by stretching their legs and massaging any soreness. With the second bell, the Sangha rises. With the third bell, the friends bow to one another from the waist and turn to the right to begin the centuries-old practice of walking meditation. The pace is very slow: one step for each breath. That is, one step on the inhalation, one step on the exhalation. This is an opportunity to incorporate conscious breathing—of merging our attention into our breathing—into one's physical movements. Walking meditation is a wonderful way to segue into practicing conscious breathing throughout the day, integrating breath practice into everyday activities like waking up, washing one's face, opening a door, preparing and partaking in a meal, even driving a car. We walk gently, as though massaging the Earth with our feet. A beautiful practice is to visualize yourself inhaling breath from the Earth herself, through the soles of your feet, through the lower leg, the upper leg, the lower lung, the upper lung, and then exhaling with your next step back to the Earth herself via the same route on the other side of your body. By bringing body and mind together though the simple practice of conscious breathing, we live deeply, from centeredness and calm. Living in awareness, we are more capable of looking deeply and continuously at what is happening in the present moment, and of acting appropriately.

The mindfulness bell is invited again. The bell is the signal for everyone to return to their meditation cushions as they circumnavigate the room for the last time. When each practitioner reaches his or her place, the bell sounds, inviting each person to bow to one another again in respect. With two more sounds of the bell, the sitting resumes.

Most of the Sangha continues meditation with the ancient practice of following the breath. Many are transforming a week of dispersion into a deep, calm, and gentle concentration. At this point in the evening, some of the practitioners consciously choose, with the assistance of conscious breathing, to continuously observe the other activities of the body. They focus their concentration along the entire length of the body, starting with their foreheads, and then coming into contact with their eyes, their smile, their spine, their shoulders, their heart, and so on. This continuous, gentle mental touching, supported by the rhythm of conscious breathing, becomes a kind of massage, a penetration. As sensations arise, the practitioner pauses to observe the rise and fall of the activities of the eyes, the ears, the nose, and the sense of touch. As feelings arise, they are observed. As thoughts arise, they are recognized for what they are. All without repressing, on the one hand, or fabricating or adding to the experience, on the other. Each sensation is observed with a smile, in equanimity. Phenomena rise and fall, in constant change. The practitioner observes the changes and returns to the breath.

After the second round of meditation, the friends once again rise and bow with the third sound of the bell. Everyone in the room introduces themselves and is encouraged to make a new friend during the ensuing social break. Brief announcements are made about opportunities to support a Sangha member who is hospitalized, about a Sangha fundraiser for a children's camp for those afflicted with leukemia, and about a forthcoming weekend-long regional retreat with other Sanghas in a five-state area. Tea and simple refreshments are then served as the group enjoys a casual break. It's time to catch up with one another on events of the past week, and about joint concerns and budding friendships.

Each week, after the hour of sitting and walking meditation and a refreshment break, the Sangha members remain together for an additional hour of Dharma discussion. Dharma discussions may include a group examination of a sutra, an episode in the life of the Buddha, or an exploration about how we might bring our mindfulness practice into daily life — such as mindfulness in the workplace, mindfulness as a caregiver, mindfulness in the family. In advance of the meeting, a member of the group volunteers to facilitate the discussion. His or her efforts will not take the form of an academic lecture or religious sermon. The facilitator will, instead, compile a humble, short summary of his or her personal experience of how the sutra or discussion topic is illuminated by simple mindfulness practices based on the experience of conscious breathing. Rather than offering definitive conclusions, the facilitator lightheartedly but sincerely describes his or her experience and asks questions about the experiences of others.

In the wake of an hour of sitting and walking meditation, these discussions are rather unique. The Sangha comes from a wide variety of religious, racial, ethnic, and economic backgrounds, but among the things they have in common is a strong affinity for meditation and the miraculous way that the engagement of conscious breathing into daily life makes us calmer, more insightful, and compassionate. Without any kind of admonition or prompting, Sangha members offer insights calmly, reflecting on actual experience rather than from the intellect or what they may have read in a book.

The friends sometimes surprise themselves with what arises. The root causes of past prejudices, habits, and tendencies pop to the surface of their consciousness like a cork out of water, perhaps for the first time. The use of meditation to stop our rushing habit energies, to look deeply, and to see and understand gives rise to insights without much use of the intellect. Profound surprise can result. Surprise that mindfulness can identify the causes and conditions of our suffering. Surprise that it helps us recognize what is healing and nourishing right in our midst. Thây puts it this way: "You need the Sangha; you need a brother, a sister, or friend to remind you of what you already know. The Dharma is in you, but it needs to be watered in order to manifest and become a reality."[13]

The evening concludes within two and a half hours. The friends remove their meditation cushions and carefully put them away. Candles are extinguished, and the modest altar is disassembled. The room is once again empty. People leave together in twos and threes as spiritual friends, kalyanamitra. You can overhear plans being made to visit the Sangha member who is sick, and to help out with the fundraiser for the youth camp. You can hear one friend offering to meet with another to discuss her anguish about a pending divorce. Certain more quietly offered remarks may also be overheard. Someone will confide that they hadn't felt like coming, either because of a general sense of tiredness or dissipation or because of other demands on their time, but how happy they are to be reminded of how important it is to practice mindfulness with a Sangha, rather than alone. Others will admit that they needed the opportunity to refresh and renew their mindfulness practice with the support of others, and that they never would have meditated this week without an available Sangha. Next week, they say, they hope to do better. In response, others remark that the previous week's meditation and Dharma discussion resonated strongly with them through-out the week. The remarks most often heard are expressions of gratitude toward the Sangha itself, for its very existence, providing a weekly oppor-tunity to sustain and nourish mindfulness practice.

GETTING STARTED

It really isn't difficult to attract people to this kind of simple Sangha prac-tice. It's like the thesis of the popular American movie *Field of Dreams* (based on W. P. Kinsella's novel, *Shoeless Joe*): "If you build it, they will come." But remember, even in *Field of Dreams* "they" did not come running as soon as the little baseball field was built. The baseball players came in ones, twos, and threes; the neighboring Iowans were skeptical; and it took a long time to see and understand the baseball field for what it really was.

Conscientious people nonetheless worry, "How can I possibly build a Sangha?" Most of us don't feel qualified! We're not monks, nuns, or famous Dharma teachers. Nonetheless, if our aspiration in starting a Sangha is to make mindfulness practice available to others on a consistent basis in a car-ing way, to transform suffering and stress, and to create a spirit of sharing and mutual learning and growth—rather than to become a famous celebrity Buddhist or self-help guru on the lecture circuit—it is possible for us to succeed. The intentions of genuine Sangha-builders are described this way in the poetic *Avatamsaka Sutra:*

> Not seeking objects of desire or positions of authority,
> Wealth, personal enjoyment, or fame,
> It is only to forever annihilate creatures' miseries
> And to benefit the world that they arouse their will.

It isn't necessary to advertise or engage in a publicity campaign to begin a Sangha. Most begin as a small gathering of friends. Why not start off by creating a Sangha much like organizing a joyful dinner gathering? When we organize such an event, we invite people with certain affinities and an openness to meeting new friends. Sangha-building can begin the same way. We've all met people right in our own community who have confided in us their interest in meditation or contemplative living, people from all walks of life: at the grocery store cash register, in the workplace, at church, on the bus, at art fairs, in bookstores, at the yoga center, at the library. Why not begin by inviting two or three friends who are interested in meditation to come to your home to share the most basic practices, such as sitting meditation, walking meditation, chanting, and discourse recitation? If the collective mindfulness practice in your small Sangha gives birth to a calm, joyful, atmosphere, before long each friend will invite another friend, and soon you will have a growing, happy Sangha! After a few years, some small Sanghas have grown to eighty or ninety participants primarily by friends bringing friends! At that point, most groups find that they can afford to rent space in local churches, temples, or yoga centers.

If you approach Sangha-building in a grim, humorless, or overzealous way, people will be much less likely to attend. They may already have too many aspects of their lives that are grim, humorless, and out of control. Sangha-building can be approached with a light and loving touch, with a sense of humor.

Don't be too disappointed if, notwithstanding your best efforts and your careful selection of a Dharma discussion topic, fewer people than anticipated arrive at your Sangha on a given evening. The more you become familiar with Sangha members, the more you learn how complex their lives are and how they often have layers and layers of responsibilities. When they come to your Sangha, they come for nourishment and support. Learn to treasure their presence as a gift!

Very young Sanghas have a much better chance of success if two of three people have a quiet, unintimidating, joyous, yet totally committed and unshakable resolve to make group practice available on a consistent basis. It's important that these folks enjoy mindfulness practice for its own sake and don't try to heap demands upon others and become judgmental if others don't meet their expectations. Other Sangha participants may be facing very challenging situations either at home or at their workplace, and we need to extend to them our understanding and love.

For these reasons, Sangha development sometimes ironically occurs in inverse proportion to its leadership's overt zeal to build it. This kind of overt zeal is a "wear on your sleeve," missionary-type ambition to change the world, to convert, to be honored as an early pioneer of Buddhism in the West, and to extract praise or obligations from others. This approach just doesn't work in the contemporary West. With luck, you may attract people to your Sangha, but they will soon "vote with their feet" and never return. We must nurture the growth of more genuine communities.

There will undoubtedly be times when the logistical tasks of organizing sittings, doing mailings, preparing refreshments, etc., tend to fall on the same field builders. Nevertheless, there is no need to become discouraged, which tends to happen if Sangha attendance becomes poor. True field builders don't become discouraged. They just practice. They make sitting and walking meditation available to those who find them to be skillful means to transform suffering, and are happy to do it. That is all. They don't worry excessively about where other Sangha members are, or fret how they are not contributing. The "missing" Sangha members may be engaging their mindfulness practice with a needy loved one, with a sick friend at the hospital, or with a lonely child, utilizing the skillful means they learned from the Sangha. They are most likely consciously drawing upon the example of the Sangha even when they can't attend, and look forward to rejoining the Sangha next week.

Thây recommends patience and tolerance:

> You cannot force your insight on others. You may force them to accept your idea, but then it is simply an idea, not a real insight. Insight is not an idea. The way to share your insight is to help cause the conditions so that others can realize the same insight—through their own experience, not just hearing what you say. This takes skillfulness and patience.[14]

The practice of right speech is critical to not only building the Sangha initially but in keeping it healthy and happy as the years pass by. It is no secret that there are many dysfunctional families in the West, families whose suffering is made worse by harsh, sarcastic, disrespectful speech. Since Sanghas are made of non-Sangha elements, inappropriate speech learned in other contexts can find its way in to the way we communicate with Sangha members, and even into Dharma discussion. By remaining close to the basics of mindfulness practice, however, and remaining aware and alert to what is going on within us through the assistance of conscious breathing, we can improve the way we communicate—as speakers and as listeners. We can provide people with a second chance to become rooted in a family—this time a spiritual family.

Through the consistent practice of sitting and walking meditation, we begin to calm ourselves, look more deeply at the causes of our suffering and our happiness, and better understand our interrelationship with others. A healthy Sangha operates like a healthy family in supporting these efforts, providing encouragement at times of weakness and offering forgiveness in the wake of failure. Practice in the context of a Sangha can eventually lead to healing in a Sangha member's family. Once a practitioner can begin to understand the roots of suffering not only in himself or herself but in the parent or child, compassion blooms for perhaps the first time, and skillful means to achieve reconciliation present themselves. Thây has observed that real efforts for reconciliation must arise from the heart of compassion which naturally arises from meditating on the nature of interbeing and interpenetration of all beings.

Of course, spiritual families need to avoid falling into the dysfunctional habits sometimes found in blood families—not only inappropriate speech but autocracy, intolerance, and a tendency to shun those who do not fit a certain preconceived ideal. Rather than respond in irritation and anger, through mindfulness we have the opportunity to become aware of the suffering experienced by others, making a compassionate response possible. Sometimes we feel incapable of practicing in this way. But Thây frankly reminds us, "If you have difficulties with another person and think that she only wants to make you suffer, and that it's impossible to do anything to help her, then you are not putting the teaching into practice."[15] Recently, similar advice was offered by former u.s. Senator George Mitchell, reflecting on his years of effort to negotiate the Good Friday peace accords in Northern Ireland. "In the making of peace," he reflected with Ted Koppel, "the first thing you must do is expunge the word 'failure' from your vocabulary."

No matter how many years a Sangha has been meeting, try to view it with fresh, beginner's eyes. In fact, it is very helpful to continue viewing the Sangha through the eyes of newcomers, who often have very clear insights into the Sangha. They can see if the Sangha is a bit too grim, too hierarchical, too formal, or even too informal. Sangha-building is an art that requires us to be continually fresh and mindful. Thây states in *Touching Peace:*

> I think that Sangha-building is the most important art for us to learn. Even if we are a skilled meditator and well-versed in the sutras, if we don't know how to build a Sangha, we cannot help others. We have to build a Sangha that is happy, where communication is open. We have to take care of each person… each of us needs a Sangha. If we don't have a good Sangha yet, we should spend our time and energy building one.[16]

SANGHA PRACTICE

Sanghas include people from all walks of life, from various ethnic heritages, and different religious backgrounds. Some Sangha participants may be deeply alienated from their family's religious tradition, while others may be experiencing an uneasy feeling that their involvement in mindfulness practice means they are being disloyal to their family's roots.

Thây has observed that it is the practice of mindfulness that makes the Sangha into a real Sangha. Sometimes people are so excited when they gather together in the name of Buddhism in the West that they forget to enjoy sitting meditation, walking meditation, or other basic mindfulness practices rooted in conscious breathing. It is usually these groups of people who have the most difficulty becoming spiritual friends and functioning together for very long as a Sangha. They remain caught up in their personal notions, concepts, and opinions about what Buddhism is, rather than opting to practice and enjoy the experience. In contrast, Thây said in a recent Dharma talk, "When we come together as a Sangha, we are no longer individuals. Something happens. We become stronger, and we know better what to do, what not to do. We know the most important thing to do, or the best way to be."

Let's review some basic mindfulness practices that help transform both individuals and our communities—mindful breathing, sitting meditation, walking meditation, recitation of the Five Mindfulness Trainings (see Appendix I), and Dharma discussion.

Mindful Breathing

The practice of following our breath, sitting at ease, and inviting ourselves to smile is a radical act. The calm, ease, and release that can arise in the midst of this simple practice enables us to look deeply at the impermanence and interrelatedness of the sensations that arise in our body, our feelings, our mind, and the world around us.

Mindful breathing is the main Dharma door to the miracle of bringing the mind and the body together. After just a few conscious breaths, many people feel relief. As thoughts and emotions arise, they are not repressed. Instead, we smile at them, name them, breathe in and out through them, and watch as they arise, change, and dissipate. As described in the Chinese text of the Buddha's *Sutra on the Four Establishments of Mindfulness*, joy often arises naturally from the simple practice of following the breath without strain, just as spring water often arises from a hillside, nourishing the land below it with its cool, fresh waters.

Sitting Meditation

While nearly everyone attests to the value of sitting meditation for their physical and mental health, many people find that it is difficult to sit regularly at home, alone. Yet when we sit together as a Sangha, the same practice is so easy. Sitting for twenty-minute sessions of meditation no longer seems impossible. Suddenly, attending a Day of Mindfulness or a retreat seems effortless. This ease arises because we are supported by the presence of others.

We learn by watching other practitioners in the Sangha. For example, we learn from people who may, like us, have difficulty with the various sitting positions as they experiment with different postures. We are inspired by their ability to concentrate during meditation, and before long, we too experience a degree of calm, concentration, and insight when we meditate.

Walking Meditation

Like mindful breathing, walking meditation is a radical act. Often in our daily lives, we move awkwardly, unaware of what we are doing, compelled by nervous energy, stress, or even anger. In practicing walking meditation, ironically, we practice stopping—we walk in peace, supported by our breathing and the Earth beneath our feet. In doing so, we are able to transform that very same nervousness, stress, and anger into calm, peace, and insight.

Walking meditation, like sitting meditation, is recommended by the Buddha in the *Sutra on the Full Awareness of Breathing*[17] and the *Sutra on the Four Establishments of Mindfulness.* It is a wonderful opportunity to practice mindfulness and conscious breathing while we move. Enjoying a fresh breath with each step, we massage the Earth with our feet, uniting body and mind.

Many people find that it is difficult to come home and practice sitting meditation after a busy day at work. Sometimes, our lives seem so confined that we don't feel like sitting. Even if we were to come home from a long day "cooped up" at our desk or workstation to find the Buddha relaxing in our living room, inviting us to join him in formal sitting meditation, we might feel so restless that we'd say, "No thanks." These are the times when we may prefer to practice either indoor or outdoor walking meditation. Once we have enjoyed walking meditation, we may be able to sit with ease a bit later.

It may be difficult, however, to integrate this beautiful practice into our lives. We read about it, but we don't take the time to enjoy it. Many Sanghas organize Days of Mindfulness and retreats in the countryside, near parks, or along riverbanks. This is an easy way to include the sun, the flowers and trees, the birds, and scenic paths in Sangha gatherings. If a shaft of sunlight, a flowering bush, or a bird song requests our attention, we can stop, breathe in and out, and offer it our full, loving presence. Sangha practice is an invaluable support, providing us with a regular opportunity to come into contact with the joy, wisdom, and sanity of the simple practice of conscious breathing while walking.

Recitation of the Five Mindfulness Trainings

In his poetic biography of the Buddha entitled *Old Path White Clouds*,[18] Thich Nhat Hanh describes how the Buddha and his monastic Sangha were once invited by a lay merchant to share a meal at the merchant's home. The layman was very impressed by the mindful, graceful way in which the monastics enjoyed their meal. He inquired how a layperson, who has responsibilities to family and co-workers, could nonetheless lead a spiritual life. In response, the Buddha articulated what were initially referred to as the Five Precepts —not to kill, not to take what is not given, not to engage in sexual misconduct, not to lie, and to abstain from alcohol and other intoxicants that cloud the mind. With the intention to make the precepts more accessible to contemporary laypeople and noting that the Pali word for "precept" also means "training," Thich Nhat Hanh now refers to the traditional Five Precepts as the Five Mindfulness Trainings. He has also expanded them to make them relevant to contemporary lay practitioners.

Local Sanghas include group recitation of the Five Mindfulness Trainings in their regularly scheduled gatherings. It is beautiful and inspiring to hear these teachings, especially in the context of a group with a shared aspiration to deepen their practice and integrate the trainings into daily life. Intellectually, it is not difficult to understand the Five Mindfulness Trainings. It can be more challenging, however, to integrate them into our daily behavior. The practice of meditation and the practice of the Five Mindfulness Trainings support each other. After sharing an hour of sitting and walking meditation, the calm and insight that we experience in meditation help us to look deeply into the heart of each training. Members enrich their understanding of the trainings through small group discussions about how the trainings can be integrated into everyday life. When we embody our practice and the trainings in our lives, our practice becomes engaged practice—mindfulness in direct contact with the challenges we face in our lives.

Dharma Discussion

Sangha gatherings often conclude with a group Dharma discussion. After enjoying sitting and walking meditation together, it is pleasant to share our insights about mindfulness practice, which can focus on right speech, deep listening, habit energies, etc., and how they affect our daily lives in our family practice and in the workplace. Dharma discussions draw upon the wisdom contained in the discourses, the Five Mindfulness Trainings, Thây's many books, as well as the life experiences of Sangha members.

Dharma discussion is a way to share Sangha wisdom and experience. We bring our insights and questions to one another without pride or pretense, inspired by a desire to offer each other support. We speak from direct experience so as not to mislead fellow practitioners. Without becoming too academic or technical, we will likely find that we have practical insights to offer that are indeed helpful to others, and that others have experiences that inspire and assist us as well.

So Many Choices!

There are times when we wish that the Sangha could be all things to all people. Some would like it to be bigger, to be more inspirational. Others would like it to be smaller, to make it more intimate. Some would like its meditation periods to be longer and more "intense" in order to deepen their practice. Others would like the Sangha gatherings to be more informal and less silent so they can spend more time talking and laughing together.

If we are in a rush to make decisions about our Sangha, we may end up with intellectually contrived solutions. If we remain close to the basics of mindfulness practice and respectful of one another, a consensus will emerge. Thây has referred to this as the art of combining ideas in order to make everyone happy. If we practice wholeheartedly, it is surprising how often we see that ideas can complement and complete each other.

Of course, this type of synthesis requires that everyone let go a bit of their own preference about what the Sangha should be doing and which mindfulness practices work best. In the Buddhist tradition, preconceived ideas and strongly held notions and concepts are referred to as "fetters." The irony about fetters is that our resistance or allergic reaction toward a mindfulness practice that does not appeal to us today may, in the not too distant future, prove to be very helpful later in life, because, after all, our circumstances change and we change, too. One Sangha member suggested that we remain open-minded by utilizing a whimsical device akin to airport metal detectors. The invention, called a "fetter detector," would be conveniently placed at the entrance and people would be invited to leave their prejudices, preconceptions, fetters, and mental formations[19] at the door. If they nonetheless forget or leave one in their pocket, the fetter detector will go off. And the Sangha will not provide bowls for passing fetters beyond this point along with car keys, belt buckles, loose change, etc.! After engaging in sitting and walking meditation, of course, it is likely that the fetters won't be reclaimed by their original owners. Thây similarly suggests that every person in a Sangha needs to ask herself, "Am I caught in my harmful desires? Am I caught in my own patterns of behavior?"[20]

In short, it is advantageous to come to the Sangha with an open mind and heart. There is no need to come rehearsed, with a prerecorded message in your mind. Come to listen to one another and to help. Mindfulness practices are intended as *upaya*, skillful means. They are not ends in themselves. It is good to learn about as many upaya as possible. Someday we, or a friend, may need them.

Another way to achieve artful synthesis in a Sangha is to take turns facilitating Dharma discussions on topics of interest to Sangha members. If a Sangha member is serving as a caretaker to a friend or family member who is ill, for example, you might suggest that some day he or she lead a session on incorporating mindfulness practice into caregiving. People may be too shy or say they are too busy at first, but weeks or months later they may volunteer. Similarly, Sangha members who have suffered illnesses may offer powerful insights on how the Five Remembrances (see Appendix II) helped them transform suffering by placing it in perspective. These topics can be announced in advance in your local Sangha's newsletter.

Another beautiful, organic way that Sanghas achieve creative synthesis is by serving as the hub of an ever-growing set of concentric circles of friendships formed by those who have met each other through the Sangha. Those who are having difficulty with their families or loneliness have a way of finding each other, and through these friendships they are able to gain insights and transcend suffering. Those who are facing challenges with parenting, work, or illness tend to find each other in the same way. Even though needs, interests, and preferences differ, people are able to receive sustenance and support from each other on a regular basis and in turn contribute insights about what they have learned.

WEEKLY SANGHA FORMAT

Sangha gatherings should be structured so there is time for sharing insights with one another and getting to know each other better. Each Sangha can experiment with a schedule that meets its own needs. Many Sanghas find it possible to meet every week or every other week with a schedule that is more or less along the following lines:

1) An hour of sitting and walking meditation in three twenty-minute sessions consisting of sitting meditation, walking meditation, and a final round of sitting meditation;
2) Recitation of the Five Mindfulness Trainings, a short discourse, or a passage from one of Thây's books (this is sometimes preceded by a silent period of stretching);
3) Short social period and bathroom break;
4) Dharma discussion.

It is important not to underestimate how much our simple presence at regularly scheduled sessions of sitting and walking meditation and Dharma discussion contributes to the happiness of others. You may not be aware of it, but there will be many times when your very presence — merely the way you are, the way you smile, the way you move — is a source of strength to other practitioners. Similarly, the mindfulness of other practitioners will be a source of strength for you when you feel weak.

Through the calm and insight that arise from our meditation practice, we will be able to practice deep listening and right speech. With our practice of conscious breathing, we mindfully observe our mental formations arise and disappear. As a result, we gradually become responsive to those around us, rather than reactive. We begin to see and understand the needs of other people, and how they, like us, aspire to be well, to be safe, and to be happy.

OTHER SANGHA PRACTICES

The "Threefold Training" in Buddhism is the development of concentration (samadhi), insight (prajña), and morality *(sila)*.[21] These three interact, inform, nourish, and support one another. A local Sangha offers core elements of the Threefold Training when it includes regularly scheduled sitting meditation, walking meditation, Dharma discussions, and recitation of the Five Mindfulness Trainings and discourses.

There are other practices that can keep our Sangha vibrant. These include:

Tea Ceremony (see Appendix III). After enjoying tea and a treat (cookies or fruit) together in mindful silence, we then share our insights, songs, and poetry with each other. Through our practice of mindful breathing, we open to even deeper enjoyment of the sheer presence of one another. Drinking and eating mindfully, we come into deeper contact with the fragrance of our tea, and we taste our treat with the joy we experienced as children.

Guided Meditations. Using suggestions from Thây's book *The Blooming of a Lotus*,[22] we offer each other guided meditation practices to deepen our concentration and understanding.

Gathas. To practice mindfulness in our daily activities, we focus our mind on a gatha, or short poem, to deepen our experience of the simple acts we often take for granted. Thây's book of short verses, *Present Moment Wonderful Moment*,[23] is a source of inspiration for our daily practice. We can also create our own gathas.

Songs and Mindful Movements. Singing, chanting, and enjoying mindfulness movements together are other forms of mindfulness practice. We can learn melodies from the *Plum Village Chanting and Recitation Book*[24] and mindful movements from the *Mindful Movements* video.[25]

Flower-Watering and Second Body Practice (see Appendix III). Flower-watering is an especially beautiful form of right speech. We often hear what is wrong about how we do things. The practice of flower-watering involves looking carefully and deeply into a spiritual friend and offering an accurate reminder to him or her of what is beautiful and nourishing inside. Flower-watering can change lives and transform despair into hope and spiritual resolve. It can empower our spiritual friend to begin anew in simple but powerful, effective, and healthy ways, employing the basics of mindfulness practice on a consistent basis.

Flower-watering can be incorporated into what is referred to as "Second Body Practice," where members of a Sangha agree from time to time to look after one another. In the *Sutra on the Four Establishments of Mindfulness,* the Buddha taught us how to practice insight meditation into what is taking place in our body, our feelings, our minds, and the world around us, without repressing the experience, on the one hand, or fabricating or adding anything to it, on the other —bare attention, just seeing. In Second Body Practice we use the calm and equanimity provided by the practice of conscious breathing to look at another Sangha member so deeply it is as if they become our second body. We can look deeply and see the causes and conditions for what may be going wrong, then offer insights and suggest Dharma practices that enable them to see things differently and transform destructive habit energies. We can also look deeply into and listen carefully to their deepest aspirations and compliment them through the practice of flower-watering when their conduct is consistent with their deepest spiritual desire.

Days of Mindfulness and Retreats. Local Sanghas host Days of Mindfulness and overnight retreats to provide additional time for members to integrate mindfulness practices into their lives. These are also opportunities to mindfully experiment with new practices. The Buddha said that there are 84,000 Dharma doors, and Thây has observed that our task is to invent new Dharma doors that address contemporary needs.

If you are uncertain how to organize a Day of Mindfulness or a weekend overnight retreat, feel free to ask for help from someone who has organized such events in Thây's tradition. Lay and monastic Dharma teachers in the tradition of Thich Nhat Hanh are available to lead retreats, give Dharma talks, and transmit to practitioners the Five Mindfulness Trainings and the Three Refuges (taking refuge in the Buddha, the Dharma, and the Sangha).

DIFFERENT FORMS OF SANGHA

In the Tradition of Thich Nhat Hanh

Several forms of Sangha have been established in the tradition of Thich Nhat Hanh. A monastic community of over one hundred monks and nuns resides at Plum Village, a training center in southwestern France, at the Green Mountain Dharma Center and Maple Forest Monastery in Vermont, and at the newly formed Deer Park Monastery near San Diego, California.

During the last fifteen years, lay practitioners in over twenty-three countries have established nonresidential Sanghas which meet together weekly or monthly to share sitting and walking meditation, Dharma discussion, discourse study, and recitation of the Five Mindfulness Trainings. In addition, there are rural residential centers and smaller residential communities of five or six people who live and practice together.

In 1966, Thich Nhat Hanh and a small number of laymen and laywomen formed the Order of Interbeing, which is a kind of bridge between lay and monastic practice, with many monastics ordaining as members of the Order as well. Order members make a public commitment to live their lives inspired by the guidance of the Fourteen Mindfulness Trainings (see Appendix I), which were derived from the efforts of both laypeople and

monastics to practice engaged Buddhism during the suffering and confusion
of the Vietnam War. Order members recite these trainings together on a regular basis so that they do not lose their guidance as a source of inspiration.
They also agree, no matter how busy they are helping others, to observe at
least sixty Days of Mindfulness and retreat each year so that they can continue to have enough calm and insight to offer others. Where Order of
Interbeing members live in geographical proximity, they have sometimes
gathered, along with aspirants, at retreats and Days of Mindfulness to
deepen their practice.

In several parts of the country, local Sanghas have gradually developed
regional networks based on genuine friendship and caring. For the past
decade, they have hosted regional Days of Mindfulness and retreats attract-
ing practitioners from various cities and states. Over time, a network of
kalyanamitra—good friends in the Dharma—has developed organically to
nourish the teachings on a sustained basis over wider and wider geographical areas. The article "The Ever-Expanding Nature of Sangha Practice" by
David Lawrence (see Part Four) describes how regional practice has grown
in a surprisingly natural, continuous manner among Midwestern Sangha
members in Illinois, Wisconsin, Indiana, Michigan, Minnesota, Ohio,
Kansas, Iowa, and Kentucky over the past ten years, leading to growing networks of friendships over considerable geographic distances.

Nonsectarian Sangha Practice

If we live in a rural area, we may feel that no one nearby is interested in
mindfulness practices. Even in a city, we may not know anyone to invite to
practice with us utilizing Buddhist forms. Or we may feel that people in our
part of the country are so devoted to a certain form of religion that no one
would be comfortable experimenting with meditation-based forms of religious practice. In *The Path of Emancipation*, Thây invites us to be creative in the
art of Sangha-building should we find ourselves in such circumstances:

> I think it is possible to build a Sangha wherever you are. People
> everywhere need stability, calm, and mindfulness. The obstacle may
> be that we want to use Buddhist terms....

Listen to people deeply, using loving speech. Then you will make friends.... I think that if you learn to use this kind of language, you'll soon be able to build a Sangha.... I know that you can do it. All of us can build Sanghas wherever we are.[26]

We may want to start a Mindfulness Practice Group, five or six people practicing in the tradition of Thich Nhat Hanh, without using Buddhist-specific language or Buddha statues. If we are successful, the group may later decide to establish a Mindfulness Practice Center. These sometimes take the form of storefront, "walk-in" facilities or facilities in existing churches. They are available to the general public and provide a place where people can come to receive nonsectarian instruction in conscious breathing, sitting meditation, walking meditation, relaxation exercises, deep listening, and mindful speech. As a resource, we can contact others who have established these centers or use *The Mindfulness Practice Center Guidebook*[27] developed by the Mindfulness Practice Association, whose office is in Vermont.

Family Practice

Of great benefit to ourselves and our society is our family and workplace practice. In our family, our primary practice consists of embodying mindfulness, understanding, and compassion in our interactions with family members. In addition, we can set aside a time for mindful eating, walking in the park, or for discussing the Five Mindfulness Trainings.

Some people set aside a corner of a room, if not a whole room, as a "mindful breathing corner," and invite children to join them when they do sitting meditation. Children can be encouraged to invite the mindfulness bell from time to time to remind adults to stop and enjoy their breathing. Your family can also host a Tea Ceremony with friends, sharing songs, poems, and new insights. Thich Nhat Hanh instructs children in meditation by inviting them to collect ten pebbles, which they move from one little pile to the other as they follow each breath. He has also set a number of gathas to music, enabling children to memorize the verses in an easy, enjoyable manner. For example, both children and adults learn to follow each breath while silently concentrating on one of the following lines:

In, out
Flower, fresh
Mountain, solid
Water, reflecting
Space, free[28]

These periods of meditation for children should be appropriately short
— say, five, ten, or fifteen minutes. Offer them in the company of adults to
demonstrate support. Children also respond quite well to the experience of
walking meditation, enjoying its grace and ease.

In addition to enjoying meditation, family retreats with Thich Nhat
Hanh and local Sanghas offer children art projects, games, and an opportunity to perform skits. Children absorb the essence of mindfulness practice more readily than many adults would ever expect. Adult hubris might
lead one to think that children don't absorb much of what's being offered.
This conclusion proves wrong when the children perform their skits. One
skit, performed by the children at a Chicago retreat, was entitled "Buddha
Meets the Jetsons." In it, the children fantasized about what would happen if the Buddha were mysteriously transported to the thirty-second century and described how his mindfulness practices might address the
helter-skelter nature of life in an incredibly fast-paced future. Children
observe the dispersed, stressed-out, and frantic activity of their parents
very carefully and understand completely how mindfulness practices seek
to transform it.

Workplace Practice

We can begin creating a "workplace Sangha" by practicing love and understanding with co-workers — seeing each person as a beloved brother or sister. We can embody the mindfulness practice in our relationship with them
by practicing flower-watering in our daily interactions. We can practice
walking meditation every time we move through a corridor.

If possible, we can sit, walk, or eat mindfully together with one other person during our breaks. Some people put a screen saver on their computer to
remind them to stop and return to their breathing. Others have introduced

the bell of mindfulness and telephone meditation practices into their work-places, and have even found a way to set aside time during staff meetings.

SUSTAINING SANGHA PRACTICE

In our nonresidential and residential lay Sanghas, questions will arise about forms, such as whether or not to have a Buddha statue, the length of sit-ting time, the style of Dharma discussion facilitation, or which chants to use. Practical questions concerning the Sangha's location, finances, and lead-ership will also arise.

As we practice with a Sangha, at some point we may feel dissatisfaction, disappointment, or discouragement. We may feel that the only worthwhile Sanghas are hundreds or thousands of miles away, and that no local Sangha practice is perfect enough to be worthwhile. What should we do if we feel that, while we have a local Sangha, it is far from perfect? Thây offers this insight in *Touching Peace:*

> The principle is to organize in a way that is most enjoyable for every-one. You will never find a perfect Sangha. An imperfect Sangha is good enough. Rather than complain too much about your Sangha, do your best to transform yourself into a good element of the Sangha. Accept the Sangha and build on it.[29]

This is excellent advice. If we practice it, we will not only enhance our mindfulness practice immensely by opening ourselves up to the wisdom and experience of the Sangha, but we will also save the Sangha the unnec-essary pain and difficulty that can occur if we speak out of anger, jealousy, pride, or misperception.

Thây often says that when he is experiencing difficulty, he returns to the basics of mindfulness by practicing conscious breathing. When we are expe-riencing unease or difficulty with the Sangha, we should return to the basics of practice in the same way as our teacher. Once we achieve some calm and stability, we can ask, "Am I sure?" about our perceptions of the Sangha and the motivations of its members. Are we sure that we are being slighted or rebuffed? Or are we misperceiving what is actually happening due to our past experience in other groups, or due to our ambition to be recognized as a seasoned practitioner of meditation? We can ask, "What am I doing?" when we attempt to cause ripples in the Sangha for reasons we ourselves may feel hard to explain. We can look deeply into the causes and conditions of this kind of behavior when we engage in it and ask, "Hello, habit energy! What are you tempting me to do today?" And finally we might employ our capacity of understanding and love to ask, "How can I contribute constructively to the Sangha in a way that utilizes my degree of understanding and compassion and helps others in concrete ways?"

What else might we do to be a good member of a healthy Sangha? We might first be sure to be a good friend to others. Many people today try to practice Buddhism all by themselves in the company of only books and tapes. Yet they are often willing to let go of this anonymity because they are ready for friendship. Exposure to books is much like relying solely on handwritten roadway instructions in unfamiliar territory. One can read the street and highway names given in the instructions, yet they lack a certain reality. When we're actually in our car traveling at thirty, forty, or fifty miles per hour, the reality seen through our windshield looks nothing like what was described or what we had envisioned. At the first discrepancy between the written instructions and the actual terrain, we panic. Oftentimes, we lose faith in the written instructions altogether even though they might have been correct had we been more observant on the road.

So, what do we need besides written instructions? Most of us need information from someone with experience. We prefer to pull into a gas station and talk with someone who's been on the same road before. We want to hear how they describe the twists and turns in the road to observe their body language and expressions as they indicate how we, too, can find the way. We want them to impart not only knowledge but confidence. Above all, we want the ability to slow down the pace of instruction to match our ability to absorb it so that we may ask questions. It is much the same with books about the Dharma, and mindfulness practice. In the same way, we can, when asked, offer instruction to others based on our actual experience.

The compassion and caring extended by good spiritual friends leads to a kind of familial warmth in the Sangha that may have been missing in a practitioner's family. As Thây has pointed out, Sanghas can provide us with a "second chance" to become rooted in a family—this time a spiritual family. Those who learn to practice wholeheartedly with a Sangha often begin to mend suffering in their family at its roots by coming into contact with estranged parents, siblings, and children, and by seeking reconciliation.

Of course, there may be times when mindfulness practices seem unable to address the needs of certain people. If you begin to notice signs of severe depression or psychosis in a Sangha participant, it is important to determine if your friend is receiving adequate psychiatric or medical help and, if necessary, suggest that he or she find the appropriate professional assistance. It can be helpful to know who among your Sangha is formally trained in medicine, psychotherapy, or psychiatry to assist you in these efforts.

Healthy families and healthy Sanghas have a tolerant atmosphere that allows people room to breathe and to grow. This happens naturally if we follow Thây's advice to stay close to the basics of practice ourselves and not worry so much if others are practicing mindfulness wholeheartedly or not. If the leadership of the Sangha starts to think a little too highly of itself and becomes judgmental or critical about other members of the Sangha, any teaching offered by its senior members will seem less than authentic. Real leadership in a Sangha is not a function of who has gone to the most retreats with famous teachers, who has become a member of the Order of Interbeing, who is facilitating the most Dharma discussions, how often someone serves as the bell minder, or how well someone can recite the teachings from memory. It has more to do with who has integrated the teachings to the point where they quietly serve as exemplars of the teachings themselves. Sangha members don't often remember everything you say, but they remember how you are. So if we aspire to build a healthy Sangha, a Sangha as warm and inviting as a loving family, we don't have to draft outlines of Thây's books or memorize the sutras; we need to use more than words. We can trust that our friends will see the value of the practice, not through what we say, but through our way of being.

Where this is the emphasis, the atmosphere is light and free of dogmatism and "preachiness." We sense that the Sangha is a place where we are

invited to give rise to the teacher within us and to become the best person
we can be without being assessed or judged by others.

When we practice mindfulness wholeheartedly, we begin to notice our
own foibles and inconsistencies, leading not only to insight but also to a
healthy sense of humor! In Buddhism, bodhisattvas are known as living
beings who strive to simultaneously cultivate wisdom and compassion for
the benefit of all beings. While this isn't always easy, bodhisattvas are said
to "ride above the waves of birth and death." What prevents these "surfers"
from being tossed into the waves is the joy, equanimity, and lightness of
being that comes as a fruit of their practice. In the Zen tradition, a sense
of humor is among the attributes of many bodhisattvas. They seem to float;
they are light and free. The bodhisattva known popularly as Hotei, a kind
of combination between St. Francis and Santa Claus, offers toys and gifts
to children from his big bag, in which he sleeps at night. In the famous Ten
Oxherding Pictures of the Zen tradition, the spiritual seeker spends most
of the ten frames seriously pursuing his true nature. For frame after frame,
the lost ox representing the True Self eludes the seeker as he hunts through
the dense forest. In a blank frame symbolizing enlightenment, the seeker
realizes his True Self. Yet, the story of the Ten Oxherding Pictures does not
end with the enlightenment frame, for there is an additional drawing showing the seeker smiling and entering the dust and din of the marketplace with
helping hands. We can approach our Sangha, and our daily life, in the same
engaged, yet enlightened and joyous, spirit. It's really the light touch and
attentive caring that keeps a Sangha going.

Those who devote time and energy to organizing the Sangha should
not allow the task of Sangha-building to overwhelm them. If we do, we
might be destroying the Sangha in an effort to create it. Thây describes the
process with these friendly words of caution:

> After a period of practice, if you have some attainment and peace,
> you may wish to share them with others and establish a small prac-
> tice community. But this should always be done in the spirit of form-
> lessness. Do not be bound by the practice center you establish. "To
> create a serene and beautiful Buddha field is not in fact creating a

serene and beautiful Buddha field" [quoting the *Diamond Sutra*] means to do so in the spirit of formlessness. Do not let yourself be devoured by your Buddha field or you will suffer. Do not allow yourself to be burnt out in the process of setting up a practice center.[30]

This is very sound advice, especially for newcomers to mindfulness practice. One fruit of practicing sitting and walking meditation consistently over a period of years is that one's energy, patience, and stamina become greater and more continuous. Helping to organize events for even the most lovely people can sometimes be a bit frustrating. So we need to gauge ourselves. Don't rush into a leadership position or be pushed into one if you're not prepared for it. Remember that responsibilities can be shared. And, at the same time, be aware of the gifts that you bring to the Sangha and be as generous as you can in providing them in a mindful way.

At first, not everyone experiences the concentration and stamina which can arise from the practice of meditation. One reason is that many of us have difficulty achieving a degree of consistency in practicing sitting meditation, walking meditation, and conscious breathing in daily life. Family matters, job pressures, and illness have a way of setting in, disrupting this consistency. It is, without question, very helpful to practice regularly with a Sangha to obtain encouragement and support. Once a certain consistency is reached, our practice can bloom. And do not forget that by simply attending the Sangha gatherings, we are in turn supporting others. Your presence is essential to the Sangha. Please do not deprive your friends of an important Dharma resource. Thây puts it this way:

> It is a joy to find ourselves in the midst of a Sangha where people are practicing well together. Each person's way of walking, eating, and smiling can be a real help to us. She is walking for me, I am smiling for her, and we do it as a Sangha. By practicing together like this, we can expect a real transformation within us. We don't have to practice intensely or force ourselves. We just have to allow ourselves to be in a good Sangha where people are happy, living deeply in each moment, and transformation will come without much effort.[31]

SANGHA PRACTICE AS ENGAGED PRACTICE

Our society sends us a lot of messages, most of which invite us to consume more goods and to live fast-paced lives in the pursuit of pleasure. We all have experienced at one time or another how these pursuits—the constant search for self-gratification—leave us feeling depleted and exhausted. In this hurried state, we overlook the presence and needs of others and deprive ourselves of the happiness of being in the presence of a loved one.

Mindfulness practice invites us to experiment with shamatha, stopping. What are we stopping? We are stopping our constant search for self-gratification and choosing to dwell in the present moment. Simple practices like sitting meditation and walking meditation invite us to reclaim our birthright as human beings capable of being aware and alert. When we join together as a Sangha, we agree to share shamatha practices, notwithstanding the contrary messages being sent with such skill and persuasion in the marketplace. Thây says it this way in *Touching Peace:*

> A Sangha is a community of resistance, resisting the speed, violence, and unwholesome ways of living that are prevalent in our society. Mindfulness is to protect ourselves and others. A good Sangha can lead us in the direction of harmony and awareness. The substance of the practice is most important. The forms can be adapted.[32]

Viewed in this way, local Sanghas are genuinely engaged agents of change in our contemporary world. Our practice of mindfulness, in conjunction with our recitation and study of the Five Mindfulness Trainings, equips us to offer fresh insights on how our society can live free of greed, anger, and delusion. When we look deeply at the suffering in ourselves and our society, we may sometimes despair. Where and how can we start to be of service? In many places, mindfulness practice in local Sanghas has manifested as "mindfulness in society" in the following ways:

   1) Hosting sitting and walking meditation, Dharma discussions, and Days of Mindfulness in prisons;

2) Sponsoring Mindfulness Practice Centers, which offer a nonsectarian approach to mindfulness practice;

3) Participating in efforts to promote peace, disarmament, environmental remediation, and healing where needed most. These efforts have included Vietnam veterans' programs and retreats; protests of forest clear-cutting, the death penalty, and violence on children's television programs; animal rights and welfare activities; peace vigils during times of war; and sponsoring interfaith gatherings among various ethnic and religious groups to address the causes of international tension;

4) Assisting in flood, famine, and war relief efforts for the benefit of refugees;

5) Organizing the Sangha to visit the sick and others in need, as well as to sustain their primary caregivers;

6) Organizing programs to assist both professional and lay health-care providers in better addressing the challenges that arise in nurturing those who are ill and dying; and

7) Participating in projects to end hunger and malnutrition, raising money for local charitable efforts, and volunteering in hospitals, hospices, schools, and homes for the elderly.

Many of these activities include close cooperation with other nonprofit groups and joint efforts under the name of "umbrella" organizations.

As indicated above, Sanghas do more than sit. They rise. Members of the Sangha engage the world in many ways. They rise and go to and from the marketplace, both as laypeople and as monastics. When they are in the marketplace, they continue to practice mindfulness, and when surprises or difficulties arise, they respond in a manner appropriate to the circumstances, rather than reacting in anger or panic. Verses in the *Plum Village Chanting Book*[33] describe quite beautifully our aspiration to live this way:

I am aware that the Three Gems are within my heart.
I vow to realize them.
I vow to practice mindful breathing and smiling,

looking deeply into things.
I vow to understand living beings and their suffering,
to cultivate compassion and loving kindness,
and to practice joy and equanimity.
I vow to offer to joy to one person in the morning
and to help relieve the grief of one person in the afternoon.
I vow to live simply and sanely, content with just few possessions,
and to keep my body healthy.
I vow to let go of all worries and anxiety,
in order to be light and free.

Naysayers may assert that meditation and religious study groups make their participants narcissistic and incapable of contributing to the larger society. This is not the case. Small Sanghas can help restore a person who has been broken by the callousness of the larger society or who has been set adrift. In fact, psychiatrists and psychotherapists sometimes suggest their patients join Sanghas in order to experience more joy and sense of belonging. Learning how to bring body, mind, and breath into harmony in the company of supportive friends can be the first step to empowering a person to find his or her way back into society and become functional again. As the years go by, mindfulness practitioners can successfully transform habit energies that have hindered members of their families through the generations. You can often see this transformation in their physical appearance: their frown lines disappear and become smiles, and their foreheads are no longer knit and furrowed.

Extensive sociological research of small religious groups has been conducted by Professor Robert Wuthnow of Princeton University, author of *Sharing the Journey: Support Groups and America's New Quest for Community*.[34] This research has shown that small religious study groups generate a substantial amount of caring that extends beyond the boundaries of the group, that they have a generally positive effect on involvement in community activities, that they inspire people to become involved in helping friends and neighbors who are not members of their religious group, and that they encourage active involvement in voluntary agencies. Professor Wuthnow says,

"Probably the most important way in which small groups influence the wider community is by freeing individuals from their own insecurities so that they can reach out more charitably toward other people."[35]

Sanghas play an additional important yet often unrecognized role in social support and social change. Many Sanghas are comprised of individuals whose professional, day-to-day lives are already devoted to social service: social workers, psychotherapists, doctors, nurses, pro-bono attorneys, environmentalists, teachers, physical therapists, etc. A major problem they face is burnout. These individuals can and do turn to the Sangha for refuge so that they can continue to serve the larger community.

Thây tells an interesting story about this in his book of conversations with Daniel Berrigan, entitled *The Raft Is Not the Shore*. The story has different messages and levels, but one aspect addresses the role of the Sangha in times of social distress. The story is about an event in Thây's monastery during the colonial war with the French in Vietnam:

> I remember quite well what he [Thây's teacher] said when I was a novice. It was a long time ago, during the French occupation. We had rice for the monks, and we had to bury the rice in order to preserve it because the French soldiers came and stole it from us. We put it in big containers and buried them in the yard. One day he and a few of us novices went out to the yard to unearth one can of rice for dinner. The master was old, but he still followed our tradition that every monk works: "No work, no food." He said to us while we worked, "I'm so tired. Let's wait until after I die." We Vietnamese say, "Well, just wait until I'm dead, I won't be tired anymore." He was joking with us; all of us were sweating because of the hard work. I thought it was only a joke, but half a minute later he said to us, "Who will be the person after I am dead? Who will be the one who will not be tired?"
>
> I was struck by that and took it as a theme of meditation.[36]

The master's question may not be a question about successorship or lineage. The "one who will not tire" may not be a particular mindfulness practitioner but rather the collective Sangha. Thây often suggests that the next Buddha may be a Sangha. We all experience exhaustion and fatigue, both physical and mental, from time to time. However, in the company of a healthy Sangha, we have access to an incredible source of energy. There will always be someone who is strong when you are tired, or calm when you are near panic. In turn, you can be strong for others when they are weary or overwhelmed. In a carefully built Sangha, there will indeed always be someone who is not tired, whose practice and stability protect us from excessive weariness or zeal, who keeps us on the Middle Way, the Wonderful Path of Practice.

PART THREE

Practicing in Community

~

Here Is the Pure Land—the Pure Land Is Here 4

BY SISTER ANNABEL LAITY

ONE DAY, Queen Vaidehi asked the Buddha, "Is the place with no suffering very far away?" The Buddha replied, "No, it is not far away." And then the Buddha taught the queen how to touch the land of Great Happiness in her own heart and in her own mind.

We talk about the "Pure Land." In Sanskrit, the word is *Sukhavati. Sukha* means happiness; *vati* means having: The Place Which Has Happiness. In the Chinese tradition, it is translated as the Pure Land, perhaps because of the nature of the writings about that place. These writings put us in touch with things we call pure. The *Prajñaparamita* writings were probably composed about the same time as the *Pure Land* writings, and they say, "No defiled, no immaculate." And yet we talk about the Pure Land in Buddhism.

In the Pure Land, there are many kinds of wonderful birds. Let us think about a bird. The bird's song sounds very pure, very beautiful. But we know the bird has to eat, and the food that the bird eats becomes waste matter, which we would consider impure. The sutra doesn't tell us whether birds in the Pure Land eat or not. But if they do, there must be bird droppings in the Pure Land, which means that the Pure Land wouldn't be quite so pure. Perhaps that is why the people who composed the *Heart of the Prajñaparamita* say, "No defiled, no immaculate." We know that if there isn't defiled, there can't be immaculate.[37]

To understand the teachings of the Pure Land, we need to understand Buddhist psychology. We need to understand that the store consciousness contains all the seeds—seeds of purity and impurity, seeds of happiness and suffering. We need to learn skillful ways of touching the seeds of happiness and purity in us, particularly when we feel overwhelmed by impurity and suffering. The Buddha and other spiritual ancestral teachers have helped us find ways to touch the seeds of purity.

The Buddha gave teachings about places where there was a lot of happiness. He sometimes pointed to a city like Kushinagara, where he later passed away, and said that in former times it was a place of great happiness. He described how the people lived there in a lot of happiness. Probably some ancestral teacher put together the *Sukhavati Sutras* based on some of the things the Buddha had said about lands of great happiness.

The *Sukhavati Sutras* and the *Avatamsaka Sutra* may seem very strange when we read them for the first time. There are descriptions of trees that have jewels for their leaves, flowers, and fruit, and descriptions of water with eight virtuous qualities — clarity, sweetness, purity, coolness, limpidity, etc. These descriptions are not for us to consider intellectually. We do not read the *Pure Land Sutras* or the *Avatamsaka Sutra* with an intellectual mind. When we read them, the descriptions touch the seeds of purity in us. For instance, we do not see leaves of jewels on the trees here. In autumn, the leaves here fall to the earth, decompose, and become one with the Earth again, whereas a jewel doesn't decompose. Actually, if we look deeply into it, a jewel comes from decomposed material, because the mineral realms are also made up of the plant realms. When we walk among the trees in the autumn on this planet Earth, we see the beautiful red and yellow colors like jewels shining in the sunlight. Sometimes, though, we don't bring our mind to the presence of the trees because we are lost in our worries or regrets. When we have been reading the *Pure Land Sutras* on a regular basis, then something in the depth of our consciousness knows that a tree is very precious, as precious as the most precious jewels. So whenever we meet a tree in mindfulness, we remember that it is precious, and we can be there with it in the present moment. When we are really there in the present moment, we are already in the Pure Land.

There are different levels of belief in the Pure Land, and the highest level of Pure Land teaching is that your mind is the Pure Land — the Pure Land is available in your mind. The ancestral teachers put together the *Pure Land Sutras* with a kind of wisdom that helps us be in touch with and have the deep aspiration to be in a Pure Land, and to help build a Pure Land.

In Plum Village, we often have to write assignments for Thây. One year, Thây gave us the assignment to write about the Pure Land that we wanted to be part of. He told us to give a very clear description. What kind of trees would be there? What kind of activities would there be? Everybody wrote about a slightly different Pure Land, so we know that there are hundreds of thousands of Pure Lands. In each of our minds, there is the Pure Land, and we can go about establishing the Pure Land. You may like to write about this also. It's a very enjoyable assignment.

When we think about our own Pure Land, we have to come back to Queen Vaidehi's question: "Lord Buddha, is there a place where there is no suffering?" Out of compassion, the Buddha said, "Yes, there is." Queen Vaidehi's heartfelt aspiration to be in that place of no suffering came about because she had suffered so much. If she hadn't suffered, the idea of a place where there is no suffering would never have occurred to her. So suffering and no-suffering go together in the same way defiled and immaculate go together. They are not absolute realities; they are only relative realities. Sometimes the Buddha has to teach the relative truth in order to be compassionate, to help, and to encourage; that is why the Buddha said there is a place where there is no suffering.

We know that Queen Vaidehi would also want to help others who are suffering. In the Pure Land, we have many such bodhisattvas. The great joy of being in the Pure Land is to be near many bodhisattvas. Of course, if a bodhisattva wants to help those who are suffering, there must be people who are suffering. Therefore, in the Pure Land, there are suffering people for us to help. When we wrote about our Pure Land, many of us described how the bodhisattvas helped others. One person even had a hospital in the Pure Land.

When you come to a Dharma talk, you feel very happy. Maybe you feel you are happiest when you are sitting and listening to the Dharma, because the Dharma is deep and lovely. It is beautiful in the beginning, beautiful in the middle, and beautiful at the end. In the *Sukhavati Sutra*, they say that in the Pure Land, you are always hearing teaching of the Dharma. You don't just hear teachings from the Buddha Amitabha, the Buddha of Limitless

Light, the Buddha who founded the Pure Land. You hear the birds giving teachings, you hear the trees giving teachings. Every time the wind rustles in the trees, that is a teaching of the Dharma. Every time the birds sing, that is a teaching of the Dharma. When people hear the wind rustling in the trees, they stop and remember the Four Establishments of Mindfulness, the Seven Factors of Awakening,[38] the Noble Eightfold Path, and the other teachings of the Buddha.

"Here Is the Pure Land" is a song written by Thây in Vietnamese and translated into English. I practice this song when I do jogging meditation. If I sing it in Vietnamese, then every syllable is one footstep. I can also sing it in English and jog at the same time. It's very wonderful to be jogging in the Pure Land.

The first words of the song are "Here is the Pure Land." The second sentence is "The Pure Land is here." This is in the tradition of the ancestral teachers. "Form is emptiness, emptiness is form." We say things twice like that because our consciousness receives the first word of a sentence as the most important word. If we just say, "Form is emptiness," our mind concentrates more on the word "form" than it does on "emptiness." We then say, "Emptiness is form," so our mind is equally concentrated on form and emptiness. In the same way, if we say, "Here is the Pure Land," our mind is more concentrated on the word "here." And if we say, "The Pure Land is here," our mind is more concentrated on "the Pure Land." So the words of the song allow us to be concentrated on both.

Watering the seeds of purity in our store consciousness helps establish a good balance between purity and impurity. We have the tendency sometimes to look on everything as being impure, and we need to put the balance right. We practice watering the seeds of happiness for the same reason. We have the tendency to took on the planet Earth as a place of suffering, and we need to put the balance right by seeing the happiness also.

When the Buddha taught Queen Vaidehi, she asked him, "If the Pure Land is not very far away, if it's right here, how do I practice to be there?" The Buddha gave her a guided meditation in which she could touch the Pure Land. It's a little bit like the guided meditation that says, "Breathing in, I am a flower; breathing out, I feel fresh." He taught her to be in touch with the lotus flower in her own consciousness, the lotus flower blooming. He taught her to be in touch with the lake of the most clear, sweet water in her consciousness. In that way, she could begin by touching the seeds of happiness in her own consciousness. Then, when she was outside walking in nature, she would also touch that world and feel happy.

Each of us has the capacity to build the Pure Land a little bit in our own home, at a practice center, or in our local Sangha. We can decide what kind of environment to create. How can we arrange the sitting meditation hall in order to water the seeds of right attention in everyone who enters it?

The idea of attention in Buddhist psychology is quite important. It's called *manaskara* in Sanskrit and is one of the fifty-one mental formations. It's also one of the first five mental formations, which we call the "universal mental formations."[39] Universal means that they are always occurring, they're always there. We are always giving our attention to something. We know that we can give our attention in an appropriate way, or we can give our attention to what is inappropriate. So we have appropriate attention and inappropriate attention.

When we read the newspaper or turn on the television, we need to be very careful what we give our attention to. If we give our attention to them, they can water seeds in our consciousness that are not altogether wholesome. All kinds of information can flow into our consciousness through our eyes and our ears. We don't even have to intentionally receive that information; it may still flow in. This is the meaning of universal mental formations *(sarvatiaga)*; it is happening all the time.

So we should make our environment a place where everything surrounding us helps nurture the best, the most refreshing things in us, things that can make us and other people happy. We can all do a little bit of this work—in our garden, in our home, in our school, in our workplace. This is part of making a Pure Land.

(This article originally appeared in Issue No. 28 of the *Mindfulness Bell.*)

Offering to the Land Ancestors 5

BY THE MONKS AND NUNS OF DEER PARK MONASTERY

W E, the brothers and sisters of Deer Park Monastery, respectfully request permission to make an offering to the ancestors of this land. We are aware that without the support and energy of the land ancestors it would not be possible for us to live and practice on this land today. In this moment we make the sincere aspiration to live in harmony with this land, with all the vegetation and animals living on this land, and with all our brothers and sisters who live here and who come to visit the monastery. We are aware that the harmony between us, which we cultivate through our practices of stopping, deep listening, loving speech, and compassionate action, directly affect the land we live on. When we are in harmony with each other, we are also in harmony with the land, the plants, and the animals. Knowing that our practice of mindfulness is our greatest protection, we are determined to practice mindful breathing, mindful walking, and consuming with awareness and compassion to offer protection to this land and all living beings residing on this land. We vow not to deplete the energy of the land and her resources with our careless actions, but rather to contribute to the regeneration of this beautiful land, bringing freshness, peace, and happiness to all who come here. We resolve to plant our understanding, our love, and our equanimity on this land with our light and peaceful steps. We are determined to practice wholeheartedly so that the door of understanding, love, and freedom may be opened for each one of us.

With great respect we ask the ancestors of this land to protect us and to nourish us with your insight, deep connection, and liberation. Like young shoots of ancient trees, we look to you to know our roots on this soil. We are like stones that have broken from the mountaintop and rolled down into the valley, and now we look up to the mountain to know our origins. We ask for your guidance and understanding to show us clearly how to proceed on our path of awakening. As children of this land we ask for your great compassion to forgive us when we have made mistakes out of ignorance or arrogance and to help us reestablish a good connection with you. We aspire to learn from your weaknesses and to continue your strengths. We are aware that the talents and skills that we presently manifest are not our possessions alone, but are the result and the continuation of the sincere intentions and loving labor of our ancestors. We ask for your support and acceptance as we continue to create structures and changes in developing this new practice center. With humble hearts and willing hands we make an offering of the Deer Park Monastery to be a refreshing refuge for living beings to nourish themselves, to contribute our solidity and clarity to the world around us, and to offer the light of awareness and liberation.

We feel the presence of the land ancestors in all the natural elements around us. We know that we need only to listen to the call of the hawks and the laughter of the coyotes, to touch the red soil beneath our feet, to taste the sweet wild buckwheat, and to smell the pungent sage in order to feel our deep connection with you. We will respond with our joyful songs, our peaceful steps, and our loving looks.

Dear land ancestors, thank you for being present for us. We will always be here for you.

Our offering was made at sunset on November 3, 2001, near the entrance to Deer Park Monastery. We chanted and offered sage, incense, tea, a bowl of clear water, and a cornmeal/buckwheat cake surrounded by green herbs, fruit, and nuts.

(This article originally appeared in the Spring 2002 issue of the *Deer Park Breeze*.)

Coming Together to Realize Our True Home 6

BY KARL AND HELGA RIEDL

S ANGHA is sometimes defined as "the community that lives in harmony and awareness." Community is one important aspect of a Sangha. Sangha can be a beautiful way to live with like-minded people, to share our responsibilities, happiness, and pains with friends in the Dharma. A Sangha supports our endeavor to live in awareness. We feel at home. We are nourished and given the space and help to heal our wounds and transform our suffering.

But when we look deeper into Sangha, when we are living in it for a longer time, we realize that the real aim of a Sangha is much more. It is the process—at times, quite demanding and challenging—of transforming our whole being. What looks like a lifestyle is actually the expression of a spiritual life. True Sangha offers an environment for spiritual growth, relaxed and gentle, but deep and thorough.

To build such a Sangha, not simply a community, one needs to understand which "building blocks" are required, look deeply into the ways a Sangha works, and become very aware of which motivations the members ought to have. Out of our experience of living in the Plum Village Sangha for six years, we would like to share what we have found to be the main principles of a residential Sangha.

COMMITMENT

True commitment reflects our deep aspiration to walk on the path of transformation and liberation and to question the life we have led—with all our ideas, concepts, and desires—and the ways we secure our ego through

97

wealth, fame, knowledge, and position. It is the heartfelt desire to submit ourselves to a life where "being" is more important than "having," where the loneliness of egoism and its restrictive ways of seeing and experiencing are opened up to others and to life as it presents itself. Commitment is the joyful willingness to let go of our concepts, to expose ourselves in the process of dissolving our existential ignorance, and to come back to our true home.

Commitment means being involved, not holding anything back. This is often seen negatively as "giving up oneself" and accompanied by hesitation and fear. It may seem safer, more familiar to us to be a casual participant, to maintain our concepts and ideas and add only what feels good to us. Living in a Sangha then becomes merely an opportunity to acquire new knowledge, to receive a training, or to solve some personal psychological problems. We need to be aware of what our commitment is.

SURRENDER

To let the process of transformation happen, we need to "surrender to the Sangha," as Thây has often emphasized. This is to surrender to the practice wholeheartedly—with all our conviction and joy—and to the activities of the Sangha. Surrender is easily misunderstood as obeying or letting other people run our life. It is amazing to watch the Hydra of the ego come up at every possible occasion. Angels turn into rebels: "I'll do it my way!" Soon our initial enthusiasm fades, and we look for every possibility to take a leave from the practice. Even minor details and changes on the schedule evoke angry discussion.

Surrender is the spiritual practice of setting aside our ideas and goals and opening to new experiences, to all aspects of life, to the unknown, without opposing them. Its religious form is the prostration: bowing down, opening our hands, not holding anything back.

SERVING

Another expression of surrender is serving the Sangha. Serving means doing what needs to be done—setting aside likes and dislikes, me and you. To serve is to overcome our habitual attitudes towards work and responsibilities and to develop our concern, care, and love for others.

Serving happens when the initial idea "I am living in a Sangha" has changed into "I am living for the Sangha." But even then, selfish motivations may remain; hidden agendas may be the driving force for our actions. In this case, serving is misunderstood as taking on responsibilities. Some people feel that they alone are able to do certain things, that they must take up the burden of a specific task or even of the whole community. In due time, they burn out and become bitter. To rely on the Sangha, to step down from self-importance and accept one's own limits, does not come easily for "the doer." When serving is misunderstood as assisting the Sangha with our skills, knowledge, and energy, then positions become fixed, and members of the community are judged by their "usefulness."

True serving is to experience the reality of interbeing. Everybody actually supports everybody; there is neither dependence nor independence. It is then that we realize, "I am the Sangha."

ACCEPTANCE AND HARMONY

A fourth aspect of building a true Sangha is the willingness, even the heartfelt longing, to live in harmony with others. By cultivating our abilities to accept each other just as we are, we break through our spontaneous likes and dislikes, judgments and categorizing. We create an atmosphere of trust. Supported by the practice of deep listening and sharing, we develop a spirit of openness, where understanding grows into loving acceptance.

In our Western societies, where competition, jealousy, mistrust, and separateness prevail, their opposites — trust, acceptance, openness, and love — are deeply longed for, but it can be difficult to open to them. It is often easier to create a "pseudo-harmony" — where we are just "nice" to each other, where everybody seems to accept and love everybody — by not getting too close to one another, by not touching anything that could disturb the peace, and by closing off to those who do not "fit in."

HUMANITY AND RESPECT

To greet the Buddha in each other is possible only when we have dissolved separateness and tackled the threefold complex of comparing ourselves with others — "I am better-equal-lower." Only then do we glimpse true humility — not putting ourselves down but gracefully accepting that we need not be "somebody" or extraordinary. Ordinary is sufficient. We need not hold onto an image of ourselves or be caught in social status. If we give a Dharma talk, we sit on a platform, and if a porter is needed, we carry the luggage of a guest.

From the depth of our being, we can show respect to ourselves and others. This respect is the foundation of a peaceful life. But respect is not imposed on us as social hierarchy. We do not pay respect to a social position but to a human being. We learn from others, follow their example, and listen to their advice because we deeply honor and respect their having matured on the path. We accept others as "elders."

Again, in a society where competition and mistrust prevail, where everybody makes sure that nobody is "higher," even respect and trust are suspect. The elder principle — found in almost all spiritual traditions and at its core a maturity principle — is rejected without any consideration. This is an obstacle to building a spiritual community, a Sangha. Either a pseudo-community is created and maintained, or power games and "boss-hierarchy" consume all energy. Especially in Western societies we need to look deeply into this situation and, with the help of the Sangha, find ways to restore respect and the elder-maturity principle.

Each of these principles is in itself a door for entering the Sangha. As all these principles are interrelated, if one is practiced deeply, the others are strengthened. But if a Sangha member has a problem or a misunderstanding in even one area, the whole process of spiritual growth for that person — and to some extent for the whole Sangha — is disturbed, maybe even blocked. So it is important to be very clear about the working of a Sangha, to avoid disappointments and suffering, and to build a harmonious and happy Sangha.

(This article originally appeared in Issue No. 24 of the *Mindfulness Bell.*)

A Year of Inclusiveness
and Forgiveness

7

BY SISTER CHÂN CHAU NGHIEM

JUST BEFORE CHRISTMAS I moved from Plum Village, France — my home for the last three years — to our new monastery near San Diego, California. Compared to Plum Village, with over one hundred monastics, our Sangha (community of spiritual practitioners) here is small, with thirteen sisters and eleven brothers. I am the youngest in age of all the sisters and one of only two Western sisters. It's a big change. Because of our small size, the sense of being in a family is strong, and I quickly felt at home. There is a lot of love between us. Although we are in the U.S., this Sangha is more Vietnamese than in Plum Village, so I am studying Vietnamese more diligently. Before I left, I was not so enthusiastic about leaving my teacher and coming out to the "frontier," but I knew it would be an opportunity to grow up and really take refuge in myself. With fewer practitioners around to help sustain the mindfulness energy, we each have to take more responsibility for our own practice and for the well-being of the community.

Whereas the land that is now Plum Village was originally farmland that has been inhabited for centuries, Deer Park comprises four hundred acres of gorgeous mountain land, which nourishes me enormously. I feel I have a lot of space, and I enjoy the stillness and wildness of the land. The energy is very different than at Plum Village. There are coyotes, rabbits, bobcats, snakes, and many kinds of vegetation unfamiliar to me. I love to watch the hawks soaring, majestic against the jutting rocks, and smell the fragrant sagebrush on the mountains all around. The sun is my very good friend; I especially enjoy resting in a hammock after lunch, watching the light play through the leaves above.

I am happy to be here. I look forward to being in closer contact with my family and reaching out more to friends. I deeply desire to take root here, to contribute the best of myself to help make my Sangha stronger and happier. I also want to offer the fruits of our practice to the young people around us. I am looking forward to coordinating a retreat for teenagers this summer in Deer Park.

I wrote the following in my journal about our New Year's Eve celebration:

During the group discussion and at dinner, I felt so grateful to Deer Park and actually proud of it. I could sense from what people shared and from their energy that here we practice and share the living Dharma. The presence of Thây is real; we are not cut off. People can come and take refuge here; it is a true continuation of Plum Village. One practitioner said that Deer Park is everywhere — it is not a place, it is not only right here. It is like a window, an entrance into freedom. It is also not the people. The Sangha is not individual people; it is our practice together, the fact that we are all going in the same direction of wholeness and freedom.

I felt many times yesterday how wonderful it is to be in the presence of other practitioners as we enter the New Year. I looked around at people from so many different backgrounds — white, Vietnamese, Latino, young, old, single folks, and parents with children — and I thought, "Wow, and this is in the U.S.!" My experience of this country is so often one of division — racial, cultural, economic — that just the fact that all of us could be here and belong was so healing, so nourishing. Everyone was welcome and felt welcomed. We didn't even need to speak the same language. This is true inclusiveness. In Plum Village it is different because it is international. People come from many different countries to France, and while that is also beautiful, it's really remarkable to me that people who are all from the same country can come together, crossing so many boundaries of class, religion, race, etc.

Looking around at everyone seated in small circles in the dining hall, each with a candle in the center, I really felt I was in a family of practitioners. This is my American Dream coming true. There was a tangible energy of peace, joy, and harmony in the room.

At the beginning of every lunar New Year, Thây shares two words that we are invited to practice and learn about throughout the upcoming year. We put up these two words on red paper all over the monastery to help us remember and practice them. During this past year, Thây chose *Tha thu* and *Bao dung:* forgiveness and inclusiveness.

INCLUSIVENESS

Recently, I was sitting and practicing this meditation:

Breathing in, I calm my body.
Breathing out, I smile.
Breathing in, I dwell in the present moment.
Breathing out, I know it is a wonderful moment.

As I practiced dwelling in the present moment, I thought of all the things happening right now in the world. People are afraid, sunk in despair; people are being tortured, killed in war; people are dying from easily curable diseases, watching their children starve. We are continuing to pollute our environment, making deeper and deeper wounds in the Earth. People are living lives of overconsumption in First World countries in an effort to numb their despair and alienation.

So I asked myself, How can this be a wonderful moment, with all of this going on? For several moments I was really in doubt. I breathed. Then I saw that in this present moment there are also people on the planet doing their very best to help relieve the suffering of others. There are those with enough wisdom and compassion to know how to do this effectively. There are courageous and caring warriors willing to go through the fire, to create more justice, freedom, and peace. There are children laughing and people dancing, happy to be alive. There are people right now truly enjoying their food and appreciating all the things that make it available to them. There are people enjoying nature and taking good care of it right now, knowing that we *are* the Earth.

I thought of my spiritual teacher and ancestors who are guiding me and countless others with tremendous strength and love. I was aware of the living presence of the Buddha, Christ, which exists in each one of us, making incredible healing and insight possible.

I knew deep inside that the present moment *is* a wonderful moment, not because suffering and injustice don't exist, but because there is a path. And I have the chance to practice it with my community, to be a part of bringing more understanding and love into the world. I do not have to get drowned in the suffering and confusion. I maintain balance by knowing there is a way out, and I rejoice in its clarity and power. Suffering doesn't have to disappear for happiness to exist. If it weren't for suffering, there would be no need to practice a spiritual path, there would be no way to grow, heal, and transform.

FORGIVENESS

I had the chance to be around Thây after September 11, and I witnessed an extremely powerful example of forgiveness, of acceptance. Thây practiced calming, and then from a place of peace, he could act with compassion—not jumping to react or punish, but slowing down in order to nourish solidity and insight. In the wake of the disaster, Thây demonstrated that to forgive we must first put out our own fire, take care of our own suffering, rather than run after the arsonist while our house burns down.

On the morning of September 11, our whole Sangha was on a bus from San Diego to northern California, and we listened to the news on our Walkmans almost the whole day. We talked about it in shock, and we were very shaken up. It was unreal. As we neared Kim Son Monastery at the end of the day, I was still listening to the news, and my sister gently encouraged me from the seat behind to pay attention to the beautiful redwood trees and not listen constantly to whatever was on the radio. I had forgotten about the trees.

The next day Thây shared the news of the attacks with the whole monastic Sangha. He also invited all of us to spend the day at the beach. The beach? I thought. How can we go to the beach during a crisis like this? We have to mourn, or do something. I went anyway, and it was exactly the right medicine. It was a beautiful day, and being together was deeply nourishing. We ate lunch in small groups, watched the waves, took naps on the sand, played a funny game — something like "steal the bacon" only with a tackle element added. It was joyful and relaxing, and I felt very connected to my brothers and sisters. I found myself singing to invoke the name of Avalokiteshvara (the bodhisattva of great compassion) as I looked out onto the calm ocean. I spotted some dolphins just before we left. It was with a contented and very quiet mind that I left the beach. Thây knew we were all deeply disturbed and needed to nourish ourselves in order to be able to embrace our pain, fear, and despair.

Thây and the Sangha responded swiftly and mindfully. The upcoming public talk in Berkeley was expanded to include a ceremony for the victims of the tragedy. A public lecture in New York City was planned spontaneously for a few days later, as was a ten-day fast, a form of prayer in action. All this in the midst of a five-day monastic retreat Thây was teaching. When I was around him, he was always calm, light, and at ease. One afternoon, after several meetings and sharing with a reporter, I saw him quietly slip out of his hut and go for a walk. This was a profound lesson for me. Although there was so much to be done, so much to take care of, he did not get carried away. He practiced to nourish himself and stay grounded in the present moment. Otherwise what would he have to offer? Even as he was deeply shocked by the tragedy, he continued to practice walking meditation, to smile, to enjoy the beauty around him.

When I returned to Plum Village, several sisters and I performed a ceremony from our tradition in order to send energy and support to those suffering in New York and Washington. The words that most touch me are from the introduction: "The peace and joy of the entire world, including the worlds of the living and the dead, depends on our own peace and joy in this moment.... Once one person is able to give rise to a deep sense of peace and happiness, the whole world benefits."

Forgiveness means coming back to ourselves when we are hurt or angry to take care of our pain. It is only when we are calm and lucid that we can see clearly and respond skillfully to someone who has wronged us. When we look deeply, we can see the roots of another person's actions and know that they do not have a separate self. They did not create themselves like that; innumerable conditions came together to make them who they are. With this understanding, we can begin to forgive. Forgiveness is understanding our interdependence with those who cause us to suffer, and with all of life.

(This article originally appeared in the Spring 2002 issue of the *Deer Park Breeze*.)

PART FOUR
Sangha-Building

On Not Collecting Cows:
Sangha-Building in a Rural Area 8

BY PATRICIA HUNT-PERRY

STARTING AND SUSTAINING a Sangha in a rural area has been a wonderful and challenging experience.

In 1991, after Thây gave a retreat in the mid-Hudson Valley in New York State, I returned to the farm where I was born in a nearby rural area. Although I had been attending retreats with Thây in California since 1987, I did not have Sangha support anywhere near the farm and knew of no one in this area who was even remotely interested in Buddhism. Some considered it with deep suspicion. After the 1991 retreat it was very clear that I could not rely on sporadic retreats several times a year but needed to create Sangha where I live. It had been clear long before that that I needed a Sangha, but I was too shy to start one.

It seemed quite a challenge. I noticed the arising of one of the main hindrances — doubt, which manifested deeply within me as self-doubt and lack of confidence. Looking deeply at that and working with it became a helpful practice. I reached out by phone to my dear friend and teacher, Lyn Fine. She helped me work with the internal formations and with very practical resources, chants, readings, and ceremonies.

Still, starting a rural Sangha had its own opportunities and challenges, so we "made the road by walking."

A friend had just returned from a three-month retreat in another compatible tradition and needed a place to stay for a little while. He was willing to stay at my home for a short time, so there was one other person to start with. A small "Wanting to Start a Sangha" notice was published in the *Mindfulness Bell*, and before I had even received my issue, someone from forty minutes away called and asked what night to come. We had to decide together.

For awhile it was just the three of us. Then another friend began to sit with us. Slowly more people began to come or to phone. This happened all through the *Mindfulness Bell* and by word of mouth. A lovely massage therapist-yoga teacher in the area became a Sangha member and let other people know about our sittings.

NEWSLETTER

Soon I found it useful to start a little weekly newsletter. It reminded people of the sitting times and other events and included a reading for each week. At that time it was sent out by regular mail, which became a growing commitment, but in our large rural area it kept people connected. It helped, too, in winter months when the snow might keep some or all from reaching weekly sittings.

COMMUNITY

In a rural area the country kitchen is often a gathering place. After Sangha sittings many stay to share a cup of tea and cookies or fruit, and this helped to build our community. We are careful not to create this as an expectation, however, as some want to return home for early rising and others have quite far to drive over dark back roads.

We were happy, and remain happy, with the number of people who come, whether it is five or twelve (our typical range). Some of our members "sit with us" in their own space at the same time when they cannot come. During one snowy and cold winter two of our members had to park their cars a quarter of a mile away and walk across a dark, frozen lake—a practice not recommended after dark. On especially wintry nights, they sat with us at their home!

Since commitment can nourish us all and some people cannot come every week, we recommend making a commitment of once or twice a month so that there is some consistency. We have found it important to keep

Sangha on the same night. (Once we tried two Mondays and two Thursdays a month, which did not work for people.)

We meet in the same general area for our weekly meetings but vary the location of our Days of Mindfulness among other places within about an hour drive. Thus, some Sangha members who may not be able to come each week can host the Sangha for a Day of Mindfulness. This also helps us reach out to others who feel they live too far away to come on weeknights.

We find weekend Days of Mindfulness on a monthly basis difficult for some of our members (those with family, with weekend work schedules, etc.). Nevertheless, we offer about ten Days of Mindfulness a year. Like our weekly sittings, what's important is not the number of people who are there but the richness and flowering of our practice. There have been as few as four or five, and sometimes thirty-five when friends from other Sanghas join us. However many come is just the right number. And when no one else comes, I sit on my own.

After about eleven years our Sangha has grown, but we still remain small. We are very happy and in harmony, nourishing each other deeply and offering the practice to ourselves, each other, and others in our community or workplaces. In earlier years others were shy about leading, but we have created a very safe space and now many Sangha members lead, offer the bell, or do the readings.

MARTIN LUTHER KING, JR.

Many of the members were drawn to Thây's practice because of their social activism. Nine years ago several members of the Sangha wanted to participate in a socially active area that was consistent with their practice, and they decided to join the newly-formed Martin Luther King, Jr. Committee. This was especially inviting because of the deep connection between Thây and Dr. King. Over the last nine years the committee has sponsored a yearly event in which schoolchildren produce their own skits, art, and dances about peace and compassion. We have had the opportunity to listen to speakers such as Pete Seeger, who give a vision of past efforts and possibilities for a responsible, compassionate, and peaceful life.

NOT COLLECTING COWS

One day the Buddha and some monks were approached by an agitated farmer who said that all twelve of his cows had run away that morning. The Buddha told the farmer that he had not seen the cows, and after the farmer left, the Buddha turned to the Sangha and said, "Dear friends, do you know that you are the happiest people on earth? You have no cows to lose."

Although we live in a rural area, our Sangha has not collected cows. We still have weekly sittings (that has remained a constant for ten years no matter how many sit) and one night a month we have "Taking Refuge in the Dharma," a time to sit/walk and then read and discuss the teachings. Our newsletter is now coedited by two Sangha members and sent out monthly, mainly by email. We neither restrict nor seek large numbers. If more people come than the farmhouse can comfortably fit, we will happily move to a larger space. If not, we will happily stay where we are. We even have a treasurer now but still make our decisions mainly around the kitchen table after our weekly sittings. We focus on our practice, our loving community, and nourishing each other and ourselves in the practice. We do not seek to have unnecessary burdens—which the Buddha referred to metaphorically as "cows"—even structural cows, or too much business or busyness!

As Thây said in a 1997 Dharma talk:

> The Sangha is a beautiful community going together on the joyful path, practicing liberation and helping peace and joy come into life. The business of the Sangha is to practice liberation. It is not to build temples but to practice liberation and to train in liberation. That training, that practice, has only one aim: that is to undo the knots which tie our mind and body.

Sangha-Building 9

BY LARRY WARD

HE OR SHE who would build Sangha realizes that the blessings of Sangha are available only in the present moment.

He or she respects and celebrates the honorable lineage that is the deep root of their Sangha.

He loves the ripening understanding of the Buddha, Dharma, and Sangha that comes from contact with monks and nuns, the gift of Dharma teachers, weekly Sangha practice, regular Days of Mindfulness, and retreats.

She acts in all matters of leadership with inspiration, clarity, and helpfulness as worthy goals.

He remembers that the Sangha is fully empty of a separate self and is not the whole world or centered around one individual among many.

She practices saying "yes" deeply before saying "no" while participating in the Sangha's life of human interactions.

He walks the Noble Eightfold Path with humility, gratitude, and compassion toward all beings including himself.

Watering seeds of unconditional forgiveness wherever she goes, she rides the Sangha waves of birth and death with a calm smile and an open heart.

(This article originally appeared in Issue No. 24 of the *Mindfulness Bell.*)

Some Experiences with Local Sangha Organizing 10

BY CALEB CUSHING

What is most important is to find peace and to share it with others.
—Thich Nhat Hanh

Thich Nhat Hanh has said that if we are fortunate enough to meet a great teacher and to pose a question, it behooves us to ask an important one, the answer to which will change our life.

In 1998, at the 21-day Vermont retreat, a retreatant named Dorothy asked such a question. She first explained to a panel of Dharma teachers, in the company of four hundred lay and monastic practitioners, that it was easy to meditate in the company of other retreatants, but upon return to Jamaica, she would be alone. How could she start a Sangha in a country where she would be the only Buddhist meditator?

Thây Giac Thanh answered. She should find a pleasant, friendly spot at the beach where there was some shade, and a light breeze, and there she should sit. The waves would be her Sangha. In time, people would ask her how it was that she was so beautiful, so joyful, so easy to be around, and they, too, would be her Sangha.

I was delighted by the charming vision. It was so clear, so simple. It seemed too easy. Now, after ten years of Sangha-building, I see that the prescription was complete.

"Sangha" means "congregation" in Pali, the canonical language of the first Buddhist texts. Thây Giac Thanh's graceful definition included all the elements which supported Dorothy's practice, everything to which she might offer gratitude for nurturing her awareness. This definition recognized interdependence and impermanence and reminded her not to look only for things that are far away.

I came to practice by way of *Being Peace*,[40] which begins: "Life is filled with suffering, but it is also filled with many wonders." I knew life was a miracle, but I was frustrated and alienated. I had all the elements of a good life but no ease and little joy. I knew what didn't help me feel good: stoicism, isolation, venting, psychotherapy, medications. Devotional meditation felt like make-believe. Albert Einstein noted that the first question to ask is, "Is the universe a friendly place?" I trusted it was friendly, but I felt like a stranger.

When I saw Thich Nhat Hanh at a public lecture, his stability and gentleness were riveting. Every gesture merited attention. I still see him, extending his hand, the palm turned outward, open, exposed, empty, the fingers slightly bent as if to support a round object. It's a symbolic gesture of charity, of offering a gift.

At my first retreat, Thây mentioned that in the West people usually associate happiness with excitement, but in the East happiness is associated with calm. Peace looked good, but I experienced no ease at the retreat. When I saw people greeting old friends with hugs and smiles, I felt alone and unlucky.

I knew I had the responsibility to change by dint of my effort rather than by suspending reason, submitting to some authority. Practicing with others seemed promising, for I had no confidence in my capacity to figure out how to meditate on my own.

At the retreat, small geographically based groups met each day to process our experiences of the retreat. On the last day, one of our group invited us to gather again at her house when the retreat was over. I did, and we continued to practice together.

Over the years, this little "No-Name Sangha" grew and metamorphosed. As members moved, stopped practicing, or joined other groups, I kept returning to the homemade model of Sangha. Sometimes there were just two of us, but it became a routine, a refuge, a gift to myself, a safe resting place where I practiced looking, listening, and sharing. Like life itself, Sangha became a sacred opportunity to be present. As a Sangha brother said just last weekend, "I tended to develop isolation as a coping mechanism early in life, and for me, Sangha models openness, acceptance, and inclusiveness."

Studying with a Soto Zen teacher, reading widely, attending retreats and Days of Mindfulness, and sitting with several Sanghas, I coasted along. Once when I hit a rough spot—and knew it was a rough spot—I consulted with a visiting Dharma teacher. Something happened. I don't remember her advice; I remember her listening. I felt so moved to express my gratitude, whereupon she said, "The one who bows and the one who is bowed to are the same." Later, she suggested I consider joining the Order of Interbeing. Others had recommended it, but I thought I had nothing to offer. Now I realized it would be fortunate to be around practitioners like her, and if she thought I was worthy, I would trust her. Supported by my local Dharma teacher, I increased my study and practice and visited Plum Village, where I learned tree-hugging meditation and how to take life easy. I took leadership roles at retreats, took my role as a Sangha host seriously, and the Sangha that met at my house thrived.

We developed a Sunday morning routine of sitting in a circle, facing inward, offering some technical tips on how to enjoy sitting, breathing, relaxing, and cultivating awareness. We sat, walked, and did a guided meditation, followed by a period of sharing. After one or more hours of meditation, one tends to speak with care, to listen with care. If there were newcomers, we introduced ourselves before sharing; we ensured our stability and freshness. We spoke in turn, going around the circle, focusing on our experience of the practice. Each week, someone said something that touched someone else; over time, everyone said something helpful, and everyone was touched. Listening is a gift, too. Even shy people who think they have nothing to offer realized they contributed a lot by their deep listening, attending to their breath, listening to what was said without judgment, and listening also to what was left unsaid.

Listening gives rise to speaking, speaking supports listening. Sharing models meditation, and vice versa. As we learn to listen to others, we learn how to listen to ourselves. We hear others treat themselves with respect, patience, and tenderness. The speaker and the listener inter-are. The Sangha acts as a model for the meditator. The benefit of one accrues to everyone. Our well-being becomes the Sangha's well-being, the Sangha's well-being is our well-being. Working for the benefit of the Sangha becomes joyful.

ORGANIZING MEDITATION GROUPS

My 1921 dictionary says, "To organize is to arrange or constitute interdependent parts into a whole." Activist Fred Ross Sr., mentor to Cesar Chavez, says, "Organizing is providing people with the opportunity to become aware of their capabilities and potential."

Organizing meditation groups entails first of all enjoying the practice and being grateful for the support of others. Knowing that the answers discovered are more valuable than the answers given, we trust the Sangha's wisdom. Gathering people together, asking questions, and listening to motivations and concerns, one encourages action and next steps in conjunction with others who share the same interests. Moving forward based only on what comes *out* of people is a practice of receptivity, responsiveness, and maintaining awareness of our preconceptions and agendas.

Some process techniques build ownership. Delegating is facilitated by attending to others' interests and skills, inviting participation, and avoiding doing for others what they can do for themselves. Empowering requires letting go, risking that things may not come together. Checking in and following up are essential, but the broad picture, the overview needs to be kept in sight. It's the practice of inclusiveness. As soon as one learns something, it helps to teach it to someone else. Activities are teaching opportunities if inexperienced people are paired with those who are experienced. The means and the ends always inter-are.

The "Potluck Sangha" with which I practice has thrived, nurturing many practitioners. It has become a viable example of a homemade practice group. Here is an overview of some of the activities we've found to support us:

To begin with, remembering that we were once all newcomers, we attend to new practitioners, greeting them, introducing ourselves, making them comfortable and welcome, and explaining our activities as we go. Because our meetings are long, we got hungry, and enjoying each other's company, we began to share potluck lunches. Sitting on the floor in a circle, like a picnic, we practice eating meditation and socialize afterwards. We celebrate birthdays with cakes and presents and sometimes with restaurant banquets. We started a book study group in the evening, where we sit, take turns reading, and practice mindful listening and sharing, followed by tea and a snack. We've had a poetry night, a Valentine's project of writing letters of appreciation to each member of the Sangha, and Saturday night nature walks with a picnic dinner. We even published a collection of recipes that includes descriptions of mindful eating and affectionate limericks.

We established a Second Body practice to deepen our relationships and to support our practice. Each participant has two "bodies": a Sangha member they care for and their own body. The care was determined by mutual consent and might entail a weekly phone call or daily sitting practice. We devised a method to set up the Second Body chain, which we reconstitute each quarter.

We organize one or two retreats a year, with a planning committee that polls the Sangha to design the schedule and activities. Communication is supported by setting up a phone tree, a roster, an email group, and a calendar.

Our decision-making process has evolved to rely on a Caretaking Committee, which solicits, distributes, and fine-tunes proposals by gathering input from everyone on an individual basis, followed by meetings conducted to discuss, refine, and make decisions on a consensual basis when necessary. At the annual planning meeting, we collect proposals for activities (retreats, Days of Mindfulness, etc.), find volunteers to lead them, and schedule activities for the year.

As we have become close, we now share activities we enjoy, such as gardening, music, yoga, dance, camping, vacations—even professional services and financial assistance. Having grown confident in our abilities, we take turns hosting, leading meditation and discussion sessions, and giving talks based upon our experience in integrating mindfulness practice into daily life. Most members go to Thây's California retreats, and many visit Plum Village.

When more than twenty-five people started to come regularly, we considered meeting in a public location rather than in people's homes.

Several new Sanghas were set up by experienced practitioners who continued to attend our Potluck Sangha on a less frequent basis. In addition, we schedule Days of Mindfulness in parks, open to one and all. These attract large numbers of newcomers and provide occasions to invite Dharma teachers, monastics, and practitioners from other Sanghas to get together.

REGIONAL SANGHA ORGANIZING

As individual practice is the basis for Sangha activity, so, too, a Sangha can influence and nurture practice on a regional basis. Wishing to meet and share experiences with other Sangha facilitators, we invite far-flung Sangha hosts to gather for a day of practice, discussion, and mutual support. It's very enriching and nurturing to hear about all the ways people enjoy being together, as new hosts get good advice and encouragement from experienced ones, and old-timers are inspired by the new Sanghas.

Thich Nhat Hanh extols Sangha, and it is incumbent on the local practitioners to make Sanghas available, and to make themselves visible. Retreatants often look forward to practicing together after local or regional retreats, and this can be facilitated in a number of ways. To foster connections among retreatants, Dharma discussion groups at retreats led by Thây are often organized regionally, facilitated by practitioners who are active in local groups and who can share their experiences and extend hospitality to newcomers. Distributing copies of retreat rosters and Sangha directories is an invaluable, irreplaceable means by which people can stay in contact and build relationships after a retreat has concluded. Also, publishing and distributing descriptive material can make it easier for people to understand what Sangha practice can be like. Back issues of the *Mindfulness Bell*, copies of Dharma teacher Jack Lawlor's *Sangha Practice*,[41] and other descriptive material can have wide influence.

Individuals or groups of Sanghas can then build on their growing friendship with one another to organize regional Days of Mindfulness and retreats. Recently we invited a Nonviolent Communication (NVC) trainer to join us, which led to an ongoing study group in these methods of connecting to our deeper feelings and needs in an inclusive way.

Surprisingly, we had limited success setting up new Sanghas through sign-ups at large public events. We learned that many people want to join local Sanghas after hearing Thich Nhat Hanh's lectures, but there were not yet enough experienced practitioners to respond to the demand. Even after inviting prospective Sangha hosts to practice and training sessions, these new Sanghas, comprised of all newcomers, failed to thrive and we discovered that practice cannot be treated like a business franchise. A Sangha is a slow-growth organism. A Sangha depends on the solidity, assurance, and inspiration of at least one committed, mature practitioner. This quality cannot be created on demand. It develops at its own pace.

As my Sangha brother Glen Schneider says, "Building as we go, we lay the track with the train coming right behind us." Knowing with certainty that meditation is fruitful, we engage with others to enjoy it. In practice, in Sangha, notions of "self" and "other" disappear. Taking care of ourselves, we take care of others. Nurturing the Sangha supports us. We all have the capacity to cultivate insight; the lessons are all around, and there are innumerable supports for awakening.

I know I no longer feel like a stranger in this world, and this is due to the practice, which is inseparable from the Sangha.

Dorothy's question reflected her appreciation of the practice, her gratitude to the Sangha, and her commitment to finding support. Being inspired, she could then inspire. She received the gift from the lineage of the open hand, the gesture that offers us the treasure we already possess.

The Ever-Expanding Nature of Sangha Practice 11

BY DAVID M. LAWRENCE

IN MY EARLY FIFTIES, it was a time to re-evaluate and look at how I was living my life. I didn't understand why what seemed like "the good life" didn't translate into creativity and happiness. I didn't feel relaxed nor did I feel peace and joy. Why was it after so many years of meditation that I had not yet found some equanimity and solidity? My spiritual practice didn't lead to a sustainable way to face day-to-day living. I had feelings of fear and anxiety. My avoidance technique wasn't working any longer. My habit energy was to use my will and distractions to keep moving ahead. I had a lot of suffering because I didn't know how to stop and look deeper, to recognize what was actually happening. Over the years, these habits and fears turned into what Thich Nhat Hanh calls internal formations. I realized that I was living a spiritual lifestyle without a true practice. As difficult as this realization was, I began to understand that this process was a blessing and that I had the opportunity, with clear thinking and an open heart, to develop skillful means that I could bring to my life.

I also recognized that I needed additional support and stability. I didn't want to feel so separate. My first idea was to find a group that focused on sitting meditation with a time for some community sharing of personal practice. There were many choices in nearby Madison, Wisconsin, but I didn't want to shop around for a teacher, teachings, and some pre-imposed agenda. By chance on the campus of UW-Madison I saw a small message on a bulletin board that simply said, "Buddhist Meditation Group. Sunday morning sittings and walking meditation." I had a good feeling about this discovery and how it happened, so I decided to visit the next Sunday.

I was greeted very warmly and immediately felt comfortable. The group was mostly made up of Chinese graduate students from Taiwan. This was their regular Sunday service, something they were familiar with from their home country. The practice was two forty-minute rounds of sitting with a period of walking meditation in between. At the end, there was a devotional ritual and then a wonderful potluck. I initially wondered if my need for community and understanding was going to be met in this group because of our cultural differences and backgrounds, but I continued to participate on a regular basis and felt many benefits.

There was a couple from Europe who had begun attending this Sangha a few months before I did. After some time, my relationship with them deepened. They were very sincere and full of love. Their lives were very pure and integrated into their practice. During my times of self-doubt and confusion, they became my first "bell of mindfulness." They had attended the 1989 retreat with Thich Nhat Hanh in Illinois. Thây's writings and teachings touched them in a profound way and planted many positive seeds for all of us in the sitting group.

Thich Nhat Hanh returned to the Midwest in 1991 for a three-day mindfulness retreat in Mundelein, Illinois, sponsored by Lakeside Buddha Sangha in Evanston. Many of the Madison university sitting group attended, and we were joined by over three hundred other people from across the upper Midwest. Because the retreat was mostly in silence, the atmosphere was especially powerful. Thây's words seemed to confirm many deep understandings inside me, although I had never heard them in words before. It was the first time that I understood the deeper meaning of the mindfulness trainings and how they related to my meditation practice and daily life. It was extraordinary to be in Thây's presence. The teachings came alive just watching him. His message to us was loving and compassionate and at the same time a very forceful plea to practice mindful breathing, living, and smiling in order to transform our seeds of suffering. I was profoundly affected and felt enormous gratitude for Thich Nhat Hanh and the teachings.

Each day of the retreat we were able to meet together in small discussion groups. We talked honestly about the issues of practice in our lives. Many people told stories of how stuck they felt and how their habit energies

kept them from feeling joy and peace. During these discussions, the practice took on a new meaning for me. I understood that I had the opportunity to return to the present moment with each breath. I could stop my
endless conversations with myself and live with more ease. The group members shared the feeling of being renewed and were hopeful about their
return home with this new energy. We knew that while living in mindfulness and overcoming our tendencies was difficult, having the support of
fellow practitioners would be of great benefit. On the last day of the retreat,
Sangha groups were organized according to geographic locations. Many in
the Madison area met together and discussed ways to organize a Sangha. We
all wanted each other for support and to be together to share our experiences of practice.

Because of the goodwill that we had for each other at the retreat and the
love that we shared, I thought that this organizational process would be
easy once we returned home. Our initial Sangha-building discussions, however, revealed that people had very strong feelings about the structure and
form of the meeting and how their individual needs would be met. Issues
around meeting place, date, time, emotional safety during Dharma discussions, and the form of the practice were articulated. Many of the Sangha
members were coming from different traditions and felt that we needed an
"open way Sangha" in which these different traditions could be expressed.
Most of us didn't have the skills or experience to listen deeply. It was amazing how people's personal agendas could get in the way of the benefits of
love and understanding. It was surprising to me that the form became the
issue, not the practice. I felt that because Thây's teachings were so inclusive,
through the process of growing together in mindfulness and Dharma discussion, there would be time and space for all expressions.

After some months of open dialogue, we found that it was impossible
to come to consensus. It was decided that three separate Sanghas would be
formed so that people's individual needs could be met. It was disappoint-
ing to me because I felt like I was losing members of my new family. It was
then that the Snowflower Buddha Sangha was born. The basis of our practice would be the form used in Plum Village, Thich Nhat Hanh's monastic
community in the south of France.

Over the last ten years, the Sangha has continued to grow. The commitment and energy of our practice has created an atmosphere of trust and open communication. The people who attend know that they come to a group that is safe and nonjudgmental. There is inclusiveness and acceptance of our individual differences. We're all learning to let go and trust the process of building community. I am so profoundly affected by the insights people share during Dharma discussions. Listening deeply to what people say often opens my heart to my stuck places.

A recent issue of the *Mindfulness Bell* featured inclusiveness as its theme. Barbara Casey wrote:

> When these differences come up, we sit down together with an open, mindful intention to practice deep listening, to hear and understand the perceptions of the other. Though we may continue to hold different opinions, this sharing allows enough space for each of us to glimpse into the roots of the other's view and to feel the love and sincerity in the intentions of our brothers and sisters.... As we practice mindfulness together the love grows in the midst of the suffering, and we find the courage and tenacity to grow a strong Sangha, a Sangha with the potential to love without limits.[42]

There have been periods when it hasn't been easy to maintain the energy of the Sangha. During these difficult times, I am learning to let go of my sense of being right and to simply stop and listen. We all go through periods of doubt, judgment, and thinking our way is best. The practice of stopping reenergizes, me and I'm able once again to see the wonderful space and beauty around other people's practice. This has been deeply nourishing in my life.

During Thây's retreats in 1989 and 1991, practitioners in northern Illinois and Wisconsin developed feelings of trust and friendship. Some of us talked about the possibilities of practicing together. Our aspiration was that individual Sanghas could support each other by having combined Days of Mindfulness and retreats. With the kindness and support of Dharma teacher Jack Lawlor, Sanghas from Madison, Evanston, and DeKalb began the tradition of hosting such joint gatherings. For the past ten years, we have since enjoyed an annual cycle of at least four regional Days of Mindfulness and weekend retreats. I am astonished by the amount of loving attention and care that is devoted to hosting these events by each Sangha as they take their turn each year. Prairie Buddha Sangha, which hosts our winter Day of Mindfulness on the frozen banks of the Fox River, even provides retreatants with additional socks! Each fall, we hold a weekend retreat in Wisconsin, and each spring we hold a weekend retreat in Illinois. In recent years, the cycle of Midwestern regional events has grown to include annual retreats and Days of Mindfulness in Milwaukee, central Michigan, and southern Indiana. Sangha members will often travel for more than four hours and return home late in the evening. The benefits include a day of walking and sitting, a Dharma talk by Jack, and the pleasure of one another's participation in small group discussions, all enveloped by a larger atmosphere of mindfulness and silence.

We have also been very fortunate to have visits from Sister Annabel Laity and Sister Jina van Hengel for public talks and Days of Mindfulness in both Wisconsin and Illinois. These visits were well-attended and created more inspiration for practice and Sangha-building. The circle expanded as people from all over the Midwest attended these retreats. New people joined existing Sanghas or created new ones in their home communities.

Sangha members come to these retreats from Wisconsin, Illinois, Minnesota, Iowa, Missouri, Kansas, Michigan, Ohio, and Kentucky. I always look forward to seeing "old friends" who have attended the retreats over the years. There is an instant recognition and deep connection even without words. New people also bring a freshness to the practice. Each year, more and more people attend. In recent years, there have been approximately eighty people consistently attending the fall retreat and winter Day of Mindfulness. We belong to a regional community with harmony, understanding, and respect. We sit and walk together. We explore nature and share *haiku* poems and meals and talk from our hearts in small group discussions. We are present and supportive as Sangha members receive the Five and the Fourteen Mindfulness Trainings. We walk in noble silence under the stars and discover hidden talents around bonfires. We smile and encourage joy and laughter.

During one of our retreats, Jack performed a wedding ceremony at sunrise. We practiced walking meditation as the day emerged from the misty Wisconsin River Valley, with the sun rising on one side of the hilltop and the full moon setting on the other. We also share tears and sadness as life reveals tragedy and suffering. We are learning together to look deeply into the present moment in order to relieve the suffering in ourselves and in our community. Jack's Dharma talks inspire and give us courage to practice when we return to our work, family, and friends.

It is now eleven years since my first retreat with Thich Nhat Hanh. As I reflect, I see clearly how important and deeply rooted my relationship is with my root Sangha and my extended Sangha. My life is centered around my practice, and the Sangha is my practice. My community goes beyond my spiritual friendships and the support and protection I receive. The community keeps extending as my practice grows and becomes more solid. The practice helps me shine mindfulness on all the manifestations of my daily life. Seeing my own joy and suffering helps me to have more compassion and love for others and for myself. I have great appreciation and gratitude for all my teachers, family, and friends, who enrich and support my life. I bow to the Three Jewels—the Buddha, Dharma, and Sangha—and to the Venerable Thich Nhat Hanh.

A Little Seed Has Sprouted 12

BY ERNESTINE ENOMOTO

INTRODUCTION

WHEN I MOVED TO Hawai'i three years ago, I searched for practitioners familiar with the mindfulness meditation of Thich Nhat Hanh. I had been nurtured through many years of attending weekly Sunday sittings and retreats sponsored by the Washington Mindfulness Community (WMC), an established Sangha in the Washington, D.C., metropolitan area. The regularity of Sunday evenings spent in sitting and walking meditation supported my own practice, and so I sought a similar comfort when I moved to Hawai'i. While there were many established Buddhist temples and organizations, I found no mindfulness group in my city—only individuals scattered among the islands. So it seemed appropriate for me, having been an active practitioner and Order of Interbeing member, to establish a mindfulness community in my new locale. While this sounds simple and logical, any new endeavor takes intentionality and desire. And it doesn't happen overnight. In fact, it took me about eight months to get something off the ground. This is the story I would like to tell.

SEEKING HELP FROM FRIENDS

Mitchell Ratner of the WMC jokingly said that in moving to Hawai'i, I would be starting the WMC Far West, extending the boundaries of our D.C. Sangha. Certainly, sitting out in the northern Pacific Ocean, I felt the sheer distance from the mainland United States, remote and removed from connections and contacts, alone and isolated. The challenge of Sangha-building felt like a daunting task.

Fortunately, my friends helped. Mitchell served as a bulwark, easing my adjustment to my relocation, my new university position, and the work of Sangha-building. He offered wise counsel from his years of experience as a founding member of the Washington Sangha. He also provided references to Thây's Dharma talks from which I could draw. We talked long distance on a regular basis about the practicalities of establishing a mindfulness community.

Among my closest friends here in Hawai'i were a husband and wife who, while not mindfulness practitioners themselves, expressed interest in and support for meditation. They served as good sounding boards for ideas about starting a Sangha. We talked about whom to contact and what options might be open to such a group. We considered meeting places and how to begin, weighing the pros and cons of starting small with friends or advertising to the public. The seed of a Sangha was sprouting.

Finding a Place to Sit

In the movie *Field of Dreams*, the protagonist dreams vividly about a baseball diamond appearing in his Iowa corn field. The words echo in his head: "If you build it, they will come." I thought the same as I worked on establishing a Sangha. John Balaam from the Big Island of Hawai'i Sangha suggested that I concentrate first on finding a location. Once a place was found, then I could publicize and begin. "If you find a place, they will come."

Some persistence was necessary to find a suitable place. I looked in the immediate area, close to home and work, first at places owned by like-minded Buddhist groups and associations, and then at those of Christian and other groups. Some expressed no interest; others were willing but without suitable accommodations. Finally, I met with a pastor of a Christian church, who gave me the name and number of an ecumenical religious organization, the Spiritual Life Center, which did offer us a place, appropriately called the House of Peace. Perfectly situated in a quiet neighborhood, the House of Peace was formerly a residence built in elegant 1920s style, spacious and inviting. It was accessible, had sufficient parking, and could be used for a free-will donation. I jumped at the offer. The first Sangha sitting was on Tuesday, August 18, 1998, and indeed, a handful of people did come that very first night!

NETWORKING AND CONTACTS

The relationship that developed with our hosts, the Spiritual Life Center, was mutually beneficial. Our Sangha met at the House of Peace regularly for over a year and a half. The Spiritual Life Center also advertised our meditations in their newsletter, opening the practice to those from Christian and other faiths to join us. The center's director invited me to lead special events such as mornings of mindfulness for their members as well as our own. With interest and participation from their group, the center continues to promote mindfulness practices and serve as a resource for new members.

When we needed to find new accommodations for our Tuesday evening sittings, we connected with First Unitarian Church through one of our regular mindfulness practitioners, who was also a member of the church. The pastor was familiar with Zen Buddhist practice and had read several of Thây's books. The church now provides us a place to sit, and in turn, we offer meditation to their congregation members.

Other groups like the Honolulu Diamond Sangha, Vipassana Hawaiʻi, and the Buddhist Peace Fellowship have practitioners who share Buddhist practices yet seek to learn more about Thây's teachings on mindfulness in everyday life. I have made contacts with these groups and have been invited to talk about mindfulness practices with them. A Vietnamese family from Vipassana Hawaiʻi opened their home to our Sangha for a two-day retreat in 1999 and now hosts monthly Days of Mindfulness. That warm invitation from like-minded Buddhists encourages our Dharma practice as well as sharing across different Buddhist traditions.

TUESDAY EVENING FORMAT

Our little Sangha, named the Honolulu Mindfulness Community, follows a schedule similar to that of the Washington Mindfulness Community. Our biweekly meditation evenings begin at 7:30 p.m. and end around 9:00 p.m. We open our Tuesday evening with a guided meditation based on instructions from Thich Nhat Hanh's book *The Blooming of a Lotus.* This first sitting is followed by indoor walking meditation and a period of silent sitting. If there are new members joining the group, I offer instructions for sitting and walking; otherwise, we continue in silence. After the meditation period, we transition from silence to Dharma discussion by introducing ourselves — saying our names and "reporting on the weather" (as described by Richard Brady in his article "Dharma Discussions" in Part Five).

Following this brief sharing, we listen to a twenty-minute segment of one of Thây's Dharma talks and then open the floor for questions and answers or sharing about the practice. The combination of sitting and walking followed by Dharma discussion offers a good mix of quiet contemplation balanced with listening and talking. One group member often brings her guitar and sings songs from the Plum Village songbook, *A Basket of Plums;*[43] we have added the joy of music meditation to our practice as well.

SOCIALS AND CELEBRATIONS

Supplementing our Tuesday evening sittings, our Sangha has hosted social events like potluck gatherings. Often these are held on Friday evenings, with members invited to bring family and friends as well as a vegetarian dish to share. Less organized and more social, the potlucks have helped us know each other more personally and have encouraged family members to participate. Highlighting our first year was the celebration of the Sangha's first anniversary on August 18, 1999. We hosted the potluck at the House of Peace, sharing a huge birthday cake. On other occasions, members have invited us to their homes to enjoy a mindful dinner or dessert and tea. The connections that are fostered through these informal social gatherings strengthen our ties to one another.

SPROUTING A SANGHA

With regularity and commitment, our Sangha has endured the usual ebbs and flows of change. We moved from the House of Peace to the First Unitarian Church. We lost some regulars to new jobs, different islands, and other interests. We changed formats and added new segments. While our Honolulu Mindfulness Community remains small with usually six or seven regulars and nearly seventy on the mailing list, I believe that we grow deeper as our individual practice is strengthened by our Sangha.

Despite busy lives filled with work and family, we make time for stopping, breathing, calming, relaxing, and joining with each other in meditation. If I feel stressed over something in my work, I go to a Tuesday gathering and am refreshed. If a Sangha member speaks of difficulties with family or job, the burden seems easier with the sharing. In fact, one does not even have to share out loud to feel a sense of relief from participating together. Thây speaks about the interbeing nature of all of us, that we are not independent from each other but interconnected with all things. That essence is reinforced as we come together in mindfulness practice, meditating collectively as a Sangha.

While our little Sangha has sprouted, it needs continued attention and care to grow. But that is for the next story.

On the Path to Liberation: Insights and Experiences with Communities 13

BY KARL SCHMIED

W HEN WE SAY, "I take refuge in the Sangha," it means that we put our trust in the community of fellow practitioners who have stability in themselves. A teacher can be important, as well as the teachings, but friends are the decisive factor in our practice. It is difficult—if not impossible— to practice without a Sangha.

Ever more urgently, Thây has been stressing the importance and the value of the Sangha. This can be seen in several passages from his book, *Touching Peace*, which illustrate his view:

> It is my deep desire that communities of practice in the West be organized... as families in a friendly, warm atmosphere, so that people can succeed in their practice. A Sangha in which each person is like an island, not communicating with each other, is not helpful. It is just a collection of trees without roots. Transformation and healing cannot be obtained in such an atmosphere. We must be rooted if we want to have a chance to learn and practice meditation. I think that Sangha-building is the most important art for us to learn.... We have to build a Sangha that is happy, where communication is open.[44]

There are many different kinds of Sanghas which I have had the privilege of building and working with over the past twenty-five years. I have become acquainted both with Buddhist and Christian monastic communities, and have been able to gather a substantial amount of experience in practicing with a community living together in the manner of a monastic Sangha at our Interbeing Center in Lower Bavaria.

We all experience every day how difficult it is to maintain one's integrity and live mindfully in our modern society, one which is so heavily marked by greed, aggression, and inconsiderateness. Our life is influenced by a system which lures us—through a variety of seductive propositions—into distraction, dispersion, and artificial consumerism. It takes us over, manipulates us, and poisons our bodies and minds. A Sangha offers the opportunity for us to reflect, reorient, and return to ourselves ("I have arrived, I am home"). Through this, we obtain a new and deep connection with reality and with potential healing processes. At the same time, it is certain that nobody will find the perfect Sangha for themselves. An imperfect Sangha is good enough. Instead of complaining about our own Sangha, we should do our best to be a good member. A living Sangha can reflect change for us and in many ways illuminate the path to more harmony and mindfulness.

I have summarized my experiences with different communities—which may be of use in establishing and maintaining a network of "friends on the path"—into ten aspects:

1) Strengthen your faith in the healing power of the Three Jewels, which includes the Sangha. Work as a firm member in it. Constantly examine your own wishes, ideas, and your intention to achieve them in your community.

2) Continuity in the practice is of the greatest importance, but can only be attained when we take joy in doing it. It does not make a difference whether there are three or fifty members in the group. Meet regularly. Arrange set times for group practice and observe them.

3) Try to create an environment where as many Sangha members as possible can contribute, help, and participate. Then you will gradually overcome the status of consumer or passive listener and become an active part of a Sangha in which real friendships can develop, and where Thây's maxim, "I walk for you" can be realized. Part of this is tolerance—inviting friends who have

their roots in Christianity or other traditions, and including them.

4) Structure the meetings clearly. The agenda, short rituals, and dialogues, as well as the meditative part, should be structured and agreed upon clearly in order to avoid it turning into an informal "tea party"—as much as there should be time available for an open, relaxed conversation over a cup of tea.

5) Almost every community needs a teacher, moderator, or companion who feels responsible for organizing the procedures, for contacting friends in the meditation circle, and who is acknowledged by the participants. This is someone who walks the path of the Dharma out of a deep conviction, who doesn't merely teach it but also lives it. Group leadership based on setting up a board or a revolving system has only rarely proven to be effective, and only when there has been a core Sangha made up of friends who have a good knowledge of the practice and of the Dharma.

6) The Sangha is a spiritual family; however, it is not a warm nest or a substitute for group psychotherapy. People who are troubled and unstable due to psychological difficulties can only, in small numbers, join a stable community, be supported, and—as much as possible—integrated.

7) Conflicts—as minor as they may be—should be taken care of in good time through the "Beginning Anew" practice (see Appendix III) and possibly with an additional "Peace Treaty" (see Appendix III) in which we make a pledge to behave differently. Small difficulties should not be allowed to grow into dilemmas. We must repeatedly practice right speech and work to understand the other's point of view. We strive for a real agreement, not a half-hearted compromise due to a need for a falsely-understood harmony.

8) Since the time of the Buddha, causing a rift in the Sangha has been considered one of the most serious faults. On the other hand, fluctuation is a natural process. Here, too, Dharma is *marga*

—a path—on which each of us can proceed according to his or her own understanding and maturity.

9) Competencies and responsibilities should be defined as clearly as possible in the areas of organization and finances. We have to make sure that we do not aim to do too much, otherwise we will create a kind of "business Buddhism." For this reason, centers, large projects, and events have to be planned precisely, and the actual means of the Sangha must be taken into consideration realistically. Financial pressures and even obligations often create an unhealthy activism, and not only bring about considerable tension within the community, but actually endanger it.

10) Let's celebrate! Joy, fun, and laughter are wonderful things. The Vesakh festival in May, the Maitreya festival during the advent season, a spring or florescence party combined with an imaginatively and lovingly-prepared Tea Ceremony are wonderful opportunities to show ourselves, our mutual support for each other, and our companionship on the path.

The essential thing is for the practice of the Plum Village Dhyana school to remain clearly recognizable in our communities despite any adjustments made due to regional circumstances, and that no randomness or "spiritual mix" is created. One needs to have clear motivation in order to move toward having a conscious, awakened society. Each person begins for him- or herself, with the support of the Sangha, the necessary practice of change and transformation. The foundation of our Sanghas remains learning to take refuge in the Five Mindfulness Trainings (mindful listening, empathetic speech, generosity, responsible sexual behavior, right use of consumer goods, and respect for life) and putting them into practice in our daily lives. All of this is permeated by the energy of mindfulness and a deepening understanding of interbeing. In addition we practice deep relaxation, mindful Dharma conversations, walking meditation, eating together with the Five Contemplations (see Appendix II), and our practice of guided, quiet sitting meditation. The framework for orientation is formed by the Fourteen Mindfulness Trainings. Regular attendance at monthly Days of Mindfulness and at one- to two-week retreats (at least two per year), opportunities for which are offered at the Interbeing Center for Living in Mindfulness, are important elements for our Sangha members to deepen their practice.

Again and again, we ask ourselves the following questions: Do we have a common vision? What is it? Is our communication alive and sincere? Are our efforts authentic—real and dedicated? Or are we trying to sail safely in the lee of society, looking upon our practice as a hobby, and the Sangha as more of a friendship club and, at best, a study group? Certainly, Sangha-building applies not only to a Community of Mindful Living, but also to our biological family, to our friends and colleagues in clubs we belong to, and in our working environment. The transformation of our habit energies and behavioral patterns necessary in order to do this are practiced in our spiritual community.

As Thây explained at a Day of Mindfulness in October 1993 at Spirit Rock Meditation Center in California, "It is possible that the next Buddha, Maitreya, will not take on any individual form. Maybe he will take the form of a Sangha, a community practicing understanding and loving kindness, a Sangha which practices the art of mindful living."

We will build new communities and strengthen existing ones which show us the abundance of life and help us to understand it as a whole. In them, we learn the practice of living spiritually. This is a way of living that is oriented toward more awareness, deeper understanding, compassion, and continuous mindfulness. Our mind becomes more open, and there is more stability in the way we deal with our emotions. Inner peace, serenity, and joy strengthen us on the path to liberation.

Mindfulness
Practice Centers 14

BY JERRY BRAZA, PH.D.

MINDFULNESS, the Eastern art of learning to live in the present moment, is currently emerging in the Western hemisphere as a useful tool for enhancing well-being and reducing stress. Currently, programs on mindfulness are typically offered by local Sanghas in various Buddhist traditions. Unfortunately, many people do not have access to these programs or do not attend because of religious or philosophical differences.

Mindfulness has its roots in Buddhism, and it also is considered a perennial philosophy. Most people are completely comfortable with the concept of "present moment" awareness or the "power of now." When people look deeply into the roots of their own background they can easily connect with this philosophy. In my university class, I ask students to bring references to the concept of mindfulness from their own religious backgrounds. Most of the students have something to share such as, "Do not worry about tomorrow, for tomorrow will worry about itself" (Matthew 6:34). Mindfulness has universal applications and can be helpful to one's personal growth.

In the late 1990s, a movement to offer mindfulness as a tool for personal and collective well-being and transformation began in the United States. The Mindfulness Practice Center Association located in Quechee, Vermont states:

Mindfulness is one of the treasures of human nature. Everyone has a natural capacity to be mindful, which means to be present in the here and now, to be truly present without wanting anything else. It is only because of countless habits of thought and action we have acquired during our life as well as inherited from our forebears that we find it difficult to be present. By gently bringing ourselves back to the present moment again and again, we can relearn the art of mindfulness which is always available within ourselves.[45]

The practice center in Quechee, Vermont, states that a "Mindfulness Practice Center (MPC) or a Mindfulness Practice Group (MPG) is a completely secular, civil establishment for the practice of mindfulness in a town or a village."[46] In this context, mindfulness is practiced in a nondenominational and nonsectarian manner. All individuals are welcome regardless of their age, race, sex, or spiritual path. With this openness and a mission to create a "mindful culture," all individuals are included in a way that may not be typically found in other spiritual groups or fraternal organizations.

The "Four Qualities of a Mindful Life" developed by the MPC in Vermont form the cornerstone of Western Oregon University's MPC. These four qualities are the basis for a mindful life and the key to healthy relationships. Facilitators of the MPC are encouraged to practice and model these qualities in their daily lives. They are summarized below:

1) Compassionate Listening: We have seen clearly that in this world there are people who have the capacity to listen deeply to others and to comfort them in their pain. This capacity lies within all of us.

2) Deep Understanding: As a result of compassionate listening, deep understanding develops. We shall practice looking with unprejudiced eyes. We shall practice looking without judging or reacting. We shall practice looking deeply in order to be able to see and understand the roots of suffering. We are determined to look deeply at the impermanent and interdependent nature of all that is.

3) Compassionate Action: After listening and understanding, compassionate action is a natural outcome. We know that every word, every look, every action, and every smile can bring happiness to

others. Students, faculty, and staff are inspired by this practice, which can impact the lives of many who connect with them.

4) Being Present for Those Who Need Us: The quality of presence is the best gift we can give to another person. Mindfulness practice helps us to be present for the joy, as well as the suffering, that exists within ourselves and others.[47]

With the support of leadership from local Sanghas and other community members, a MPC or MPG is created and normally meets in a rented or donated space. A daily and/or weekly program is provided to facilitate mindfulness practice. The organizational structure is typically nonprofit, non-religious, community-run, and open to the entire community. Early morning, noontime, and late afternoon sessions are typically held to provide an opportunity to practice sitting and walking meditation along with discussion groups on the practice of living mindfully. Other activities include study groups, tea ceremonies, guided meditations, and other techniques useful in managing stress. Emphasis is placed on the physical, emotional, mental, and social benefits of the practice. Days of Mindfulness and retreats are held and may include families and children. Groups may also spend time in outreach programs to support various community projects.

An ideal environment for a Mindfulness Practice Center is a campus community. Inherent in academia are many stresses that can affect the quality of life for faculty, staff, and students alike. Every college and university could benefit from a space where members of the campus and surrounding community can calm and renew themselves. The Mindfulness Practice Center offers such an oasis.

The MPC that is housed in the Student Health and Counseling Center on the campus of Western Oregon University offers a daily mindfulness practice from 12:00 to 12:30 p.m. each weekday. The center offers support through student facilitators who have been trained in mindfulness practice and make themselves available to participants. The practice of mindfulness offers an opportunity to reduce stress, increase concentration, enhance relationships, and find more peace and joy in one's personal and professional life. Practicing together as a group offers support and encouragement in the process.

The center at Western Oregon University is founded as a part of a national movement to bring "mindfulness," or present-moment awareness, into the academic community. Our long-term goal is to develop a national model for other universities.

For additional information and a copy of a booklet on how to develop such a center, visit: www.wou.edu/mindful.

Part Five
Sangha Practice

~

A Rare Haven 15

BY SUSAN O'LEARY

SANGHA IS ORDINARY. Being in community is a simple practice you create by showing up, by slowing down, by listening—to yourself and to others, to your breath, to your heart.

Sangha gives a form, a way of being. To practice breathing as others breathe. To practice being silent as others are silent. A social practice of silence, Sangha is that rare haven in worldly life where you come together on purpose to not talk, to not say, but to be. And to return home.

As we practice the silence, sitting in two straight rows, member facing member, we come to feel what it can be to create community. We come to know each other through our practice. If you are first turned inward, turned to yourself, then when you look outward you see others with simpler eyes, a surer breath. You realize how others create your practice, for without the other Sangha members showing up, maintaining the continuity, there is no community to rely on. As you sit, you increasingly give thanks for this presence.

Sangha, too, is Dharma. It is discourse, the seeds of knowing refined into practice. For after sitting, we *do* talk, and we take turns leading talking, but this is a speech preceded by silence, a speech recognized by bows. And so we come to hone speech, to parse it, to try to speak the one true sound that comes from the breath. Because if you know when you speak that others are truly listening, you may have something very different to say. Perhaps simplicity that comes from the heart. Perhaps difficulty or pain that the evening allows to be spoken. Perhaps an understanding the evening sit has awakened. Perhaps thanks.

If you keep coming to Sangha long enough, you may come up against difficulty in the Sangha community. Sangha is not separate from life; it is life. Sangha is a place where you can practice trying to be present with discord and letting it settle. To see what you, yourself, bring from your past that is present with you now in the discord. To try to see with new eyes, with your breath, with an open heart.

Sangha is repetition, as the breath is repetition. Years of the practice community come into your body as a knowing. The chants that memorize themselves and whisper to you during the day. The invitation of the bodhisattvas to move to an understanding so caring that it dissolves boundary. The foundation of the mindfulness trainings, bedrock in life.

As you come back — week, month, year after year — Sangha becomes a grounding, a gratitude. It is an impermanent physical presence you can return to again and again to know who you are. To begin anew.

It exists in life and is of life.

It is the heart's world home.

Intergenerational Practice 16

THE CLEAR HEART SANGHA has been meeting for about ten years. Over that period of time, we have grown to have about thirty-five to forty members. We have experienced the blessings of Sangha life—watching the transformations in ourselves and others, developing trust and confidence in the Sangha wisdom, and enjoying the shared strength and joy of practicing in community. Our members range in age from young people in their late teens and early twenties to septuagenarians. One member commented that having participated in various groups her whole life, she particularly appreciated that this was the first one that seemed to encompass such a diversity of ages, socioeconomic strata, sexual orientations, interests, and backgrounds.

We are also very fortunate to live in a university community and have had students from Brown University and the University of Rhode Island participate in our Sangha. They are so bright, sincere, and thoughtful. They are very interested in the Dharma and bring freshness to our Dharma discussions. One of our senior members said, "They are our future, they give us hope." Another described it as "a real gift" to practice with the students. Many of the students who attend are involved in political science. They are very knowledgeable and committed to social action. Some of them have appreciated gaining a different, nonideological perspective on social change as well as a different view of causality and nonattachment to outcomes. The students have brought us a lot of information and helped raise our awareness about sustainability and mindful consumption. One member felt that the students had raised her consciousness and inspired her to learn more about the global economy. She also appreciated the students taking part in various demonstrations for social change, in which she was unable to participate due to her life circumstances. She felt that they were representing her and she felt deep gratitude and respect for them.

The students seem to enjoy the loving kindness of a family away from home. In the midst of their hectic, academic lives, they appreciate stopping, calming, resting, and healing. The practice of meditation itself helps them respond more skillfully to the stresses of college life and allows them to experience peace and quiet. One student stated that "college campuses are some of the hardest places to practice." He appreciated the concrete practices that bring stability. He felt that "they were very beneficial and a really positive alternative to binge drinking" which he was observing other students turn to in order to cope.

Some have really enjoyed the practice of deep listening during the Dharma discussions. One student said, after his first visit, that he was so moved by being listened to. It was a novel experience to have all the time he needed to express himself, to not be rushed and to be heard. A student who has gone on to work for peace in the nation's capitol said that he often thinks of Thây's talks about the power of deep listening. He has found that practice to be extremely transformational in some of his work in Washington, D.C.

One student commented that she really appreciated the opportunity to explore spirituality outside of the context of a church. Along with the spiritual nourishment the Sangha provides, one student commented that he appreciated the tea, the cookies, and the fresh fruit!

Having students and faculty be a part of our Sangha has also opened the way for nice exchanges. They helped to organize an Honors Colloquium on Peace and Nonviolence at the university and invited one of the Tiep Hien Dharma teachers to speak. Some of the Sangha members have been invited to lead meditations or to simply sit with the students at their weekly meditations on campus. We have also been invited to introduce and lead walking meditation at their annual daylong meditation retreat.

The role a Sangha can play in student life was described beautifully by a former student who recently wrote of his experience, "The Sangha became an anchor for me, and brought much needed rhythm and perspective into my hectic college existence. I remember most vividly the energy I felt as we all sat together, smiling in silence. In the Sangha, I found emotional and spiritual support as well as deep connection with older generations—things that previously had been missing from my life in college. I found refuge after a long week of giving such priority to my intellectual self. It was where I returned to my center, to my suffering, and my joy. The relationships that I found there continue to be some of the most precious of that period in my life."

Our Sangha has also been very fortunate to have Maple Forest Monastery and Green Mountain Dharma Center not too far away. We took a Sangha field trip to the Dharma Center for a weekend retreat. After our retreat, one of our members, who is a long-time practitioner, observed that every tradition in which he has studied taught the importance of mindfulness, but it wasn't until he had spent time with the monastics that he truly understood its direct application in every moment of daily life.

Over the past year, we have deepened our relationship with the monastics. In April, we helped to organize a Regional Day of Mindfulness, and four monastics facilitated the day for us. Because it was regional, the monks and nuns could visit with all of our Sanghas at one time and we could get to know them, as well as our neighbors, a little better. It was pure joy. It is a gift for those of us in the lay community to be able to strengthen our practice with those who embody it. It also gives all of us an opportunity to get to know and understand each other better so we can support one another.

To be with the monastics and experience how they live is a deep teaching. They are aware of their capacities and do not take on more than they can reasonably and joyfully complete. They bring the same mindfulness to play as to work and accept huge responsibilities with complete confidence that they will be supported and assisted. It is very beautiful to see how everyone tries their best to support everyone else in being the best they can be—to develop all their skills and gifts to the fullest, because that's what is best for everyone. To be a part of that is to directly experience the Four Immeasurable Minds —loving kindness, compassion, sympathetic joy, and equanimity.

Here at the Clear Heart Sangha we feel deeply grateful for all of our friends along the path, and we are really enjoying interbeing!

Dharma Discussions: Practice and Community 17

BY RICHARD BRADY

THE BUDDHA often described his teachings, the Dharma, as a raft that could carry his students to the other shore, to liberation. Today practitioners can learn about this raft from Dharma talks given by contemporary teachers, from the sutras, and from other Buddhist writings. In Dharma discussions we support each other in deepening our understanding of the teachings, in developing an understanding of our experiences in the light of the Dharma, and in finding practices through which we can apply the teachings to our lives. Dharma discussions are a fundamental part of Sangha meetings, mindfulness retreats, and Plum Village life. At their best they embody qualities of group meditation, enabling us to enter a common place of quiet in which to stop, to listen deeply to ourselves and each other. How can our Dharma discussions provide a better space for us to be in contact with our own inner Buddhas and to feel invited to ask for and give support?

In his Plum Village question and answer sessions, Thây responds to questions from his personal experience of Buddhist teachings. In doing so, he helps to make these teachings come alive and be accessible to retreatants for use in everyday life. Dharma discussions have this same goal: enabling participants to see connections between their experience and Buddhist teachings, to be, as the Buddha said, "lamps unto ourselves." To accomplish this, participants need to look within and share from their own experience. Leaders can encourage reflection by asking questions. In a recent discussion, for instance, a participant asked about the meaning of "true self." I responded by asking if he were requesting that people share their personal experiences of being in touch with their true selves. His "yes" led to some deep sharing about vulnerability, compassion, and self-acceptance and avoided conceptual answers. After the Washington Mindfulness Community listens to a tape of Thây, we begin the Dharma discussion that follows with a reminder: We now have an opportunity to share where the talk has touched us, to share something from our practice, or to share some success or some difficulty to which others can speak.

When facilitating new groups, I sometimes mention at the onset the importance of periods of silence. I have observed a connection between the depth of the Dharma discussion and the quality of the silence from which it emerges. Too often the silence can vanish, one sharing following immediately after another as if there were some pressure to keep the discussion going. These are the times when inviting the mindfulness bell feels particularly appropriate to me. Occasionally a period of silence stretches on to the point where it begins to feel unproductive. My ability to see when and how best to facilitate reflects the degree to which I am present. It can be difficult for me as the facilitator to decide whether to try to return to the previous discussion or to move on to new concerns, to ask the group a question or to share an experience of my own.

Group members occasionally address questions directly to me or another facilitator. When I'm the facilitator, I like to sit back, listen, and learn. Knowing that anyone in the group may have a helpful response to a question lessens my temptation to jump in and teach. When we do answer such questions directly, group discussions can turn into two-person conversations with an audience. One way to avoid this is to invite others to answer first. However, I am inclined to enter a discussion if it has lost contact with Buddhist teachings, perhaps asking how the Dharma might be of assistance. If the discussion has become absorbed with the teachings in a disembodied way, I might ask whether someone has an illustration from his or her life.

Dharma discussions have several important functions in addition to deepening participants' understanding of the Buddha's teachings. In large mindfulness retreats, especially silent ones, discussion groups are home base for many participants. Some retreatants inevitably get in touch with painful emotions, and their Dharma discussion groups are frequently the one place they can go to for help. In large Sanghas like our Washington Mindfulness

Community, where organizational work is often performed by a relatively small core group, Dharma discussions provide others an important opportunity to be known by the community.

Before each of our Sangha's Dharma discussions, we go around the circle giving our names, our home communities, and, if needed, requesting a ride home. This simple practice brings everyone into the discussion. Introductions are even more important in retreat settings, where many participants are strangers. During a recent Plum Village summer opening, Eveline Beumkes gave me a very helpful variation on the usual introduction: the weather report. After participants told their names, home countries, and arrival days, they described their internal weather. Some gave bare-bones reports: stormy with a few rainbows. Others described the nature of their storms and rainbows. Some chose not to use weather images and simply reported their emotional state. These reports allow group members to feel safe and open the way for further sharing. They establish connections between each participant and the group and between group members. Weather reports also give the facilitator an opportunity to see where the group is. Once during the introductions, several newcomers commented on their great tiredness. As the facilitator, I was in a position to validate the common feeling of tiredness and invite sharing about that.

After a discussion during the recent summer opening at Plum Village, a newcomer shared with me that she did not feel ready to speak but hoped she would next time. During that particular session several of the participants had shared three or four times. I decided to begin our next one by suggesting that we could all encourage more participation by each sharing only once, waiting to speak again until all had had a first opportunity. This time my quiet friend was the first to share. She thanked me afterwards for my encouragement. I don't know whether we ought to make such suggestions routinely, but we might at least make them privately to Sangha members who speak frequently.

Creating an atmosphere where all participants feel invited to share is a major challenge for facilitators. Over the past four years Washington Mindfulness Community Dharma discussions have grown in size from about ten to as many as thirty participants. When the number exceeds twenty, we divide ourselves in two. I have found that even in smaller groups there are people who virtually never speak. In one Plum Village Dharma discussion, I asked which members of the group had already received the Five Mindfulness Trainings. When half the group raised their hands, I suggested that they all might have helpful responses in the following discussion on the trainings. Almost all did. When I look back on Washington Mindfulness Community Dharma discussions, some of the ones I feel best about are the few in which none of the senior members of the community felt called to speak. What a strong message—the more senior members sitting quietly listening, empowering every member to share his or her own experience of the Dharma!

Last fall our Sangha had several very special Dharma discussions. The first occurred at our Sangha's semiannual family and friends getaway weekend where we had a discussion about the Sangha. We began by going around the circle, each person sharing what he or she had been looking for in first coming to the Sangha, what had worked well, and what new direction he or she wished for. Every participant, newcomer and old-timer alike, spoke from the heart, many affirming their connection to the Sangha. We experienced a deep sense of community. Now our Sangha is working to make this experience an enduring reality.

The Importance of Right Speech and Humility 18

BY NGUYEN DUY VINH

IN THE BOOKLET *Sangha Practice* published by Parallax Press, lay Dharma teacher Jack Lawlor observes:

> Presently, our society does not offer support or encouragement for simple contemplative practices. The importance of being a part of a community that supports our spiritual life cannot be overestimated. What does a good spiritual friend do? She is truly present with others and listens with an open heart and mind, free of prejudice and harsh criticism. He looks deeply to see what is best in others and encourages its development. She seeks to understand the "weaknesses" that may be manifesting and artfully does her best to water the "good seeds," the inherent virtues and strength in her friend. He observes right speech—speech that is free of intolerance and sarcasm—which is vital to creating a sense of friendship and family.[48]

This short paragraph describes important qualities needed to build a harmonious Sangha. We are lucky if we have a good number of people who possess these qualities at the beginning of the Sangha-building phase. Usually, our capabilities of deep listening, tolerance, and right speech at the start are quite weak, and we are very clumsy in our ways of doing things. We bring with us our own problems, our own views, and our own internal formations. Our perception is often dictated by our judging mind. Our ego is sometimes very big, and we care mostly for our own agenda. We need a core number of brothers and sisters who sacrifice their time and material resources to give the Sangha a good start until we have enough members with a strong commitment. Slowly and steadily, we will reach the "cruising speed" phase. People in the Sangha start to know each other a bit more. Some friendship and solidarity begin to develop, and the Sangha becomes stronger and healthier.

The Sangha must be ready to cherish all contributions without judging. The Sangha must be sincere in its advice. Advice should come from our own experience and suffering and not from our intellect, from our loving heart and not from our analytical brain. We must also learn to be humble and take all criticisms with an open mind, willing to do better ourselves and to improve ourselves in the practice even if the criticisms may at times be unfair to us.

Our happiness is not personal; it is related to other people's happiness. How can we build a harmonious Sangha if there is not mutual respect and reciprocal understanding and love? We must learn to see that we are not the only ones who suffer in this world. We should practice to be thankful and develop our gratitude to all the wonders we receive from our surroundings.

In order to improve Sangha life, we can start with ourselves. Through diligent practice, we will become more and more inclusive and loving. We will be able to listen deeply and take good care of our friends and loved ones.

(This article originally appeared in Issue No. 24 of the *Mindfulness Bell*.)

Walking on Ice 19

BY JACK LAWLOR

Even the Buddha's Sangha experienced difficulties. His cousin Deva-datta once attempted to divide the Sangha and lead it himself. The Buddha could not mediate a dispute over etiquette between the Precept Master and the Sutra Master at Kosambi—at least not initially. The *Upakkilesa Sutta*[49] describes how the bhikshus at Kosambi were "quarreling and brawling and deep in dispute, stabbing each other with verbal daggers." The Buddha's verse on this dispute reveals how keenly he observed what was happening:

> When many voices shout at once
> None considers himself a fool;
> Though this Sangha is being split
> None thinks himself to be at fault.
> They have forgotten thoughtful speech,
> They talk obsessed by words alone.
> Uncurbed their mouths, they bawl at will;
> None knows what will lead him to so act.

> "He abused me, he struck me,
> He defeated me, he robbed me"—
> In those who harbor thoughts like these
> Hatred will never be allayed.

For in this world, hatred is never
Allayed by further acts of hate.
It is allayed by non-hatred.
That is the fixed and ageless law.
Those others do not recognize
That here we should restrain ourselves.
But those wise ones who realize this
At once end all their enmity.

Many Western Sanghas have also experienced difficulty. Ordained teachers in various traditions have engaged in sexual misconduct and selfish financial practices, and disputes have arisen out of personality differences and opinions on how the Sangha should be "led." In response, we often want to reach beyond basic mindfulness practices to resources from other venues, such as conflict resolution techniques used by businesses or other spiritual traditions. If carefully modified to address the people involved, these can sometimes help lessen difficulty in a Sangha, but there are limitations on how much relief we can reasonably expect from organizational solutions, except with respect to extreme behavior and abuses. A healthy, happy Sangha ultimately depends less on structures than on consistent mindfulness practice and true concern and affection for each other.

Simple practice helps us penetrate the limits of conceptual thought by deepening our insight into our own and others' motivations and needs, thus enabling us to transform our behavior and nourish the Sangha. Practicing in a Sangha that concentrates wholeheartedly on basic practice, it becomes easier to let go of some of our favorite ideologies and concepts—including our concepts of what Sangha should be like. The *Diamond Sutra* boldly asserts that "Buddhas are called Buddhas because they are free from ideas."[50]

We are invited to participate in a Sangha with an open mind and heart. We should not leave a Sangha merely because it occasionally uses practices that do not appeal to us. A practice that does not appeal to us today may be of great help in the future. Practicing as a healthy Sangha involves a collective decision to practice wholeheartedly each time the Sangha convenes. As Thây reminds us, happiness is not an individual matter.

The calm and peace produced by our mindfulness practice provides insight when uncertainty, impatience, or anger arise in us. With mindfulness, we are better equipped to watch these states arise and fall. We are able to respond to the actual circumstances we are in, rather than react as if compelled by habit energy. From this space, this freedom, the practice of right speech—so critical to any healthy Sangha—becomes possible. We find little use for gossip or sarcastic speech, which causes so much suffering in a Sangha. During a past tele-Dharma talk to North American members of the Order of Interbeing, Thây reflected:

> Causing division, juggling for power, juggling for influence, opposing each other are just the symptoms of lack of practice. You can apply mindfulness in every moment of your daily life. We should not put a lot of energy into how to organize or structure or how to settle things, as in politics. The main thing is the practice. The practice is the first thing. We should set up organizations on the basis of our practice, not the other way around. If we use our intelligence to organize our daily practice, we can get nourishment, healing, and transformation every day, and we can help our brothers and sisters do the same.

Following this advice can be difficult. It is more entertaining to play with ideas about how to graft Western organizational models onto Buddhist life. Buddhism and Western culture already interpenetrate and inform each other. But successful integration will happen more as the result of our collective experimentation with living mindfully and practicing in small local Sanghas than as the result of structure imposed by hierarchy. Some folks get so caught up in ideas and concepts that they slowly abandon their own daily mindfulness practices. Veteran practitioners cannot cheat on daily practice and hope to remain mindful—even in the name of Sangha-building or spreading the Dharma in the West.

Balancing mindfulness practices and the desire to help is like walking on ice. Sometimes the ice is hidden or even invisible. In the Midwest, we call this "black ice." In some places it is safe to walk, but inches away it may be extremely slippery. If you fall, you learn the true meaning of dispersion. Despite the difficulty, I recommend walking on ice as a mindfulness practice. It teaches us something about life as a layperson, as an organizer and facilitator of a local Sangha. Sometimes conditions are ideal; sometimes they are not. Sometimes we can see the obstacles and difficulties; sometimes, even if we try to look with our Sangha eyes, they remain hidden. When the going is slippery, it is best to slow down and return to the basics of breathing and walking. When we do, those with us are much safer, and we become less dangerous and less frustrated with the slippery, uncontrollable conditions of daily life.

When a lake freezes before a snowfall, you can sometimes look deeply into it through the ice and see the lily pads and roots of last summer smiling at you from below the frozen surface. When we slow down and face our difficulties, illuminating them with mindfulness before we speak or act, we may also find that much below the surface is revealed.

The Buddha never lost faith in Sangha practice. Not long after his enlightenment, he built his first Sangha, and he continued Sangha-building for forty-five years. He interacted with Sangha members from every stratum of society: kings, princes, princesses, wealthy men and women and their over-privileged children, paupers, outcasts, and criminals. But, he learned from all of them, and this learning is evident in the deepening of his teachings as his Sangha practice continued. The wisdom body we share today as "Buddhism" is a result of this collective interaction. In the wake of the difficulties of the Sangha at Kosambi, the Buddha found three monks practicing as a small Sangha in the Eastern Bamboo Park. He was favorably impressed with how considerate they were of each other and asked how they succeeded in "living in concord, without disputing, blending like milk and water, viewing each other with kindly eyes." The monks' response, recorded in the *Upakkilesa Sutta*, inspires us even today:

Venerable sir, as to that, I think thus: "It is a gain for me, it is a great gain for me that I am living with such companions in the holy life." I maintain bodily acts of loving kindness towards them both openly and privately. I consider: "Why should I not set aside what I wish to do and do what these venerable ones wish to do?" Then I set aside what I wish to do and do what these venerable ones wish to do. We are different in body, venerable sir, but one in mind. Whichever of us returns first from the village with almsfood prepares the seats, sets out the water for drinking and for washing, and puts the refuse bucket in its place. Whichever of us returns last eats any food left over, if he wishes. He puts away the seats and the water for drinking and washing. He puts away the refuse bucket after washing it, and he sweeps out the refectory. Whoever notices that the pots of water for drinking, washing, or the latrines are low and empty, takes care of them. If they are too heavy for him, he calls someone else by a signal of the hand and they move it by joining hands, but because of this we do not break out in speech. But, every five days, we sit together all night discussing the Dharma. This is how we abide diligent, ardent, mindful, and resolute.

The living Dharma is in the details of living mindfully and attentively, aware of the needs of others and allowing our understanding to bloom into direct manifestations of wisdom and compassion. In the classic Mahayana text *The Way of the Bodhisattva*, Shantideva advises:

Those desiring speedily to be
A refuge for themselves and other beings
Should interchange the terms "I" and "other"
And thus embrace a sacred mystery.

When we practice this way and recognize that others share our spiritual aspirations, it is easy to be truly present with others and to regard them as our kalyanamitra, our spiritual friends. Ananda once remarked to the Buddha, "Half of this holy life, Lord, is good and noble friends, companionship with the good, association with the good." The Buddha reflected for a moment and then responded, "Do not say that, Ananda. Do not say that. It is the whole of this holy life."[51] When faced with disputes within our Sanghas, we must return to the basic practices of mindful breathing and walking and ask ourselves the question the Buddha posed to the bhikshus at Kosambi:

> Breakers of bones and murderers,
> Those who steal cattle, horses, and wealth,
> Those who pillage the entire realm—
> When even these can act together,
> Why can you not do so too?[52]

(This article originally appeared in Issue No. 24 of the *Mindfulness Bell*.)

Beginning Anew: 20
Opening the Heart Practice
for Individuals, Sanghas, and Society

BY LYN FINE

"WE ALL NEED LOVE," Thich Nhat Hanh reminds us in the *Mindfulness Bell* issue dedicated to Sangha. "Without enough love, we may not be able to survive, as individuals and as a planet." He continues, "It is said that the next Buddha will be named 'Maitreya,' the Buddha of Love. I believe that Maitreya might not take the form of an individual but as a community showing us the way of love and compassion."[53]

Yet as we form Sanghas, lay and monastic, residential and nonresidential, we bring into our Sangha practice our experiences and expectations from our families, our religious root traditions, our experiences with other groups, our internal formations, and attachment to views. There are times when our attachment to our own views and images of what a Sangha "should" be is strong. There are times when we are caught in our feelings of hurt, frustration, exasperation, or disappointment triggered by the tone of voice or behavior of another Sangha member. Our expectations and needs are not met, and images that we didn't even know we had are disappointed.

Taking refuge in the jewel of the Sangha, "the community that lives" — or goes in the direction of living — "in harmony and awareness" is wonderfully nourishing, but how do we learn to cultivate a community showing us the way of love and compassion? What causes and conditions contribute to the manifestation of peacemaking and peace-building in these times?

The practice of Beginning Anew (see Appendix III) has been offered as a practice since the Buddha's time. In its traditional and contemporary forms, it is a skillful means, when practiced on a regular basis, for opening the heart and deepening Sangha and other relationships. Sister Annabel describes the practice of Beginning Anew in this way:

> In India in the sixth century bce, the monks and nuns practiced the Pavarana Full Moon ceremony at the end of the rainy retreat and also in conjunction with the precept recitation ceremony. *Pavarana* is sometimes translated as "invitation," as it is a time when monks and nuns invite one another to tell them of their shortcomings. Monks and nuns have continued to the present day doing very much the same ceremony before the twice-monthly precept recitation ceremony.... The effectiveness depends on our depth of commitment to listening and speaking with our whole heart. If we do not practice deep listening and wholehearted speaking, the ceremony can be superficial.... Traditionally, there is no Pavarana ceremony for lay families. But why should lay men and women not enjoy all the benefits which monks and nuns enjoy, even if it means modifying the ceremony in certain respects?...We have translated Pavarana as Beginning Anew...To disclose or uncover our regrets, our hurts, and our shortcomings is wholesome because it helps us to begin again.[54]

One lay Sangha described its practice of Beginning Anew after a painful split in the group, which had been meeting for a number of years:

> Members of the Sangha have worked over the past months to establish a process of peacemaking, conflict resolution, and Beginning Anew, based on Thây's teachings. We are still fine-tuning and modifying the forms as we try them out.
>
> Each month we have a new moon ceremony. We begin with "watering each other's flowers." Slowly and joyfully, we express our appreciation of one or more Sangha members for something they have done or an aspect of their way of being. In the second phase of the ceremony, each of us takes responsibility for our behavior that may have caused suffering to a member of the group or the Sangha.

This is received in silence, as other Sangha members practice deep listening. In the third phase, we each invite feedback from the others. Perhaps we have been unaware of a behavior in ourselves that has caused problems for someone. After some silence, other members of the Sangha may give feedback, which is received in silence, unless further clarification is needed.

This new moon ceremony is based on two prior steps of conflict resolution. Whenever there is some difficulty between members of the Sangha, the first step is for them to meet alone together, to speak and listen deeply to each other. If they are not able to complete the reconciliation process, the second step is for them to request a fair witness from the Sangha to meet with them. The role of the witness is to hold loving energy for them and, where necessary, to intervene to assist them in listening to each other with open hearts. If the conflict is still not resolved, it is brought to the new moon ceremony and addressed by the whole group. At this time, both persons describe, without blaming the other, their perceptions of the problem. We meditate on the issue as a group, and then we make suggestions for reconciliation that the two conflict members can agree upon. If the conflict begins to pervade the Sangha at large, a friend of the Sangha, a fair witness from another Sangha, might be invited to facilitate open dialogue, but we have not had to try this yet.

All of these procedures depend on the goodwill of everyone in the group. The forms alone are not enough to ensure stability and reconciliation. They are only a skeleton that must be fleshed out with loving compassion, right intention, and skillful speech. The new moon ceremony has helped us feel safer and more trusting. We have begun anew as a Sangha to heal ourselves from the wounds of separation and loss, so that we may grow and be strengthened as a community of practice.[55]

Of course, each Sangha needs to consider a variety of factors in determining whether to proceed with Beginning Anew in this fashion. It is important to first arrive at a consensus. There may be people experiencing difficulty with one another who are not comfortable with using this skill-ful means at a given time. The use of the complete ceremony might be trou-bling for those facing psychological difficulties or who are in an excitable state of mind. It may be awkward to expect newcomers to participate in the ceremony or to use it in the context of a newly-formed Sangha where peo-ple have not become familiar with one another and developed bonds of trust. If a Sangha is in harmony with the use of Beginning Anew for the first time, it may be possible to find a Dharma teacher or seasoned practi-tioner familiar with the practice to serve as a facilitator.

Nonresidential lay Sanghas in which I have participated have practiced Beginning Anew with the general format of flower-watering, beneficial regret, sharing hurts and difficulties, and ending with gratitude and flower-watering, as described above. It is helpful to begin with just flower-water-ing, and then, as trust deepens, the other elements can be added. It may be advantageous to conduct Beginning Anew in the context of a residential retreat or after several rounds of sitting meditation, when our conscious minds have had an opportunity to settle down through the practice of con-scious breathing. Sometimes, especially when people do not know each other well, we encourage each other to water the flowers not only of peo-ple present in the room, but also of people in our lives who are not pres-ent—family, friends, coworkers, even political leaders. Sometimes, but not always, lay Sangha practice with Beginning Anew includes the recitation of the Beginning Anew chant, either by one person, by the group as a whole, or in "round-robin" style.

Modifications of this Beginning Anew format have sometimes arisen out of the needs of a particular group. One Sangha, for example, began with a flower-watering circle in council format (go-round with a talking stick, no cross-talk). Then Sangha members had the option to speak when they felt moved to do so, to offer flower-watering, regrets, or hurts—but they also had the option to invite another person into the center of the circle for a one-on-one ten-minute maximum Beginning Anew dialogue, in which they exchanged flower-watering, beneficial regret, and sharing of hurts in the language of nonviolent communication. The person invited into the center had the option to say no. This modification of the format worked well as a means to provide for what had been expressed as a need by several people in the initial council go-round for a "back-and-forth" alternative to the more usual guideline of refraining from cross-talk. Encircled by the compassionate listening witness of the Sangha, several pairs of people were able to open their hearts and share deeply with each other, bringing them again in touch with the reality of love, kindness, and compassion in their relationship.

In my experience, the Beginning Anew Sangha practice is usually scheduled for the week before the recitation of the mindfulness trainings, but in lay Sanghas we have also sometimes simply included a brief flower-watering and beneficial regret meditation and sharing just before the recitation of the trainings. At an Oregon State Penitentiary Sangha Five Mindfulness Trainings Transmission Ceremony in which ten men received one or more of the trainings, it was especially powerful to include an opportunity for sharing in the form of Beginning Anew just after the transmission.

Beginning Anew practice at the workplace can be wonderfully nourishing and beneficial. Because of the feeling that there is not enough time, or that sharing in this way is not appropriate for the workplace, it can sometimes be difficult to initiate a "workplace Sangha" with a consistent practice of Beginning Anew. At one workplace, however, we were able to set aside time every week to "check in" with each other in a Beginning Anew format. This served us very well on a continuing basis. Also, when communication became stuck at one point, one person was able to write a "peace note" to another (see Peace Treaty and Peace Note in Appendix III), and a special Beginning Anew was scheduled. Another person was invited to be a witness and sound the mindfulness bell from time to time, while the person who was feeling hurt and the person who had acted unkindly, however unintentionally, spoke and listened to each other truthfully and compassionately. The "crisis intervention" aspect of this Beginning Anew worked well in part because of the previous ongoing nourishing experience with the regularly scheduled "non-crisis" Beginning Anew sharing.

To begin anew in our lives after an experience of deep hurt—loss of a beloved one or a loving relationship, betrayal of trust, an experience of humiliation and shaming—is not easy. In these moments the energy of mindfulness is not always strong enough to let go of the internal formations and feelings of terror, frustration, disappointment, rage, and grief from the past, to touch again the reality of love. Vulnerability and insecurity are present, and there can be great difficulty in releasing oneself from being caught in the past experience of hurt or injustice. These life experiences and the way we relate to them sometimes challenge our harmonious practice with our Sangha. We may need more love, attention, and caring than the Sangha has resource currently to provide.

The general approach of Beginning Anew can also be adapted to interactions between two individuals. One Sangha sister, some time after her separation and divorce, wisely invited her ex-husband to sit together with her in a beautiful garden so they could share together in a time of deep listening and speaking from the heart. It was not easy to do this, she said, but she did not want either of them to remain imprisoned in bitterness and resentment for the rest of their lives. With the help of a mindfulness bell, they took turns to listen to each other and to offer each other flower-watering (appreciation) and beneficial regret. Then, with this listening and speaking as a foundation, they began to share with each other in non-blaming, nonviolent communication, some of the hurts they had experienced during their previous fourteen years of marriage to each other. They ended their time in the garden with flower-watering. The divorce remained, but transformation and healing of each person's inner landscape occurred. The process was not easy, but in the end, they were freer to continue their lives with joy, to go on to build new loving relationships, and to be at peace with the new form of their relationship.

In my experience, the individual practice of Beginning Anew, the Sangha practice of Beginning Anew, and the societal practice of Beginning Anew inter-are. Individual, Sangha, and society Beginning Anew practices are mutually supportive. The individual and the collective inter-are. The individual is a Sangha—Beginning Anew helps us to deepen the peace and harmony within this Sangha. As the visioning statement of the Mountain Lamp Community in Washington, under the guidance of lay Dharma teacher Eileen Kiera, says, "We touch within ourselves a place of refuge that is always there, but gets covered over by our everyday lives of planning and worries." As we continue to manifest new ways to refresh our individual Beginning Anew practice, we open our hearts and begin anew with more energy and less effort with our Sangha brothers and sisters. As we continue to manifest new ways to refresh our Sangha practice of Beginning Anew, our heart of understanding opens and we also begin anew with ourselves.

What If Nobody Shows Up? 21

BY IAN PRATTIS

IT HAPPENS. That unanticipated moment when you—the facilitator—are there, and nobody shows up. I remember with a mixture of anxiety and humor the first time this happened. One fall evening I had cleaned the meditation room, set the cushions in a neat semicircle in front of the simple altar, meditated beforehand, and made sure the notes for the Dharma talk were ready. And nobody showed up. At first I thought friends were just a little late, but thirty minutes past the hour convinced me that nobody was coming. I was disappointed and remained so until two beautiful beings caught my attention. My dog, Nikki, and my cat, Lady, were sitting patiently close by me in the meditation room, waiting for my attention. They were fully present, only I was not. When I did notice them, I smiled. Only then could I look deeply at my thoughts. What, in fact, was disappointed?

My ego, expectations, habit energies, and mental formations—these were all certainly disappointed. Yet the moment I smiled to my loving animals, the disappointment began to fade away. I was left with the insight that of the many elements necessary for a Sangha facilitator, on this night it was Equanimity with a capital "E" that I needed most to nurture. After inviting the bell for Nikki, Lady, myself, and absent friends, I meditated on the Four *Brahmaviharas*[56]—the Buddha's teachings on love—with a particular emphasis on the fourth one—equanimity.

The following evening the doorbell rang at 7:00 p.m., and two friends from the Sangha came in, followed by another three, then five minutes later by another four. I welcomed them with surprise at seeing them. They were puzzled by this welcome, then told me that this was our Sangha evening. I had prepared for them the day before in error! We all laughed until the tears rolled down our cheeks when I told them the story. Our meditation and gathering that night became known as the Night of Warm Smiles and Quiet Chuckles, as once again Nikki and Lady joined us.

Not surprisingly, after meditation our discussion was about equanimity. Of how we can so easily get caught in our projections and mental formations when equanimity is absent. Also we shared at length our experiences of its interconnection with love, compassion, and joy — the remaining trio of the Four Brahmaviharas. To make these qualities come alive, we all knew that our practice had to become more skillful, drawing on one another's support.

There are many other things I could write about the Pine Gate Sangha practice — our hikes in the forest, finding a quiet place for a Dharma talk, and then on to a waterfall for a silent and mindful lunch, and the generosity of Sangha members as they take their practice out in an engaged manner. The Sangha practices in the true spirit of engaged Buddhism, introducing mindfulness practice into city schools, forming Citizen's Coalitions to protect the city environment from inappropriate development, and undertaking peace marches to bring about an end to war. The other groups in these coalitions are quite happy to find a meditation group at their core, and I do believe we assist them with our steadiness, especially as one Sangha member created and monitors their website. There is so much more — yet for me the Night of Warm Smiles and Quiet Chuckles after the Day When Nobody Showed Up provides a benchmark for the qualities actively cultivated during this time. Whenever I talk about the Buddha's teachings on love, usually at our Christmas gatherings, the Sangha revisits this benchmark.

There is a story about equanimity that I would like to tell.

There was once a rishi who lived in a remote part of northern India. Many people from the surrounding villages were drawn to this kind and compassionate holy man. They felt the clarity and love in his talks, which were drawn from the universal wisdom tradition of the *Vedas.* His teachings and guidance became part of the fabric of village life, and he conducted daily and seasonal prayers and ceremonies to honor the Earth and sacred traditions he had immersed himself in since childhood. His spacious hermitage was set apart from the villages. It was like the central hub of a great wheel, the congregating point for the surrounding communities. He was honored and revered for the gentle manner in which he brought people to their own deep, quiet communion with God.

One morning a group of elders from the villages slowly approached, looking very grim and angry. They were accompanied by a young woman and she was visibly pregnant. Arrisa was her name. Arrisa had always brought flowers to the hermitage, and her soft eyes, laughter, and elegant demeanor gave a special grace to the gatherings there. With downcast eyes and hesitant speech, Arrisa stated publicly, in front of the elders, that the rishi was the father of her unborn child.

The rishi paused in what he was doing and looked at Arrisa with deep compassion and love in his eyes. He was silent for a while, then simply said, "Very well." The elders left one by one, feeling deeply betrayed in the trust they had placed in the rishi, and they and their villagers did not return. Arrisa stayed at the hermitage in a separate room, and not once did the rishi rebuke her for her falsehood. She took upon herself household and garden responsibilities. At the time of her confinement, several women from her village came to assist with the birth. They saw the separate living arrangements, but brought neither offerings nor respect to the rishi. To all this the rishi simply said, "Very well."

A healthy son was born to Arrisa, yet she was tormented by what she had done. She took wonderful care of the hermitage, the farm animals, and the garden, growing the most beautiful flowers ever seen in that region. She saw how the rishi continued with his daily prayers and meditations. He diligently and joyfully conducted the seasonal ceremonies just as before. No one was present except for Arrisa and her son, or so she thought. Then she noticed how the farm animals would come closer to the hermitage and sit nearby when the rishi gave his teachings. He spoke to everything, to the birds in the trees, the insects rustling in the grass, the whisper of wind, and the animals gathered close to him. His heart was full, just as before, and he was happy to be with whatever was there.

Arrisa could stand it no longer. One morning she told the rishi that she was taking her son to meet the village elders and to tell them that the father of the child was a young man in a neighboring village. He had left the region to join the army and was posted in a faraway location. The rishi looked at her with the same compassionate eyes and simply said, "Very well."

Afterwards the elders and villagers began to return to the hermitage, full of apologies for their judgments, and for abandoning the teachings, saying how much they had missed his guidance and kindness. To all this the rishi merely smiled and simply said, "Very well." Arrisa and her son continued living at the hermitage. The father of her child returned to the region and married her. He asked the rishi if he could stay at the hermitage with his new wife and child and serve the rishi as his attendant for the rest of his life. The rishi looked at the young man with the same loving and compassionate eyes that he had presented to Arrisa. And we all know that he smiled and simply said, "Very well!" His equanimity had revealed the truth of everything.

To build and maintain a healthy Sangha requires many elements and virtues, not the least of which is equanimity. I think of this as a strong binding quality for the Pine Gate Sangha, which directly and gently guides us to love, compassion, and joy. The Buddha's teachings on love, no less.

PART SIX

Practicing with Young People

The Flowers of Our Sangha: Practicing with Young People

22

BY DAVID DIMMACK

YOUNG PEOPLE'S programs usually include singing, pebble meditation, and the practicing with the bell of mindfulness. The primary song and pebble meditation are based on a gatha from *The Blooming of a Lotus*:

Breathing in, I know I am breathing in.
Breathing out, I know I am breathing out.

Breathing in, I see myself as a flower.
Breathing out, I feel fresh.

Breathing in, I see myself as a mountain.
Breathing out, I feel solid.

Breathing in, I see myself as still water.
Breathing out, I reflect all that is.

Breathing in, I see myself as space.
Breathing out, I feel free.

In pebble meditation, each person makes a pouch and finds five pebbles to place in it. Each pebble represents one phrase of the gatha: In/Out, Flower/Fresh, Mountain/ Solid, Water/Reflecting, Space/Free. When it's time to meditate, the pebbles are taken out of the pouch and placed in a pile. Then each person picks an "In/Out" pebble, holds it, looks at it, breathes with it, imagines the phrase In/Out, and then sets the pebble in a new place. With the next pebble each person does the same, thinking, "I am a flower, I feel fresh," and then places the pebble with the first pebble. Slowly each pebble is transferred, one by one — looking, holding, breathing, and remembering. The pebbles are then returned to the pouch or the meditation is repeated. Children of all ages can learn to meditate this way.

We often sing the Two Promises to help develop understanding and compassion (see Appendix II). Betsy Rose's tape, *In My Two Hands,* has many songs children enjoy that are accompanied by hand gestures. Music, song, and story are essential to a young people's program.

Each young person also practices being bell master. When calm and ready, the bell master stops and bows to the small bell, slowly picks it up, holds it in the palm of his or her hand, raises it to eye level, and looking at it, imagines he is holding a precious gift in his hand. Then using the small wooden stick, she taps the bell to wake it up and let everyone know it is time to be still and quiet. With a full stroke, a long, beautiful tone is invited. Everyone enjoys three full breaths and returns to what they were doing more refreshed and aware.

Young people also enjoy orange meditation (see Appendix II), drawing, craft projects, discussions, reading, storytelling, improvisational skits, interactive games, free play, stretching, tumbling, hiking, jokes, and just hanging out. Often, they present songs, skits, drawings, or Dharma recitations to the Sangha. A program tends to be more successful when loosely structured, giving the children time to focus on their own projects. Inviting visitors — Monks, nuns, musicians, or storytellers — is another fun way to help cultivate the seeds of mindfulness in these tender young sprouts.

A young people's program reflects the positive attitude of the Sangha. Feelings of trust and cooperation grow among everyone involved. Young people welcome the slower, gentle rhythm of the meditation and retreat process, away from television and other fast-paced gadgets.

Local Sanghas can create similar programs. Playfulness and mindfulness need not be separate; breathing and smiling, as well as a balloon or a funny hat, work wonders. As the Greek scholar Phaedrus said, "The mind ought sometimes to be diverted that it may return to better thinking." A leader only needs to provide a few simple activities, be devoted to gentle play, and be willing to be a little foolish. Let the collective playfulness of your Sangha be your guide.

(This article originally appeared in Issue No. 20 of the *Mindfulness Bell*.)

Cultivating Family Practice in the Sangha 23

BY MICHELE TEDESCO

Two years ago, I presented to the community at Plum Village
a very special vase of flowers. It took me about fifteen minutes
to arrange it in front of the community. The whole community
was breathing and smiling while I arranged these flowers.
But that vase of flowers was quite different from any other vase
of flowers I have arranged, because that evening the flowers that
I arranged were children. Each child is a flower. Adults should
remember that children are flowers to be taken care of in order
for joy and happiness to last. — *Thich Nhat Hanh*

E very time adults practice together, we have an opportunity to present
the Sangha with just such a vase of flowers made of our children. We
may not be skillful at flower arranging, because the practice is new to us. We
may be afraid to handle the blossoms for fear they are too delicate or the
bright colors may offend some community members. We are afraid the vase
may tip and fall loudly, causing some to lose their mindfulness momentar-
ily. We are afraid of discord in the Sangha. As with any new skill, we must
overcome fear of failure to make the first attempts. If we are mindful and
diligent, we will learn to be skillful flower arrangers.

My husband and I are fortunate that our Sangha supports our learning
to arrange our beautiful flowers — Christopher (15), Giovanni (7), and
Gabriela (5) — in front of them on a regular basis. Indeed, over the past two
years, the Sangha has encouraged us. Many have seized the opportunity to
practice with our children. Because of this, our family, our practice, and our
Sangha have reaped many rewards. As a family we are able to practice together

and feel the support and love of our community. Our Sangha benefits by having the vibrancy of youth to inspire us and provide other ways to practice.

Even within my beautiful Sangha, however, some parents do not include their children in our community practice. There is nothing unique that makes our three children more accessible to the practice, but they are the only children who attend functions regularly. I know this must be similar in other Sanghas as well. I have spent much time and energy trying to figure out "why" in order to help people understand that children and Sangha practice can go together—even if it is a little messy sometimes.

This past spring, I decided that instead of bringing children to the Sangha, I would bring the Sangha to the children. In May, we had our first Kid's Mini Day of Mindfulness. The day was a great success, not because everything happened perfectly—of course, it didn't—but because it simply happened. Ten children, from one to fifteen years old, attended with at least one parent. Even five members of our Sangha who do not have children participated by taking on activities through the day or by simply leading around a restless one year old—a beautiful contribution of support for the mother. Here is the schedule we used:

10:00 a.m.	Arrival and Opening Circle
	Introductions
	Orientation for kids and parents
10:30 a.m.	Planned Physical Activity: Mindful Games
10:45 a.m.	Snack (provided)
11:00 a.m.	Dharma Talk: What Is Mindfulness?
11:30–Noon	Parent Breakout Group:
	Mindfulness in Parenting
11:30 a.m.	Songs: "Breathing In, Breathing Out"
11:45 a.m.	Story Time
Noon	Lunch
12:30 p.m.	Free Play
1:00 p.m.	Meditation:
	What Is Meditation?
	Bell Meditation

1:15 p.m.	Art: Looking deeply at a flower, then drawing it
1:45 p.m.	Closing Circle: Sing songs for parents Closing comments by the children
2:00 p.m.	End of Day

During orientation I explained the symbolism of the Buddha statue on our small altar. Some parents and children knew very little about Buddhism; some practice another religion as their spiritual foundation. To alleviate any discomfort they might feel, we made it very clear that the statue was not the Buddha but a symbol of his wisdom and enlightenment. I explained that we show respect to these qualities, and to this potential within ourselves, when we bow. Also, we oriented the children to the bell and used it as a gathering sound.

The mindful games, led by one of our "less-young" Sangha members, consisted of carrying beans in a small spoon from one pot to another. If they spilled, they had to start over. In another game, the children held the edges of a parachute and tried to keep balls rolling on it. In both games, the children discovered that the slower they went and the more they concentrated, the more successful they were.

In the Dharma talk, we talked about their experiences in the games as applied to the idea of mindfulness. Cultivating mindfulness was our theme for the day, and the games gave the children direct experience of its benefits. We also discussed how to be mindful with parents, siblings, and friends. Even the youngest children understood these experiences of mindfulness.

During story time, another less-young Sangha member read some of the Jataka tales. Then, one of the mothers taught the song "Breathing In, Breathing Out." The children drew pictures of some of the concepts in the song: mountains, flowers, water, space. While the children were doing this, I threw in a parent discussion group almost as an afterthought.

The parents' discussion turned out to be a wonderful, nurturing experience. We asked questions and shared experiences. We opened by reading and discussing a longer version of the quote at the beginning of this article.

Most importantly, I wanted to give the parents some simple, useful, practice tools. First, I encouraged the parents and children to use the bell when emotions are high, to bring the family back to its breath. Another tool I find very effective is using the word "mindful" with children, for example: "Susie, was it mindful to yell at your brother?" Finally, I gave the parents copies of the Five Contemplations (See Appendix II). Reciting the contemplations before a meal, announced by a bell, can add meaning and closeness to this daily family activity.

During lunch, we introduced the practice of the contemplations. The bell was invited, and the contemplations were recited. Then there was another bell, and we took a few breaths before we ate. To deepen the practice of mindful eating, I asked the children to take one bite of their food and chew it ten times, counting their chews. During the meal we invited the bell a few more times to remind them to count their chews.

Meditation was presented to the parents and children as simply quieting your body and mind. We practiced bell meditation. Everyone closed their eyes and listened to the beautiful sound of the bell. When they couldn't hear the sound any longer, they raised their hands. All the children enjoyed a turn at inviting the bell, especially the one year old, who invited it several times. At first, I thought it was a mistake to put meditation after free play, when energies are at their peak. It did take a few minutes to settle down, but this was good training for the children. After all, mindfulness is most useful when things get crazy.

The last activity was art. Toni Carlucci, an art teacher whom we are fortunate to have as a Sangha member, is discovering wonderful ways to cultivate mindfulness through art. First, she showed the children some seeds and seedlings. Then they walked around the grounds and looked at all the plants and flowers. Toni spoke to the children about how, through looking deeply and mindfully, they could see that the earth, rain, and sun are in the plants. Next, they made a three-paneled drawing of the seeds in the ground, a seedling, and a plant in full flower with the earth, sun, and rain in each panel.

In the closing circle, we came together one last time. We looked at the art projects, and the children sang their new song. Each child was encouraged to say something. The point was to hear everyone's voice even if the only thing they had to say was, "I don't have anything to say."

We had a full day, yet everyone—parents, children, and other Sangha members—came away with a deepened sense of mindfulness for themselves and their families. In other words, children's and family practice works.

I encourage every Sangha with families and children to plan some special time like this, even if you have only one or two children. Don't worry. If you start this practice, more will come. It is easier than you think. You may be surprised by the talents and energy your Sangha members bring to this project. Don't expect the kids to practice like adults. This is a different kind of day. Instead of Noble Silence, encourage the practice of Noble Not-So-Loud. Be prepared to abandon a plan if it is not working with your group. Be flexible. If four hours are more than you can handle, try two hours. Have parents and children practice together as much as possible through the day, especially during the Dharma talk, the meal, and meditation. It is important that parents and children are on the same page in the practice so that it continues at home.

Deepening family practice in your Sangha will add a new and vital energy to the Sangha as a whole. As your spiritual community broadens itself in this way, its strength will grow, making a deeper well from which all members can drink.

(This article originally appeared in Issue No. 27 of the *Mindfulness Bell*.)

Generation Present Moment: Mindfulness Camp for Teenagers at Deer Park

24

BY SISTER NHO NGHIEM

I T WAS ONCE SAID that, "This generation will be Generation Y," that there is no hope for the future, that we as teenagers have failed and will continue to fail to fulfill the hopes and dreams of our ancestors, our parents, and our teachers.

Deer Park's teenage mindfulness camp defies everything said above. We, the teenagers, have proven not only to ourselves but also to the world (as a community, as a Sangha) that we have the capacity to continue on the path of understanding and love instead of consumption and ignorance. Deer Park has truly created a "Pure Land" for teenagers to take refuge in and to be a part of.

On the first night of the mindfulness camp, we had the opportunity to sit down together in groups of three or four to get to know each other. To me, such a simple act was incredible—to sit down and talk to each other with open ears and open minds despite the fact that we didn't know a thing about one other. In that very meditation hall were people who share the same aspiration as I do: to carry out the hopes and dreams of our ancestors, of ourselves, and of our future.

The following day, we were awakened at 6:30 a.m. by numerous sounds of the bell, which I thought was a great way to wake up! We gathered together in the Oak Grove to do morning exercises. After that, we were off to conquer the mountains of Deer Park (in other words, we went hiking). About an hour into the hike we all took a break on the rocks to have breakfast with one another. After having breakfast together, we hiked to a vast field where we heard what we thought were a lot of rattlesnakes. We sat together on the rocks and listened to Sister Ha Nghiem. She first shared with us a story from the book *Old Path White Clouds,* then a very simple but powerful Dharma talk. She spoke about how our minds could be compared to gardens. The things inside our minds are like seeds, and every day we water them unknowingly. After that talk we were a lot less fearful of the rattlesnakes, knowing it was watching movies that had watered our seeds of being scared of these slithery beings.

I consider the hike to be the peak of the experience, because in many ways we had to work together to get through the natural obstacles of the trail. Holding each other's hands, sharing our water bottles, and warning each other about the trail ahead, we were eager to accomplish this hike together, as one. In the midst of the hike, everyone was anticipating 3:00 p.m. At that time we were scheduled for the practice of Total Relaxation. When it was time, we all gathered in the meditation hall to lie down. Two minutes after Sister Thang Nghiem had invited the bell about half the room was dead asleep. That's what I call total relaxation!

That same night we had a bonfire at the site of the bell tower. It was time for us just to be together, knowing it was our last night. We sat around the fire, heard stories, sang songs, and cracked a few jokes. After all the excitement simmered down, the full moon rose over the mountains. It was then that we all learned the true beauty of the moon. I had never really enjoyed it before that night; it was just something that happened every month, but I was not much aware of it. I realized that night that to see things without being aware is a great shame.

For many people, that night was their first session of moon meditation. It was very quiet. All that was heard were the sounds of everyone breathing and the flickering of the fire. The moon was especially bright, and the atmosphere of community was present. As an adolescent, having these feelings—of peace, happiness, and harmony—is very rare. We cherished these moments together so much.

The camp was very authentic. It gave us the opportunity to sit together and share our hopes and dreams, our fears and sufferings. We had the ability to speak freely and to know that we weren't going to be judged. Everyone was sincerely nourished, if not by the brothers and sisters or their peers, then simply by the environment. I have seen so clearly that we will NOT be Generation Y, but generation NOW. Someone once said, "A single star can light the dark, a single smile can warm a heart, a single hand can lift a life, a single voice can speak the truth, and a single life can make a difference." If one single person can do this, imagine what a Sangha of teenagers can do.

Deer Park has cultivated seeds of compassion, seeds of love, and seeds of understanding in us, and has watered them so skillfully. Each teenager who was a part of this camp has left with a new garden full of beautiful, blooming flowers. There is only one thing that I would change about this camp: the length. I wish it were a bit longer. I am glad to know that Deer Park will continue being here for everyone young or old. To feel such feelings of peace and joy is a great gift, and every day I am at Deer Park, I am offered that gift. The present moment is a gift. That is why it is called the "present" moment. Thank you for being present.

(This article originally appeared in Issue No. 29 of the *Mindfulness Bell.*)

My True Home 25

BY TRACY COCHRAN

O N THE FIRST NIGHT of my seven-year-old daughter, Alexandra's, first Buddhist retreat, Thich Nhat Hanh smiled and looked into her eyes as few adults ever look at children. Although he sat very still on a stage, the Vietnamese teacher seemed to bow to her inwardly, offering her his full presence and inviting her to be who she really is.

Alexandra threw her jacket over her head.

"Children look like flowers," said the man who was nominated for the Nobel Peace Prize by Martin Luther King, Jr., in 1967. His voice was soft and bittersweet. "Their faces look like flowers, their eyes, their ears...."

Surrounded by scores of monks and nuns who had traveled with him from Plum Village, the French monastic community that has been his home since his peace activism caused his exile from Vietnam, he lifted his eyes from the little flower who was huddled, hiding her face, in the front row. Before him sat 1,200 people who had gathered in a vast white tent on the wooded campus of the Omega Institute for Holistic Studies in upstate New York. Thây, as he is affectionately known, had convened us for a five-day retreat dedicated to cultivating mindfulness through practices such as sitting meditation, walking, and sharing silent meals.

As the Master talked about the "freshness," or openness and sensitivity of children, I couldn't help but be struck by the way Alexandra was ducking for cover. He extolled freshness as one of the qualities that each of us possesses in our essence, our Buddha-nature. Alexandra, shrouded in nylon, was reminding me that true freshness isn't limited to those moments when we feel happily and playfully open. It often means feeling raw and vulnerable. I wondered if it had been a mistake to bring her here, to risk exposing her to the way we really are.

During the retreat, children and adults came together during different parts of the day. In addition to sharing meals and a daily mindfulness walk, the children clustered at the front of the stage for the first twenty minutes of Thây's Dharma talks, which he carefully framed in simple, poetic images that children could remember. I brought Alexandra hoping that contact with Buddhist practice would stimulate her imagination and awaken her own wisdom. I thought she could be inspired by the various techniques Thây described, such as listening to the sound of a bell that can call us back to "our true home."

"My true home is in Brooklyn," Alexandra whispered. She had peeled off her covering and lay stretched out on the floor with her head in my lap, jittering her foot to convey how bored and impatient she was. On the first night, most of the other children nearby were sitting cross-legged, quietly, and listening with what seemed to me preternatural attention. Alexandra was muttering to herself and writhing around on the floor like a big, unhappy baby. I wondered if she had some mild form of autism that had escaped detection.

Seventy-three-year-old Thich Nhat Hanh was sitting directly above me, embodying a mountain-like stability and compassion. A monk on the stage winked at Alexandra, and a pretty young nun dimpled up in a fit of silent giggles. The people around me were friendly and relaxed. I felt like a terrible mother to be judging and comparing my daughter in these gentle conditions. It was almost as if the spirit of nonjudgmental acceptance that surrounded me was triggering a perverse reaction, drawing out my darkest, meanest thoughts. I felt like a vampire who had stepped out into the sunlight.

As we made our way back to our little cabin, the power went out all over the Omega campus. And a light turned on inside Alexandra. We stopped on the path, unsure which way to turn. I had left the flashlights behind. Alexandra took charge.

"Let's go back to the visitors' office," she said, leading the way. A kindly man on the Omega staff gave Alexandra a candle and walked us to our cabin.

"You knew just what to do," I said as I tucked Alexandra into bed. "That was good thinking."

"I hated to think of you wandering around in the dark," she said, beaming in the candlelight.

The next day Alexandra asked, "Mommy, is Thich Nhat Hanh a man? Like, does he have a penis?"

Yes, I offered, he was an ordinary man but he was a monk. That meant that he lived for the happiness of others, so he might seem different. My answer felt vague and wimpy, not as real as the question.

The following day in the dining hall, I discovered how deeply traveling with your own pint-size Zen master makes you feel aware of yourself, and how apart. The majority of the people there were moving about with a kind of underwater grace, practicing silence. We parents struggled with the task of filling trays and settling children while trying to remember to stop and breathe consciously when the mindfulness bell sounded.

Alexandra and I sat at a table in the dining hall facing a table decorated with pumpkins.

"Mommy!"

I whispered to her that we were supposed to try eating silently together.

"This is not my experiment," Alexandra reminded me. "I don't want to do it, because I have a question."

"What's your question, Alexandra?"

"Is a pumpkin a fruit or a vegetable?"

"A vegetable."

"Why are you being so mean? Aren't you supposed to be happy?"

The interconnection of all phenomena is a constant theme of Thich Nhat Hanh's. He speaks often of "interbeing," the actual state of reality that, once recognized, nurtures compassion and empathy. As people ate in silence around us, I remembered an incident that had happened several weeks earlier. Alexandra was going through a phase of pondering how she was related to the first person who ever lived and to all other people.

"Every living being is connected," I had told her as I was putting her to bed one night. "The whole universe is alive, and what you put out in the world is what you get back. If you put out love and kindness, you tend to get love and kindness in return."

Alexandra and I had decided to put the little purple bike with training wheels that she had outgrown down on the street for someone to take. She crayoned a sign that read, "Whoever takes this bike, please enjoy it, love Alexandra."

She had been full of anticipation. The next morning she bolted out of bed and ran to the window.

"Mommy, my bike is gone!" she'd said, as radiant as on Christmas morning. "Somebody took my bike!"

The concept of the web of life was alive and breathing that morning. But by the end of the day, not surprisingly, she had moved past the shimmering magic and was applying the cause-and-effect practicality of a kid.

"So when do I get something back?" she asked.

David Dimmack, a longtime student of Thây's, was the volunteer in charge of the children's program on the retreat. He taught the kids the "Flower Fresh" song, the theme song of the Community of Mindful Living. At the beginning of a Dharma talk one morning, they all got up on the stage together and sang to Thich Nhat Hanh and the rest of the Sangha.

"Breathing in, breathing out," sang Dimmack and the children.

"I am blooming like a flower, I am fresh as the dew.

"I am solid as a mountain, I am firm as the earth. I am free."

When I stood in the back of the tent, watching the children on stage, it was impossible for me not to compare it to Sunday school.

Dimmack has called the songs "entrainment," matter-of-factly acknowledging that sometimes teaching just comes down to presenting ideas in a way that gently and gradually makes an impression, like water wearing away rock. At the same time, though, he emphasized that there was a constant creative tension in the children's program between teaching and allowing, between imposing structure and letting the kids be.

Mark Vette, another student of Thây's, works as an animal psychologist and lives on a ranch in New Zealand. Vette had the inspired idea of teaching the kids to use dowsing rods made of bent coat hangers and pendulums made of little pieces of wood.

"Here's the dowsing prayer," he said to the group of us gathered on a big meadow in the center of the campus. "May I let go of the things that are known and embrace the things that are unknown." After the kids tired of looking for water and chasing each other ("Lead me to a dork!"), many of them settled down to find their place of "inner power." (The kids liked the word "power" better than "peace.")

"Pendulums and dowsing rods seemed to be a perfect way to introduce them to their own intuitive sense," said Vette, a sandy-haired, athletic man who by the end of the week had completely captured my daughter's heart. "In the bush, these things work because we really already know where that lost animal is or where north is. And the kids can use it in the same way to learn to meditate, to find their center or their true home."

One day, during walking meditation, I began to get an inkling of what it is to find my true home. Every day the children, who left the Dharma talk after the first twenty or thirty minutes, were invited to meet up with Thich Nhat Hanh and the grown-up students as they flowed out of the Dharma hall to walk toward the lake. On one beautiful azure day in late October, those of us who were with the children watched Thich Nhat Hanh walking toward us from the Dharma tent, leading his multitude: 1,200 tall Americans dressed in bright Polartec colors following a small figure in brown.

No sooner had Alexandra and several other children joined to walk up front with Thây than she split off to scamper to the top of a leaf-carpeted hill.

"I'm going to roll down this hill!" she shouted to another girl. "Come on!"

It actually awed me that she was so unselfconscious about shattering the silence. Alexandra rolled down the hill, sounding like a bear crashing through the forest.

I dropped my head and trudged along. Suddenly, I noticed Thich Nhat Hanh gliding along, like a mountain on rails, almost next to me. His face looked calm and fresh, while mine ached like a clenched fist. Alex had raced ahead to the water's edge, where she stood waving and smiling at me. I felt a pang of love for her and really experienced how the voice of my heart was being drowned out by a welter of negative thoughts that seemed to come from somewhere in my brain that didn't even feel organic—more like a robot, a split-off part of me mechanically repeating bits of old programming.

Aware as I now felt, I was haranguing myself that really good mothers didn't get swamped by nasty reactions. Good mothers, my mind chided, were capable of unconditional love.

The bell calling for mindfulness sounded. I knelt down in the warm sand. The bell rang again, and a third time. I picked up my head to see an old man's hand gently stroking a familiar head of thick ash-blond hair. Thich Nhat Hanh and my daughter were sitting side by side. It slowly dawned on me that it was Alexandra who had just rung the bell calling the rest of us back to our true homes. Thây had been inspired to pick Alexandra, the loudest kid there that particular day, to sound, or "invite," the bell that called everyone else to silence.

At that moment, the ideal of unconditional love seemed nothing but a brittle concept, a fetter. I felt I finally comprehended what Thich Nhat Hanh meant when he said that acceptance is understanding and understanding is love.

"I was throwing sand and I looked up and he was looking at me," she explained later. "He was kind of smiling. He waved for me to come over and sit by him. He didn't say anything, he just showed me how to ring the bell."

Back in Brooklyn, as Alexandra and I slipped back into our daily routines, I wondered from time to time what effect, if any, a week of mindfulness training might have. Then, one night many months later, I was fuming about some frustration.

"Breathe, Mommy," said Alexandra. "Just relax and breathe and return to your true home."

(This article originally appeared in the Spring 1999 edition of *Tricycle*.)

Hovering with Your Children 26

BY JULIA BURNS

ONE OF MY FAVORITE ACTIVITIES is hanging out and watching my children, just watching, not necessarily doing anything for or with them. Often, I sit at the antique wooden table in our kitchen and look out our picture window at their activity. This window frames the life work of my children engaging in play. By sitting and slowing down, this staying in the present has created our best moments as a family. I have discovered that when I am still like a flower, my children come to me and hover. They hover over and around me like bees. And I sit and watch as we savor the nectar of being together, balancing their fullness and vigor with my own quiet reflection and wonder at their grace. The power of this silent meditation yields calmness and healing for everyone in the family.

Pick one day a week to experiment. I take one "day off" a week. It is on this day that I have the greatest opportunity to hover. When my children come home from school, I sit on the sofa and let them come to me. I am not in the basement doing laundry or typing on the computer. I don't run errands or answer the phone. We don't choose an activity. I just sit and observe their movement—skateboarding and basketball, practicing piano or completing homework. I receive their thoughts and listen to their mind's chatter instead of my own.

As you are sitting, letting your child's life and activities unfold around you, your mind may continue to chatter. As you sit on the sofa holding your daughter, your eyes wander to your favorite houseplant, which is wilting because it needs water. Your job is to continue to sit and hold your daughter. Turn off the message that the plant will die if it is not watered today. Your steady demeanor becomes like the light from a tower, beckoning your children home. You create safety and harmony through your energy. You will hear and learn about new dilemmas in their lives as you sit and watch them resolve their differences with each other without any interference.

"It's my turn, now. I want to talk," my little girl said last night.

"Okay," I said. "Momma and Daddy won't talk about this grown-up thing anymore. What did you want to say?"

"I don't know, nothing. I just want to be able to, if something comes up," she said, obviously feeling left out of our adult conversation.

Pay attention. Stop your movement, your phoning, your cooking, your planning the school picnic or church bazaar. Stop and attend to your family's motion as if in meditation. Be in awe of them and their higher beings. Stop and be still in their jumping. Hover and let them hover. You will find great happiness and delight when you jump into the stillness of your family.

(This article originally appeared in Issue No. 29 the *Mindfulness Bell*.)

PART SEVEN

Engaged Practice

Profoundly Grateful: The Experience of Organizing and Participating in a Sangha Support Group

27

BY LAURIE LAWLOR

What distinguishes the healthy from the ill—which is
a more significant division in any society than class or gender
or possibly even homelessness—is that the healthy consider
feeling well to be the normal state of things.
—*Inga Clendinnen*, Tiger's Eye[57]

W HEN ONE OF OUR longtime Sangha members living in Chicago was
diagnosed with a rare form of leukemia, a group of approximately
twenty volunteers from the Evanston-based Lakeside Buddha Sangha visited him at home and in the hospital for six months until his death in late
December 2001.

What was unusual and challenging about the situation is that this particular Sangha member had so few family members either living nearby or
involved in his day-to-day care. Art had no spouse or companion living
with him. Fiercely independent all his life, he faced what looked at first like
a long, lonely road.

The desire to accompany him on this journey—wherever it might
lead—was made in a very spontaneous way by the Sangha. How this
effort occurred, why it happened, and the long-term effects the experience
has had on the Sangha are all worth observing, and we are still reflecting
on it. Perhaps our experience may be useful to other groups meeting the
challenges of helping and providing companionship for members facing
illness or death.

The idea to begin a somewhat organized effort to make sure Art had regular visits evolved for the same reasons that anyone offers support for another human being in need:

Because you have a tender heart.
Because it is asked of you.
Because you are afraid.
Because you can make a difference.

These words of encouragement were helpful mindfulness bell reminders to me as the sporadic visits to Art blossomed into almost daily coverage by some member of the Sangha.

The beginning tasks were simple but urgent. We wanted to find out who would like to volunteer and what they'd like to do. We needed information beyond names, addresses, phone numbers, and email addresses. A member developed a simple questionnaire that was passed out at the sitting asking people what they'd like to do. Requests included: make phone calls, run errands, visit Art, do household chores for Art, send cards or books, etc. The questionnaire asked if individuals would like to go alone or with another Sangha member. The last item stated: "I would be comfortable thinking that I could be involved: (a) once a month, (b) once every several months, (c) once a week, (d) once every several weeks, (e) not very often." Room was left at the bottom for individuals to add personal comments.

After gathering the completed forms, we were able to get a good idea of how many people were willing to help, how much time they'd like to help, and what they'd prefer to do. We made a calling list with names of volunteers and their phone numbers and a detailed description of Art's location at home and at the hospital. We included his various phone numbers and described available public transportation. Someone volunteered to act as a rotating telephone liaison to call people from the list to set up a weekly schedule. The idea was to make sure there wouldn't be five people coming on the same day and then nobody the rest of the week.

Little by little, the disease began to take its toll in insidious ways. Like so many individuals confronting cancer, at moments Art felt certain he had beat the disease. Other times he seemed clearly despondent. Yet he always tried to keep up the most optimistic outlook—even as his progress began to resemble a crazy roller coaster: up one minute, down the next.

For several of the volunteers, Art's illness was their first opportunity to get to know him. An excellent conversationalist on wide-ranging topics—from photography to Chicago politics—Art was always eager (especially on his good days) to discuss almost anything. He loved to talk. A cheerful, generous presence, he made a point of not complaining. He knew, I think, that the group was a kind of lifeline. He wanted us to come back.

As he moved back and forth between the hospital outpatient clinic and home again, he needed a driver. He found one in an old friend from his former church. When he was too weak to go up and down the three flights of steep steps in his three-story apartment, we made extra keys so that he would not have to climb down the steps to let visitors in to see him.

Early visits were a way for Art to keep in touch with Sangha members and feel connected. We ran errands and occasionally took him out to lunch or helped him deliver his car for repairs. We made pit stops at his favorite bakery to pick up coffeecakes for his favorite firemen at his neighborhood station. He needed groceries. He needed a prescription. He needed to return books to the library. These were all errands that Sangha members performed.

When Art felt strong enough, he made it to limited meditation sessions. This was clearly difficult for him, however. Soon he had to give up driving anywhere alone—something he always loved.

What Sangha members brought on their visits varied from jokes and homemade soup to books and an attentive ear. When the chemo destroyed his appetite, we brought him his favorite smoothies. Each person who came had their own strength to offer. When the disease began to ravage him with ferocious intensity and many of us felt frustrated that we could not do more, one of the members reminded us, "We cannot individually be a perfect friend. But together we create a perfect friend." That outlook brought a great deal of comfort to many of us.

Some Sangha members found that going with another more experienced volunteer eased some of the fear or anxiety they might have had. It was interesting to see how one friend could then help another who might have been anxious about hospital visits. It was a little like a chain reaction in building non-fear.

We also gained a great deal of strength throughout this entire period attending the weekly meditation sessions. Beyond providing the nourishment of practicing walking and sitting meditation, it was also a place where people who had been visiting solo had a chance to reconnect with other volunteers and support one another.

Efforts were made for people to connect by phone during the week. Some volunteers met for coffee just to "touch base" and provide each other with helpful listening. Because there was rarely a family member available to field questions and concerns about Art's situation when his attending doctors were visiting, it was often very difficult to know exactly how he was doing. We depended solely on what he was willing to tell us. We soon learned that he gave different information to different people. While on the phone he might glibly proclaim he was going home "any day now" for physical therapy; with another visitor, he might soberly discuss his concerns about a living will.

During the last month, it became clear that the people who were volunteering to support Art now needed to be supported themselves in a more organized manner. Each week, time was set aside before the Sangha formally convened to give people time to share feelings, experiences, and perceptions of his needs—whether that meant seeking information about hospice, figuring out how to contact his grown children, or locating a social worker at the hospital who might have resources available when Art went home.

While we were lucky to have a few people with actual hospice training, most of the volunteers were new to watching a friend be transformed by illness. Some of us had loved ones die in hospitals. Others had avoided hospitals whenever possible. Yet we were all working together as a team.

Some of us found that we could sit, and wait, and watch. We talked about how each of us tried to find a way to use an alert inner eye to know what to do at the bedside. Sometimes Art wanted to talk. Sometimes he slept. When Art had questions—spoken and unspoken—we tried not to rush in with answers. We discovered that when we listened well, we would know the right time to talk.

For me, practicing walking meditation on the way from the parking lot to Art's hospital room was immeasurably helpful. In this way I could focus my energy and try to find some kind of inner spring of calmness and acceptance. Before I entered the room, I would do "doorknob meditation" —turning the doorknob and breathing, knowing I was about to enter a new space where anything might happen. I also benefited by doing some kind of physical activity—like swimming—on a regular basis. Other volunteers used tai chi, yoga, or a long walk. Keeping a journal was also helpful to me and others. We all tried to help each other, reminding each other not to burn out.

What was so helpful about our support as a group was the realization that all of us had to empty our minds of preconceptions. We could not worry about what might happen next. We simply had to devote our full attention to Art and give him what he needed most—total acceptance. We were all deeply aware how difficult this gift of acceptance was to deliver. One of our discussions centered on how our personal agendas sometimes got in the way. As one member said, "We try to do the right thing when all he wants is for us to be there with him while he goes through his changes."

Courage and restraint became our new watchwords. We discovered that it takes courage to be present for pain—no matter what—and that it takes restraint to stay grounded in our own breath and not react with old habits. Letting go meant letting go of any special role we felt we had as "helper." What was so marvelous about the last weeks with Art was the realization that genuine, compassionate helping comes from inside us, from the spirit. We didn't "do" anything. It just happened.

As Merrill Collett says in *At Home with Dying,* "Death demands that we question our lives. Caregiving offers as the answer an unbounded experience of being. The light of the dying reveals our greatest wealth to be life as it is."[58] So here was the paradox: giving care to the dying gave new life to us.

Just before Christmas, Art's two adult children arrived from out-of-state and took him home, which is where he wanted to be. He died a few days later. The Sangha had a moving ceremony and chanted the *Heart Sutra* forty-nine days after his death. It was attended by nearly fifty people. Everyone involved—the larger Sangha as well as the steady group of volunteers—

had an opportunity to mark his passing and to share their own thoughts and feelings. One volunteer wrote, "The experience we shared of being with Art was one for which I am profoundly grateful."

Art transformed all of us.

Sangha-Building in a Massachusetts Prison: An Interview with James G. 28

BY BROTHER PHAP LAI

After being released from nine years in prison, James attended the 2001
retreat at the University of California at San Diego with Thich Nhat Hanh.
He spent the winter retreat in Plum Village in 2001–2002. He practices
with the Phoenix, Arizona Sangha. Fellow retreatant Ben Boucherat (now
Brother Phap Lai) talked to him about developing Sangha in prison.

Question: Jim, can you say something of your background and your life
before prison?

Jim: Well, that's not what I want to talk about so much, but let's see. I'd been
in a twenty-year marriage. My wife and I split up when the kids were in their
teens. We have one son and two daughters; they're all out in the world now.
I taught martial arts, and before that I was in the Navy from 1958 to 1962.
That's when my drinking got heavy, in my twenties, though I started
younger. When I was six years old I would drink whiskey to numb the pain
of the beatings from my stepfather. I didn't drink or do drugs in prison, not
that you couldn't do that stuff, but I'd had enough of that particular realm
of suffering. I'm still attending AA. I haven't touched alcohol or drugs for
ten years now. I know I can't if I want a meaningful life.

Question: When did your interest in Buddhism begin?

Jim: I'd been inside about five years when a fellow inmate asked me to help
him set up a Sangha. I knew nothing about Buddhism or meditation, but I
read about the Four Noble Truths. This got to me: suffering exists. I could
go with that. And there's a way out. Try it and see. If a teaching works for
you, great; if not, then you can leave it. I had some funny ideas at the time.

I thought eventually I'd learn to levitate over the walls and escape. When I came across the idea of emptiness I thought I'd make myself invisible and escape that way. I didn't realize then that I was going to discover compassion for my fellow inmates and for myself or that these teachings would help me escape from the prison in my head, the prison of fear and isolation. I didn't used to like myself, but I like Jimmy now. At first I was just in it for myself, but that changed over time.

Question: What brought about this change in your heart? How did that develop?

Jim: It took time, and it started with insects, pigeons, squirrels, and cats. I began to notice their hunger, their suffering, and their beauty. Caring about them, being with them, transported me to a different world. If there was a wasp in the cell or day room, I wouldn't let anyone kill it. I'd have it crawl up on my finger and take it to the window. It gave me something to care about, to connect with. We all need that connection to nature — it's a human need. Through this and trying to get something going with the Sangha I started to like myself, and then I started trying to understand the suffering of others. I started to care about the inmates. I still have a hard time when I think of some of the guards. A lot of resentment and anger comes up about things that were done. I realize I've got to work on this, and Plum Village is a good place to start.

Question: Can you tell us the story of how your Sangha was set up?

Jim: Before we began we knew it was going to be an uphill struggle, but we had no idea how steep. It was in going through that, doing it, that the brotherhood began. We spent months writing to Buddhist organizations before we finally got a response from the Shambhala Center in Colorado. Then a few of us sat in the half-lotus position outside the office of the director of programs to get him to talk to us about receiving a visit from a lay Dharma teacher. Many months later it was cleared, and a successful meeting was held in the waiting room of the barbershop. Eventually, a teacher was allowed to come every two weeks.

In the meantime we were trying to get a room to meet in. The Native

American group offered us their room twice a week. So with rolled up coats for cushions, we seated ourselves in this room for the first time. It felt like a true beginning, and we continued to meet like this twice a week. We sat in front of a small picture of the Buddha pointing to the Earth in response to Mara's demand: "Who can bear witness to your enlightenment?" In the following months a Spanish friend made an amazing two-foot-high statue from a picture using cardboard and toilet paper for papier-maché. Since we're rationed to one roll a week, we'd had a hard job getting the paper, bartering for it with coffee and cookies. We "painted" it with coffee syrup smuggled from the chow hall. Similarly we acquired some bowls for rice and water offerings and came up with a small table to put things on. We covered a library book with blue paper to represent the Dharma. Our Sangha had a beautiful-looking altar. After three months or so the Department of Corrections took the statue, saying it could be used to hide drugs or weapons. They agreed not to destroy it and gave it to a Buddhist nun who visited us on occasion. A friend's wife drew us a beautiful picture of the Buddha to replace the statue.

Parallax Press and Wisdom Books were kind in sending us damaged books. I must have read four hundred books in the five years before I got out. We were sent books and videos of Thây, and I was impressed by the clarity and the simplicity of his teaching. I could really understand it. I don't know if Thây has any idea how much help he's given to people inside. We made other contacts with Buddhist teachers, some of whom came in. I'm so grateful for their time. For us it was golden to have these visits, especially to have something on a regular basis. To be able to have regular visits is a crucial factor.

Question: You've told me your Sangha friends called you "Mother Hen." What was that about?
Jim: They called me "Mother Hen" because I took such care of the room we had. I wasn't satisfied with the routine cleaning the inmate cleaners gave it. The others didn't mind so much, but I would say, "We have important guests; we're inviting the Buddhas, bodhisattvas, and deities to be present." I gave up my breakfast so I could clean the room. That way there was no

argument; it was clean enough because I had made sure of it. Even some of the guards would take their shoes off before coming into the room.

Question: What advice would you give to people in prison thinking of starting a Sangha?

Jim: Go for it. We did it, so you can. If there are a couple of people dedicated to change and ending their suffering like the Buddha taught, it'll happen. By formimg a Sangha you create a legacy that money can't buy. You have to be willing to stand up for your rights and be prepared to be punished and ridiculed for this. It took years of going through the courts before we were given the right to be vegetarian. Perhaps I've made it sound tough. Well it is, but there are good times too, and everything you go through is worth it. As Thây says, "A lotus cannot grow on marble, it needs the mud." You get a tough time from everyone, but in the end you get respected and you get protected because it's something genuine going on and people respond to that.

Going through this you get strong, and with the practice and the different way of thinking that Buddhism gives you, you have some calmness. This calmness can help people. One time we heard that one of the prisoners was pretty upset because he had been refused his last chance of parole. We put the word out that he should come and see us. He came to the room, and I was there sitting in front of the shrine. He was desperate and, feeling he had nothing to lose, he had the intention of killing someone. I said, "Before you do anything you might regret, try to calm yourself down, sit down here with me and breathe with me for a while." He did this and in ten minutes he'd calmed down and began to talk. He expressed his fear over the fact that he was going to die in prison and would be spending the rest of his life behind bars, that he would never get to be with his family, his kids outside. He cried. In the end he was all right, and later on he thanked me.

Another bit of advice is to watch out for ego: "This is my Sangha, I started it," "I did this," "It was my idea." Ultimately it's the petty squabbles, the infighting that can destroy a Sangha, not the pressure from outside. You've got to keep coming back to the source, the heart. You have to practice being inclusive. Anybody that was genuine and wanted to pratice with us we let in. I didn't think of the man's crime, I thought of the suffering. There was a he/she (a man who feels he is a woman) and a gay man that wanted to be in the Sangha. There was some argument and we were given a hard time, but we accepted them because the Sangha's not about discriminating.

Question: What would you like to say to the Department of Corrections now?

Jim: I'm learning. They're under a lot of pressure, and it's not a question of blaming them. The director of programs who was reluctant to help us ended up making sure we had what we needed. I think he saw something good, and he did what he could to help. I am grateful to him.

But the system is set up to warehouse men and make money. There are two million people in prison in the u.s. Each costs around forty thousand dollars a year to house, and very little of this money is going into rehabilitation, which is where the investment is really needed to start reducing the re-offending.

There's a need to recognize human needs, like having contact with nature. There should be counseling and educational opportunities available. I was able to complete a degree just before they stopped providing this possibility. There needs to be more openness to the spiritual needs of inmates in general.

Buddhism teaches that ignorance creates suffering, that we suffer and we cause others to suffer. There's a lot of ignorance in the whole system. Thây says that if people offend against society we may sometimes need to lock them up to protect society, but these people need our help, not punishment. We cannot simply go on equating justice with punishment and think that solves the problem. In fact, the problem is getting worse. A change of attitude, a change of heart is needed, not just in the Department of Corrections but in the judicial system, the state governments, and the general public.

Embracing Diversity in the Mindfulness, Diversity, and Social Change Sangha

29

BY CHARLES KING

Welcome to the Mindfulness, Diversity, and Social Change Sangha.
Our Sangha was created during a retreat in the fall of 1997 by People
of Color and social change activists. Our desire is to create a space
where anyone can come together for mutual support and mindfulness
practice. Our intention is also to offer people of diverse social identities
a safe, welcoming and participatory Sangha where they can feel at home
and in community.

Our practice is based on the teachings of Thich Nhat Hanh,
a Vietnamese monk of international recognition and honor.

We welcome people of all faiths and practices who wish to explore ways
to heal the interconnected forms of injustice and oppression through the practice
of mindfulness and to find a place to rest and reexamine their daily lives.

As a grassroots Sangha we don't have a regular Dharma teacher,
so we encourage and actively seek participation by all members in
planning and offering Dharma teachings.

THIS PREAMBLE IS READ at the opening of every weekly meeting at our
Sangha, which is nearly five years old. The Sangha was founded with
awareness that most convert Buddhist communities in North America
reflect the demographics of the dominant culture—their members and
leaders are predominantly middle- or upper-class heterosexual people of
European ancestry. As we attended retreats, Zen centers, and Sanghas, we

have been disappointed that the participants do not reflect the rich diversity of our communities in Northern California and in Oakland, where our Sangha meets.

We believe that aspects of traditional forms of practice and structures of power in Buddhist practice centers and Sanghas often discourage people of diverse backgrounds from feeling welcome and participating fully. Only through conscious examination and awareness of these practices can we recognize elements of the "isms" (able-ism, ageism, classism, homophobia, racism, sexism, etc.) that may be excluding or alienating many people who would otherwise join us on the Dharma path. The founding members of the Mindfulness, Diversity, and Social Change Sangha took up the challenge of creating a Sangha that would be mindful of these "isms" and aspired to develop practices that would clearly welcome and empower people who have often had the experience of being marginalized and disenfranchised in North American culture. In addition, inspired by the tradition and teachings of Thich Nhat Hanh, they sought to encourage and support socially engaged Buddhism, by providing a community and a refuge for practitioners who are committed to social activism.

Our practice is based on the teachings of Thich Nhat Hanh and other mindfulness practitioners. We welcome people of all faiths who wish to explore mindfulness practice as a way to help heal the interconnected forms of injustice and oppression, from global threats of militarism and environmental exploitation to everyday, habitual forms of racism, classism, sexism, and other 'isms' which cause such painful separations in our human society.

This statement appears in the handout that introduces new members to the Sangha. It is important to make it clear that members of the Sangha share awareness of the strong habit energy in the dominant culture to create divisions of "us" and "them," divisions that cause suffering and undermine the experience and realization of interbeing. It is important that new members of the Sangha feel that we are open to discourse about these sources of suffering in the world and in our Sangha family.

PRACTICES THAT SUPPORT DIVERSITY

The multiple objectives of the Sangha include:

1) practicing meditation in community
2) learning about practices and teachings from Thây that promote mindfulness
3) providing opportunities for members of the Sangha to share
their experience and struggles in mindfulness practice and
social activism
4) providing opportunities to discuss issues of importance to
the Sangha community
5) supporting one another in our mindfulness practice and social
activism

In order to accomplish these varied objectives, a format has evolved over
time with input from many Sangha members. Four topics are rotated each
month. The following description appears in the Sangha's "Guide for Facilitators and Bell Inviters":

There are four generic topics that rotate. Each has its own
purpose and some variation on the generic structure. Each
type of presentation is followed by discussion in the council
circle format.

1) The first Monday of each month we reserve time to recite the
wonderful Five Mindfulness Trainings. Thich Nhat Hanh suggests to those who formally receive the trainings that they
practice recitation of the trainings at least once per month. We
offer the recitation ceremony as a way to support this practice.
We use the standard recitation ceremony; facilitators may
chose to shorten the ceremony by skipping certain parts of
the ritual. The full text of the ceremony can be found in the

Plum Village Chanting and Recitation Book and in *For a Future to Be Possible*, both by Thich Nhat Hanh. There are also copies of the full recitation ceremony as well as an abbreviated version available in the Sangha materials. We usually distribute copies of the abbreviated ceremony so that participants can read along.

2) Forms of Practice sessions are for the purpose of introducing to the Sangha practices that cultivate mindfulness during our meditation and in our daily lives. Previous presentations have included: Using the bell, singing as a form of practice, metta practice (loving kindness meditation). These may be practices from the tradition of Thich Nhat Hanh or from other Buddhist or other spiritual traditions.

3) Open Dialogue sessions provide a time to share our thoughts with each other, in the moment and without a preestablished agenda, communicating mindfully in a circle what is on our minds and in our hearts regarding our practice, on our cushion and in the world.

   In Open Dialogue, the facilitator's role is to encourage participation of all Sangha members and to summarize the themes and topics that are emerging in the circle. Generally, this is done each time the talking piece circles back to the facilitator. The facilitator and bell inviter work together to maintain a mindful space that promotes deep listening and expression of diverse viewpoints.

4) As Thich Nhat Hanh has encouraged, the Sangha is committed to supporting and practicing socially engaged Buddhism. Meditation in Action sessions provide an opportunity for members to share with the Sangha their involvement and interest in topics of justice and social change. The purpose of Meditation in Action sessions is to raise our collective awareness of justice and social change issues that are of concern to

Sangha members. Meditation in Action sessions are also an opportunity for us to cultivate the mindfulness we need to maintain compassion, strength, and solidity in our social change efforts. The Sangha strives for a balance between increasing our awareness of suffering and maintaining our mindfulness and compassion while we do so.

5) In months with five Mondays, the extra Sangha session may be used for an additional session on Forms of Practice, Open Dialogue, or Meditation in Action. Otherwise, the Sangha has traditionally used these weeks to listen to audiotaped or videotaped Dharma talks by Thich Nhat Hanh, followed by a discussion in the council circle format.

As a grassroots Sangha, we only have a Dharma teacher available to lead the Sangha about once a month. Over the past couple of years we have been delighted to enjoy the teachings of Lyn Fine, True Goodness. Otherwise, our meetings are facilitated by members of the Sangha. We actively encourage members to participate as facilitators and bellkeepers. The "Guide for Facilitators and Bell Inviters" was written to help newer members to take on this role with less trepidation.

The Meditation in Action sessions provide a particularly useful vehicle for increasing involvement of Sangha members. Many do not feel comfortable taking on a role that they view as ordinarily occupied by a monk, a nun, or an ordained Dharma teacher because they do not see themselves as experts on matters of practice. However, members of our Sangha often do have expertise and passionate interest in some topic of social injustice or social activism. When our members share their knowledge and wisdom, the Sangha benefits in several ways. The Sangha honors the special knowledge, courage, and social change efforts of the presenter. The presenter feels recognized, validated, and empowered. The Sangha learns about a source of suffering in the world and about actions that each individual can take to help reduce that suffering. The Sangha learns to practice deep listening and compassion in the presence of suffering. In addition, the discussion that takes place in the council circle format provides an alternative to the usual debate that occurs when controversial political and social issues are discussed. Over the years the Sangha has heard about a wide range of topics, to name just a few: the Fair Trade movement, the incarceration and pending execution of Abu Mumia Jamal, the impact of the U.S. embargo on Iraq, a firsthand account of conditions in Kosovo during the U.S. bombing, a firsthand account of conditions in Nike factories in Thailand, the impact of treating cattle with bovine growth hormone, the discovery of cemeteries of African American slaves in New York City, the impact of the Prison Industrial Complex and California's Three Strikes Law, and peace efforts among Sanghas in Israel and Palestine. Inviting social activists to come and speak to the Sangha has provided an opportunity to connect with and to support the efforts of others who are also pursuing a mindful path toward social change. For example, we have welcomed Diana Lion of the Buddhist Peace Fellowship to talk about prison ministry, and filmmaker Ellen Bruno to share and discuss her documentary, *Sacrifice*, about the plight of girls from Burma who are sent to brothels in Thailand.

COUNCIL CIRCLE FORMAT

Unfortunately, mindful listening and right speech are not always practiced in groups that gather for the purpose of social activism or for mindfulness practice. Without structures that promote these Dharma practices, the dominant culture's traditional methods of discourse commonly prevail. These methods usually include frequent interruptions and overtalking, domination of time and precedence in speaking by white males, and little space for those who speak slowly, deliberately, quietly, or less aggressively. These factors tend to exclude the voices of people from groups that are disempowered in our society. Even well-intentioned, mindful Dharma discussion groups at our retreats and Sanghas often replicate these dynamics. We believe that adherence to the council circle format for our Dharma discussions has helped to cultivate the deep practice of mindful listening and to promote diversity by creating space for everyone to speak and to be heard. This practice allows for safe expression of diverse viewpoints, a principle that is at the heart of the Fourteen Mindfulness Trainings. Again from our guide for facilitators:

> For our discussion we will use the council circle format. As we pass the talking piece around the circle, each of us in turn will have a chance to share their thoughts on this topic without interruption. We use this format to encourage deep listening and mindful speech. If you receive the talking piece, and you do not wish to speak at that time, just pass it on to the next person.
>
> **Sharing our Discussion Time:** The facilitator and bell inviter can work together to encourage equitable use of discussion time. A bell can be a useful reminder that it is time to yield the talking piece and return to deep listening. The facilitator can also make comments suggesting that all members allow others time to share their thoughts.
>
> **Talking out of Turn:** The purpose of the council circle process is to facilitate mindful speech and deep listening. The facilitator may remind participants of the value of waiting to speak or waiting to get a response to their remarks or questions. While some members may find it awkward not to have more immediate dialogue, we have found much wisdom in the council circle process.
>
> **Levels of Emotion or Intensity:** Sometimes Sangha members will have strong emotional reactions during our discussions. The facilitator may suggest a bell or a brief period of silent meditation to allow us all to return to mindfulness.
>
> **Offensive Comments:** All Sangha members have a responsibility to be open and honest to the best of their ability. This includes telling others if they have offended you with their speech or actions. This is part of the Fourth Mindfulness Training. The facilitator has an additional responsibility for creating

a safe environment in which diverse people feel at ease by maintaining the council circle process and by practicing right speech in his or her presentation.

ALLIES

The Sangha has benefited from efforts by the broader Buddhist community to address obstacles to diversity in all of our Sanghas. One day in November 1998, practitioners from many Sanghas and traditions gathered at a conference in Berkeley to discuss manifestations of racism in Buddhist communities. An outgrowth of this conference was a series of monthly meetings organized by the Buddhism and Racism Working Group to discuss how practitioners can help to heal racism and increase diversity in our Sanghas. Members of our Sangha were active organizers and participants in these events. They brought back their wisdom, insights, and compassion and helped to keep the dialogue alive in our Sangha.

At this point I will speak from my personal experience about important lessons that I learned in these forums and in our Sangha. I speak from my perspective as a European American male, from a middle-class background, with an advanced graduate education. I learned that it is not enough for me to be open, accepting, and tolerant, in accordance with my liberal values. I learned that I could no longer sit back and expect that People of Color or other oppressed groups would raise the important issues about racism, sexism, or homophobia when such issues needed to be addressed. I realized that if I want to enjoy the benefits of a diverse Sangha, then I also need to do the hard work to assure that these issues of "isms" get addressed in a way that makes the community safe and welcoming for everyone.

I learned what it means to be an "ally"—someone who takes responsibility for welcoming and supporting people from diverse backgrounds in an environment that may feel unfamiliar and threatening for them. I learned that it did not matter whether I did not feel qualified, authorized, or sufficiently skilled to fulfill this role. I decided it had to be my responsibility to learn how to be an effective ally, even if I made mistakes, sounded ignorant, or suffered awkward and embarrassing moments in the process. I learned that I had to take this responsibility even when I wished that someone else would do it or doubted that I was the right person for the job. I still struggle with these questions: Should I be facilitating the Sangha tonight? Am I qualified to speak about this topic? Should I be writing this article?

HAVE WE SUCCEEDED?

Not to my satisfaction. We do have a more diverse Sangha than most, even here in Northern California. We have many active gay and lesbian members. There have been Sangha sessions where the majority of practitioners were People of Color. There have been meetings when I looked around and I realized that I was the only white male present, causing me to reflect on how this experience of being in the minority is rare for me, but it is the norm for People of Color and gay, lesbian, bisexual, or transgendered folk when they attend Buddhist events. I have found that the diversity of our Sangha has enriched my own experience and practice.

As in all Sanghas, members come and go. I have especially strong feelings of disappointment, and sometimes failure, when African American, Asian or Asian American, Latino, or young members disappear. I wonder what more we can do. I certainly believe that elements of able-ism, ageism, classism, homophobia, racism, sexism, and other prejudices are present and still influencing our Sangha in subtle and detrimental ways. I hope that we will continue to strive to recognize these influences, to name them, and to find ways to heal the harm they have done. I hope that we can all learn better ways to be allies. I hope we can learn from our Dharma brothers and sisters in other Sanghas who share our intention to be continuously open to new practices that honor and promote diversity in our Sangha communities.

The author would like to acknowledge the founding members of the Mindfulness, Diversity, and Social Change Sangha and subsequent members who have been especially instrumental in developing the format, guidelines, and practices of the Sangha: Rosa Zubizarreta, Lawrence Ellis, Lauri Rose Tanner, Kym Kuzmic, Lee Maddox, Don Marx, Susan Greef, and Olga Grinstead. I am especially grateful to Lawrence and Olga for their review of an earlier draft of this article; their thoughtful suggestions contributed greatly to the final version.

Directing the Mind towards Practices in Diversity 30

BY LARRY YANG

O PPRESSION IS A DIFFICULT CONCEPT to embrace, and it is a difficult experience to explain. Oppression is an intense form of suffering that often elicits seemingly immediate reactions from individuals, whether they be the target of oppression or the instigators of oppression. For people who are directly wounded by the violence of racism, sexism, homophobia, classism, or other forms of oppression, the pain may be so great that it is difficult to examine on the moment to moment basis that Dharma practice asks of us. For people who perpetrate oppression or who are not the direct targets of oppression, the pain may not be acknowledged, seen, or even understood.

And yet, it exists. And it separates us from each other—in ways that harm the quality of life of all beings. So, what to do? How do we consciously move towards the suffering, from wherever we are at, with the awareness and intention *and* compassion that the Dharma has taught us?

The intention in developing these trainings is to break down the concept and experience of oppression into some salient components. The invitation offered is to begin by transforming a piece of oppression, rather than being intimidated by the vastness of its suffering. Dharma practice is often presented as an incremental and cumulative process. The practice of diversity is also such a process. The hope is that this process can invite us into taking these important steps to transforming our experience with oppression in deep and meaningful ways.

The practice of these trainings is an opportunity to begin the journey towards narrowing the experience of separation. As humans, we all partic-

225

ipate in the harmful behaviors that these trainings are addressing. We all have been the perpetrator and victim, at one time or another. These trainings are for all of us, not just for any particular group or community. And in our conjoint practice is the vision, hope, and possibility of both cultivating non-perpetration of oppression and increasing the compassion in how we live our lives and understand each other.

Entering into the trainings can be done many different ways. They can be used in contemplative meditation practice and as themes for inquiry in individual practice. If used in a Sangha, they can serve as guided meditations and intentions, or the beginning of mindful conversations. Related to this is the possibility to use one or more of these trainings as guiding principles during critical discussion, conflict resolution, mediation, or other sacred dialogue.

Thich Nhat Hanh's Fourteen Mindfulness Trainings of the Order of Interbeing were an invaluable inspiration and nourishment of these trainings in diversity. The First Mind Training in Diversity is a variation of Thich Nhat Hanh's Third Mindfulness Training about freedom of thought. Since culture and identity are often made up of beliefs and views, this felt like the best place to begin the trainings. Thây has written: "Many of today's problems did not exist at the time of the Buddha. Therefore, we have to look deeply together in order to develop the insights that will help us and our children find better ways to live wholesome, happy, and healing lives."[59] This encouragement and suggestion for our Dharma practice becomes especially important with issues of diversity.

Trainings of the Mind in Diversity

1) Aware of the suffering caused by imposing one's own opinions or cultural beliefs upon another human being, I undertake the training to refrain from forcing others, in any way—through authority, threat, financial incentive, or indoctrination—to adopt my own belief system. I commit to respecting every human being's right to be different, while working towards the elimination of suffering of all beings.

2) Aware of the suffering caused by invalidating or denying another person's experience, I undertake the training to refrain from making assumptions or judging harshly any beliefs and attitudes that are different or not understandable from my own. I commit to being open-minded and accepting of other points of view, and I commit to meeting each perceived difference in another person with kindness, respect, and a willingness to learn more about their worldview.

3) Aware of the suffering caused by the violence of treating someone as inferior or superior to one's own self, I undertake the training to refrain from diminishing or idealizing the worth, integrity, and happiness of any human being. Recognizing that my true nature is not separate from others, I commit to treating each person that comes into my consciousness with the same loving kindness, care, and equanimity that I would bestow upon a beloved benefactor or dear friend.

4) Aware of the suffering caused by intentional and unintentional acts of rejection, exclusion, avoidance, or indifference towards people who are culturally, physically, sexually, or economically different from me, I undertake the training to refrain from isolating myself to people of similar backgrounds as myself and from being only with people who make me feel comfortable. I commit to searching out ways to diversify my relationships and increase my sensitivity towards people of different cultures, ethnicities, sexual orientations, ages, physical abilities, genders, and economic means.

5) Aware of the suffering caused by the often unseen nature of privilege, and the ability of privilege to benefit a select population over others, I undertake the training to refrain from exploiting any person or group, including economically, sexually, intellectually, or culturally. I commit to examine with wisdom and clear comprehension the ways that I have privilege in order to determine skillful ways of using privilege for the benefit of all beings, and I commit to the practice of generosity in all aspects of my

life and towards all human beings, regardless of cultural, ethnic, racial, sexual, age, physical, or economic differences.

6) Aware of the suffering caused to myself and others by fear and anger during conflict or disagreement, I undertake the training to refrain from reacting defensively, using harmful speech because I feel injured, or using language or cognitive argument to justify my sense of rightness. I commit to communicate and express myself mindfully, speaking truthfully from my heart with patience and compassion. I commit to practice genuine and deep listening to all sides of a dispute, and to remain in contact with my highest intentions of recognizing Buddha nature within all beings.

7) Aware of the suffering caused by the ignorance of misinformation and the lack of information that aggravate fixed views, stereotypes, the stigmatizing of a human being as "other," and the marginalization of cultural groups, I undertake the training to educate myself about other cultural attitudes, worldviews, ethnic traditions, and life experiences outside of my own. I commit to be curious with humility and openness, to recognize with compassion the experience of suffering in all beings, and to practice sympathetic joy when encountering the many different cultural expressions of happiness and celebration around the world.

"Metta as Diversity Practice," developed by Larry Yang, can be found in Appendix II.

PART EIGHT

A Taste of Community Life

The Cambridge Sangha 31

BY MURRAY CORKE

THE CAMBRIDGE SANGHA in England ccame together as a result of a close friendship between a small group of people who had previously practiced together in a different tradition. The commitment to practice of this core group has created stability and resulted in a regular program of Days of Mindfulness, evening sittings, and local retreats. Our shared practices, based on Plum Village forms, are simplified to suit our needs. The size of each local event has been largely self-regulating, with about twelve to fifteen members as the number most people are comfortable with. The more events we held, the more we saw our numbers increase. As we grew, we budded off into a new Sangha at the edge of our geographic area, which we helped to get started.

Flexibility and commitment to the practice have been very important in holding our Sangha together. We meet mostly in members' homes and have a general rule that the host does not facilitate the event, as this spreads out the energy better. We have regular meetings at fixed times that continue regardless as to how many people come, and there are no fixed expectations of the outcome. There is an open door—everyone is welcome. People stay because they wish to and are always free to leave. Newcomers seem more likely to come again if we do not make them feel different from others and do not offer them too much help initially.

We use consensus to make decisions that affect the Sangha. We are grateful to outside Tiep Hien (Order of Interbeing) facilitators for helping us to resolve personal differences that have arisen within our Sangha.

We advertise our Sangha only through national Sangha events, the national Website and contact address, and the *Mindfulness Bell.* Newcomers also arrive through personal contacts and contacts at Plum Village.

The Sangha has been strengthened by members attending national retreats and Dharma Training events, and by visiting Plum Village. As the Sangha has grown we have been able to offer bursaries to support members in these activities. We have worked, both as individuals and as a group, on larger projects such as organizing national retreats and events. Members of the Sangha go regularly into prisons to facilitate meditation sessions and share the Dharma with inmates interested in Buddhism.

The active involvement of two local Vietnamese Tiep Hien members has added to the richness and diversity of our practice together.

Our Second Anniversary Tea Ceremony 32

BY MITCHELL RATNER

ONE RECENT Wednesday evening, like every Wednesday evening, members of the community began arriving just after 7:15 for the mindfulness practices evening. Leaving their shoes and coats in the holistic health center's waiting room, they climbed two flights of stairs to the attic meeting room. The first people to arrive pulled out the mats and cushions and arranged them in a rectangle along the room's periphery. The large meditation bell was set out and the room was transformed into a small meditation hall with space for twenty people to sit.

The early arrivers sat quietly on cushions, facing the blank walls and windows. In a few minutes the room filled. At 7:30 the bell was invited three times to begin the meditation period. Twenty-five minutes later, it was invited once again to end the meditation. People massaged their legs and turned around.

As bell master, I informed the group that this evening was special. We would have a Tea Ceremony to celebrate the second anniversary of the Still Water Mindfulness Practice Center located in Takoma Park, Maryland. After a brief introduction to the Tea Ceremony for a few newcomers, the group waited silently downstairs while the tea servers set up. Several minutes later a bell sounded, the Sangha members came up the stairs, one by one, and were welcomed to the Tea Ceremony. Once everyone was settled, flowers were offered. "In gratitude we offer these flowers to all Buddhas and bodhisattvas, wise men and wise women, throughout space and time." Then the ginger-lime tea, homemade cookies, and clementines were passed on trays from person to person. After reciting a gatha, there was silence, except for the crunching of cookies and the sipping of tea.

After most of the cookies had been mindfully nibbled, as tea master, I invited people to share: "The questions for tonight are: What has Still Water meant to you? What difference has our community made in your life?"

One after another, members of the community bowed to the group and spoke. Many of the comments were about having a home or a haven, where the practice of mindfulness was understood and appreciated. Valerie said:

> My feelings about this place are that it is so wonderful to have a community like this, a Sangha like this, where I feel safe and embraced by mindfulness. I think someone coming here for the first time can have the sense that this is a place of peace and presence, safety and trust. That is a very rare and precious thing today, particularly in this city.

From Joan:

> When I remember it is Wednesday and I can come here, there is this sense of haven.... [I value being able] to come and experience it and also to connect with those same feelings when I am not here, during my daily life, which is not so peaceful.

Another theme that people mentioned during the Tea Ceremony was the quality of the sharing, a sense of being fully accepted in this group. Sharron told the group about her first morning:

> I will never forget the first morning that I came. I had been looking for a Sangha for a long time. I got Mitchell's number from the Internet, called him up, and then came one morning at 6:30. I will never forget the feeling when we all turned around and everyone bowed and everyone was smiling at me. It just made me feel so good. When I left I was thinking, "This is the first time since kindergarten I've been in a room full of people who were smiling at me."

Chelsea talked about her experience of the Dharma discussions:

I really enjoy sharing with everyone. Everyone is so open. You don't have to wonder or worry or think, What did they mean by that? I'm just very glad to be here.

Marie talked about the openheartedness of the Still Water community:

Still Water is a ballast. I can leave whatever it is I am doing at home. The roots go down deep, soak in the energy during our sitting. Then what we discuss strengthens my roots, helps me to open up and then keep that openness. . . . It is truly incredible to have a place so safe that these feelings can come up from deep, deep down. It is a real gift of the Sangha.

Peter wrote a poem about his experience of morning sittings.

Still Water

A place I have learned
that cars passing by
can ebb and flow
        into its waters and out
with the beauty of a sunset and sunrise.

Sharron talked about how for her, as a young adult, the community provided role models:

One of the things that is particularly amazing about Still Water as opposed to other places I've practiced is that there are a lot of parents here. When my partner and I think about having children we know that there will be people we can call on or ask questions of. People here are good role models as dads and moms, taking care of themselves as well as their families. I think that is extremely rare.

Joan talked about a night the community explored art and mindfulness.

One of the memories that stays with me is the night we did body diagrams. I had a very pregnant body at that time. I drew a little fish inside the diagram, and very big breasts. There is no group of strangers I would do that with. The drawing has been up in my art room ever since. It is a wonderful memory of Still Water honoring my pregnancy.

Once the sharing began, it flowed, and there was more than can be included here. I took a few moments to thank everyone for sharing and for supporting Still Water these past two years.

I noticed, also, how much the community has matured. During the first six months, Dharma discussion sharings frequently began with "I don't know much, but...." or "What would a Buddhist say about....?" Now sharings begin with statements like, "The way I've learned to practice with anger is...." or "Having learned to calm down, I am better able to deal with...." The community as a whole often radiates a stability and confidence in the practice. We have succeeded in creating a place in the city where mindfulness can be honored, supported, and nurtured. We have become a concrete manifestation that this is possible.

The anniversary celebration ended with a Still Water MPC rendition of the Plum Village song "I Have Arrived, I Am Home," first in Plum Village–style, measured and stately, and then a second time with an upbeat tempo, clapping, and impromptu percussive instrumentation, as rousing as a jazz version of "When the Saints Go Marching In."

We ended with hugging meditation.

Amici di Thây Sangha 33

BY ROBERTO DEL MASTIO

I FIRST ENCOUNTERED Buddhism in 1975 in Nepal when I lived there for six months. Upon my return to Florence I read and started to translate anything regarding the Dharma. In 1979, the first monastery of Tibetan Buddhism in Italy was founded by Lama Yeshe in Tuscany. After a few years, I felt that since this monastery was two hours away from Florence, laypeople could profit a lot if there was a place in town where they could meet during the week. So in 1983 my wife and I decided to start a Sangha in Florence. We contacted the few Florentines we knew from the monastery and we printed a very vibrant poster that we pasted all over town announcing the first meeting. That fall there was a Dharma Center in town! From 1983–1988 we helped organize many important events, retreats, and conferences to get as many people in touch with the Dharma as possible.

In 1988 my wife and I decided to pass the "seats" of Director and Sangha-Builder to others because we felt there was something missing: we had not yet found our teacher. Following this there were three years of loneliness and sad feelings. Then like a miracle, for my birthday, a friend gave me a book by Thich Nhat Hanh, *Peace Is Every Step*. It was love at first sight! The next year Thây came to Italy and after the first Dharma talk we knew that we had finally met our teacher. The guide that we had wished to meet in the depth of our hearts was right there in front of us. Fully present because he was "there for us," breathing mindfully, a real full-time Buddha.

I know now that to meet your root teacher, it is the most precious gift and the greatest joy that life can offer. So, now, how to explain the desire, the force that came from inside and pushed me to share the Dharma with as many sentient beings as possible? I began to make a list of the people from Florence that I knew were interested in Buddhism and all the people I met at the first retreat of Sister Annabel in Italy. Then I contacted them and asked if they wished to start to develop our mindfulness together. And in 1993, Amici di Thây Sangha was born in Florence.

I believe that the moment we decide to practice steadily, no matter what, we have made the first step towards building a Sangha. We must feel that we do this for us, not for others, so that when we inform people that on a certain day and hour we will be meditating, we will be there. To be present is fundamental. Now, after eight years, we meet every Tuesday and hold Days of Mindfulness every month and a half. We sustain each other with our practice. We know that we must hold hands, we all have ups and downs and only a strong Sangha can help us to keep our practice alive. In our Sangha we are all leaves on a tree, none is more important than the other, old practitioners, new practitioner or future practitioner, we are all doing our best to keep the Dharma tree alive and that's what counts. In our Sangha nobody pretends to teach anything to others, we just listen and breathe because we know that things will happen at the right moment by themselves.

I try to share my personal experiences and encourage others to do the same. Nobody pretends to teach anything to others, we just listen and breathe, because we know that for everyone things will happen at the right moment all by itself. Opening our heart to others helps everybody. For me a lighthearted, joyful atmosphere is most important. A sad practitioner builds a sad Sangha. For this reason I bought red clown noses that we put on when someone feels sad. Wearing this nose and looking at ourselves in the mirror helps a lot! (We also sell it to newcomers to help the owners of our building pay for heating and electricity.) I believe that the Amici di Thây Sangha is now a cozy place to share positive and less positive experiences of life, a place where we do our best to awaken our mindfulness.

A Sense 34
of Sangha

BY ELLEN STUEBE

I T'S BEEN THREE YEARS since I first encountered the term "Sangha." I was attending a bush retreat led by teacher Khanh Le Van, and as she spoke the word, she gave a generous sweep of the air with her open hand. I looked at where she had gestured for a clue to the meaning. What was that word? "Sun-guh"? Does that mean the air? The ambience? The breeze? Or had she indicated a certain important person sitting before her in the hall? Maybe it was another word for a retreat, or a method of meditation, or the bell at her elbow. Perhaps it was a *mantra*.

These days I use the word "Sangha" frequently in my own daily life. Traditionally, I understand it to mean the monastic community. In a contemporary sense, it has come to represent any group of people practicing the Dharma. And on a personal level, it is the word I use to describe the bunch of friends with whom I practice the teachings of Thich Nhat Hanh. We call ourselves the Lotus Buds Sangha. Khanh Le Van is our teacher, and the group of people I met at the retreat are now my Dharma brothers and sisters.

But an intellectual understanding of Sangha is a poor substitute for experience. Just as Sangha-building takes place on a physical level, it must also take place in the hearts and minds of each member. My own sense of Sangha began when I first joined the Lotus Buds. People smiled at me when I arrived and I felt truly welcome. I looked forward to each week in the knowledge that I would be with like-minded individuals. In particular I looked forward to the cup of tea we would share after the meditation and the chance to talk about our lives and the practice. Nowhere else in my life had I been embraced in this manner. My confidence grew. I felt I could truly be myself. I was beginning to get a sense of the word "Sangha."

Before long I found myself involved in many aspects of Sangha life. I instigated a weekly recitation of the Five Mindfulness Trainings and enjoyed leading the singing every now and then. My relationships with other Sangha members grew more relaxed, and we often told jokes and laughed as we drank tea. Every now and again Sangha members were invited to share something of their practice in a talk to the whole group. On several occasions I offered something of my personal practice. In this atmosphere of understanding and support, I began to allow my weaknesses, my confusion, and my attachments to be revealed. The ensuing feeling of freedom was extraordinary, and I found that my understanding of Sangha continued to grow steadily.

One day my teacher called me at home to inform me that someone in the Sangha had made a formal complaint about me. I was shocked. "A complaint about me?" Anger, frustration, and indignation rose in me instantly. In my own heart and mind I felt at peace with all my Dharma brothers and sisters. But the reality remained—in an unmindful moment I had hurt someone's feelings. Attempts to arrange meetings to resolve the issue were thwarted, and before long I felt as though I were in a torturous limbo. On meditation nights I skulked in late and held back for fear that I might be offending people by my sheer presence. This, I thought, was not what Sangha was about. My sense of Sangha had obviously been mistaken. I wondered if I might have only imagined the sense of support and cohesion. I felt lost and confused.

For two months I did not attend our Sangha and practiced alone. At first I could no longer remember why I was practicing at all. Sitting by myself seemed pointless. Yet my sense of Sangha had also lost its meaning. As time passed a new vision of Sangha began to grow within me. I realized slowly, painfully, that in fact the Sangha had not failed me—but my expectations had. My attachment to notions of perfect harmony, while optimistic, was unrealistic. Clearly this was a group of people like any other, with as many opinions and feelings as there were members. Instead of allowing the Sangha to be what it was, I had attempted to make it what I wanted. Rather than working with the challenges, I had run away from them.

On returning to the Sangha, I was embraced wholeheartedly. The issue of conflict was never "fixed," but in its own time died into the great spaciousness of forgiveness. I began to notice subtle changes in the way I viewed the Sangha and my role within it. Recognizing the interbeing nature of the group, I saw that a Sangha was far more than the sum of its individual parts. It was ever-changing and expansive. It seemed to have a life of its own. Rather than the static concept I had first imagined, it was a real, living, breathing entity. I may have been part of it, but it was also part of me.

Opening gradually to this new realm, the Sangha's magic began to reveal itself in unexpected ways. When Khanh, our teacher, was away for some weeks, we rallied 'round to share the planning and responsibilities, finding creative ways to approach our weekly meditations. Guitars found their way to our singing sessions. We went out for late night pizza. Our monthly recitation gathering began to find new form. I could now see that the Sangha was in fact a microcosm of life. Dharma brothers and sisters moved away. New members brought fresh questions. Some of us got married. Others broke up. We faced sicknesses and growth spurts and crises of confidence. In the midst of the chaos, a solidity began to return for me. And with it, a deeper understanding of this thing called "Sangha"—its offerings, its limitations, and its power to transform.

I recently attended another of our bush retreats led by Khanh. I felt I knew what to expect of this Sangha experience. This time, however, my mother was present, and we found ourselves sharing a room. Mum sat near me at meal times and winked at me during noble silence. She appeared behind me in the meditation hall and spoke enthusiastically in Dharma sharings. When I awoke, there she was. At night I couldn't sleep for her snoring. "Your mum is fantastic!" my friends were saying, but I wasn't so sure. Dharma brothers and sisters I had heard of, but Dharma mothers? Then, as I watched her practicing deep listening, singing with all her heart, and finally, taking the Five Mindfulness Trainings, I realized I had simply reached the next step of Sangha understanding. I was being asked to embrace a still wider sense of the word. Wonderfully, this time it included my very own mum.

After three years of Sangha experience, you would perhaps expect that my understanding of the word should be complete. True understanding comes slowly. Just when I think I can define Sangha, it becomes something else entirely. In building my own sense of Sangha I have been forced to abandon old concepts in favor of here and now experience. In this way I continue to uncover what Sangha is, what it is not, and what it might be if I could only let it.

Looking back to the day when I first heard the word, I realize that from my space of not knowing, I had touched its true meaning. "Sangha" does mean the air. It does mean the ambience. It is the breeze, the person before us, the retreat, a method of meditation, and the bell. It could even be our mantra.

Feeling the Sangha 35
in Nijmegen

BY JAQUELIEN VAN GALEN, EMMY VAN DEN BERG,
AND JAAP BROERSE

O UR SANGHA MEETS in the library of a small, old village monastery near Nijmegen, Holland. The monastery is situated in a beautiful, hilly forest that has surrounded us for hundreds of years. It is a splendid environment for walking meditation, and the library's good atmosphere also invites us to meditate together.

We meet once a month, sometimes for an afternoon, sometimes for the whole day. Our meetings are special; members of the Sangha call them inspiring, nourishing, healing.

So what makes our Sangha so special?

We are just ordinary people, but we feel a special tie to one another. We may not meet very often in daily life, but more and more we are coming to know what moves each other deep inside. It is the feeling that we are surrounded by islands of mindfulness connected by thin strands of concern proceeding from our shared dedication. We are all inspired by the practice of mindfulness, especially as taught by Thich Nhat Hanh.

For many of us, our Sangha meetings are a monthly gift. We meet on a Saturday, coming from all directions, some traveling for a couple of hours. Many people attend regularly, but we are often joined by newcomers. Everyone is welcome; there is no discrimination.

A few members arrive a half an hour early to prepare for the arrival of the others. The library is invited to become our Sangha room. A draped cloth becomes an altar. People place on it objects that might inspire the group: a small statue of the Buddha, a picture of Thây, a candle, a picture of Jesus, a stone, a leaf, anything with special meaning to the one who puts it there. Someone arranges flowers and candles in the middle of the circle we will form together when we sit to meditate or gather for the Dharma talk. The arrangement may include flowers from someone's garden, a few leaves, or a wreath of ivy — always selected with love and laid down with attention. Others make coffee and tea, and a collection box is set out for donations to cover our expenses and to support projects in Vietnam.

When the others arrive the room is already filled with mindfulness, and those who enter feel welcome. The atmosphere is still and full; there is talking, laughing, and greeting. We enjoy the intimacy of being together — the silence, the synergy.

When we sit down the first thing we do is to give our name. We know and feel then that we are present, welcome, and together. We normally continue with sitting meditation, *kinh hanh* (walking meditation), then another period of sitting meditation. Thereafter we accept the forest's invitation to enjoy walking meditation. The trees help us find the rest we are looking for, and they connect heaven and Earth. The Earth holds us up, she relieves our sorrows, and we massage her with our feet.

When we come back to the Sangha room we drink tea and talk until the bell invites us for the Dharma discussion or Dharma talk. Here everyone can share their experiences and feelings. The form is not important. As one asks to speak, the others listen with care and attention. Often someone tells a story about practicing Thây's teachings or of some personal life experience. Others read poems or sing songs. We always end the meeting with a short meditation.

The friend who began our Sangha some years ago — with all the modesty that characterizes him — is a major support to our group. He radiates heartfulness and welcome. He attends to what is needed without giving the impression of being in charge. He is leading from within and allows things to unfold without clinging to forms or rituals. This atmosphere of openness and freedom invites others to contribute easily.

Last year's December meeting was very special for our Sangha. That month always focuses on the approaching Christmas, an important feast in the root tradition of most of us. No one specifically organized the meeting; we simply gathered in mindfulness and allowed things to unfold as they were meant to. We spoke from our hearts and listened mindfully to each other. There were personal stories, poems, and songs. Someone brought chocolates with beautiful little greeting cards; another shared delicious homemade apple pies. We enjoyed singing with one another—both sutras and Christmas carols accompanied on the piano and the guitar. We each lit a candle and described to whom we had dedicated it. It was a beautiful day. We felt very much united, and we still talk about it.

We see our Sangha growing in all aspects and are very hopeful. Our Sangha is a community of mindfulness, love, and caring. Thây has said that the Buddha of the future is the Sangha. We sometimes feel that in Nijmegen.

Building a Sangha Is a Team Effort 36

BY NGUYEN DUY VINH

WHEN WE RECEIVE the mindfulness trainings and vow to take refuge in the Three Jewels, we commit to take care of ourselves and bring joy and happiness to others. The mindfulness trainings constitute our ideals and the basis of our mindfulness practice. Taking refuge in the Three Jewels—the Buddha, the Dharma, and the Sangha—we know that these commitments cannot be accomplished without a good teacher, a true teaching, and supportive friends—a Sangha. The Sangha is essential, for without it our practice will slowly fade away. Thây has compared nuns and monks who leave their Sangha to tigers that abandon the forest and are soon caught by hunters. Without a Sangha, lay practitioners too will be caught by the traps of our environment and our habit energy. But building and maintaining a Sangha can be challenging. To succeed, you need committed people and, in the long run, companionship, camaraderie, and solidarity.

Throughout the years I have had many memorable encounters with the members of our Sangha, all of which strengthened our relationships. In November 1997, several brothers and sisters from Ottawa and Montréal traveled to Vermont to meet Thây and to attend the inauguration ceremony of Maple Forest Monastery. Before we left Ottawa, we listened carefully to weather forecasts of snow and wind, but they didn't sound too bad. By the time we were out of Montréal, however, a blizzard had started, and driving became very difficult. It took a tiring five and a half hours to reach Woodstock, Vermont, normally a two-hour trip. When we arrived, we discovered that Thây's talk had been canceled due to the storm. Fortunately, we had a cell phone and called for directions to Maple Forest Monastery. Driving up the steep, slippery road, we were forced to abandon our cars and walk. After forty-five minutes, we were lost and exhausted. We phoned again and learned we were almost there. Ten minutes later, we saw a huge barn with light inside. We arrived very late and tired, but joyful. We also found that through our hardship, our solidarity and friendship were strengthened.

Small things can serve to bind us together as well. I recall when our sister Brenda Carr invited the Sangha to a formal recitation of the Five Mindfulness Trainings at her home. After a very difficult childbirth, Brenda had been ill for some time. That evening, I was particularly moved to see Brenda put on her brown Order of Interbeing coat for the first time. (The coat was a kind gift from the Toronto Vietnamese Sangha.) The recitation that night was vibrant with sincerity and commitment. We eleven practitioners were honored by Andre and Brenda's beautiful six-month-old daughter Karuna.

I recall also the sorrow our Sangha experienced late last December when our sister Annette Pypops passed away after two years of fierce struggle against breast cancer. Strengthened by Montréal's Maple Village Sangha, we organized a chanting and prayer ceremony for Annette, answering the wish she expressed before she died.

All these moments of joy, hardship, and sadness bring us together, allow us to know each other a bit more, and enhance solidarity and friendship within the Sangha. The Buddha himself taught that such friendship and solidarity is very important. Once, the Buddha found a sick monk who had been left alone while the other monks went on almsrounds. After caring for the unwell monk, the Buddha instructed the returning monks: "Friends, if we do not look after each other, who will look after us? When you look after each other, you are looking after the Tathagata."[60]

In applying the Buddha's teaching to Sangha-building, we often find that our primary difficulty in enhancing Sangha relationships is tied to how each of us organizes his or her own life. We are busy with professional and family life. Most of us spend eight to ten hours a day working to earn our bread and butter. In current Western society, it is not easy to work part-time unless we have a liberal profession or our needs allow us to live simply. The struggle is even more difficult when we have a family to support, especially with young adults of university age. But, we must find time to take care of our Sangha friends who are in difficult moments—illness, accident, loss of beloved ones, job loss, etc. A Sangha's success depends on its members sharing time, energy, and material resources with each other. The well-being of our Sangha affects our own well-being, and vice versa.

(This article originally appeared in Issue No. 24 of the *Mindfulness Bell.*)

Planting Seeds of Peace in the Middle East 37

BY MEMBERS OF THE ISRAEL SANGHA

Two members from the Israel Sangha took the initiative, with the support of several members of the Sangha, to create and coordinate a project called "Peace Begins with Myself." (Plum Village, New Hamlet, August 6th, 2001.)

OVER THE PAST FEW YEARS, Thich Nhat Hanh has suggested more than once that Palestinians and Jews sit together in meditation and that they practice deep listening and sharing of each other's suffering. Thây's suggestion planted the seeds of a dream.

A few weeks ago, several Israeli practitioners began the process of realizing a dream they had in their hearts for a long time. Separately, these people had dreamt the same dream, and the conditions were right for them to meet, share ideas and begin to make it a reality. That dream was to bring a group of Jews and Palestinians together in Plum Village. Now that this group has been here for two weeks, Thây has asked us to share our experiences with you.

Over a period of two weeks, we have had meetings—almost daily—attended by a mixed group of about fifteen Palestinians and Jews, and supported by attending monks and nuns, including Sister Chân Không, Sister Annabel, Sister Jina, Thây Doji, Brother Iver, and Brother Phap Minh.

The meetings generally lasted for two hours, sometimes longer. Sharing was in English, Hebrew and Arabic, depending on who was sharing, with translation always present. The pace and format of the process were guided by the monks and nuns, under the guidance of Thây. All of the meetings were recorded.

During the first few meetings the group members were encouraged to focus on deepening their personal practice and nurturing their own grounds of stability, along with the rest of the international community at Plum Village. We ate, walked, and practiced together in mindfulness.

After a few days of nurturing our inner peace—calming our bodies and minds—the process of deep listening began with a session with Sister Chân Không. People in the group shared feelings of despair and anger and asked for guidance on how to use the practice to deal with their feelings. Sister Chân Không shared her experience in dealing with her own anger and despair and finding inner peace and clarity during the Vietnam War.

One evening, we practiced walking meditation in the forest in the Lower Hamlet where we joined together in a Beginning Anew circle with Sister Jina and watered each other's flowers. The next day we began a series of meetings in which we practiced sharing and deep listening. Over the course of the meetings, each person had the opportunity to speak mindfully and to share his or her personal story. Our stories were often interwoven with the suffering of our ancestors and those in our present community.

The bell of mindfulness was invited between each sharing, as well as when the sharing became very emotional. This helped us to return to ourselves to get centered.

The Palestinians spoke about their difficulties as Israeli-Arabs, the discrimination in Israel, and their inferior status in relation to Jews, the Israeli government, and the police. They spoke about their fears of being uprooted from their homes because they are a minority in a Jewish state. They shared their experiences of discrimination by the government that does not permit them to build homes in their villages or to develop their land. They spoke about the land that had been expropriated and given to Jews.

The Palestinians who live in the West Bank and Gaza talked about the distress that has been going on since the first intafada (the Palestinian uprising and clashes) in 1987, the humiliating treatment they experience from the Israeli army, the difficult conditions they live under, and their poverty. They shared about the deportation of many of the Palestinians who lived in Arab villages and towns during the 1948 war, and about being scattered around the world, uprooted, unwanted, and homeless. They spoke of hatred for those Jews that took away their home.

The Jewish members shared their difficulties in struggling to protect a state surrounded by enemies, about their great fear of others wanting to destroy them, about difficulties in differentiating between the Palestinian citizens in Israel and the neighboring Arabs who are considered to be enemies, and about life in the shadow of constant fear: fear of terrorist attacks in the streets or on the buses, and the fear of further wars. As a result of this fear, there is a lot of violence and aggressive communication. Jewish members shared that Israeli society is mentally disabled and suffering from disconnection from itself. It also suffers from apathy and a lack of understanding for the other side. They shared that many Israelis want peace and not war, but that they distrust the intentions of the Palestinians.

Jewish members shared about the Holocaust and genocide of their people in Europe by the Nazis, a trauma that is imprinted on every Jewish soul and which effects their behavior. They also talked about being homeless, in exile, for two thousand years.

The main emotion expressed was fear.

Many of us had participated in Israeli-Palestinian dialogue in the past, but the process in Plum Village was different in that it involved neither dialogue nor a search for solutions. It was a practice in compassionate listening, without commentary and without judgment. And when we shared we were encouraged to use loving speech.

The sense of safety provided in Plum Village and the presence of the teachers created a safe space for sharing and listening. One wise brother said, "If we don't transform, we transmit." Each one of us, in our own way, underwent transformation.

We would like to share the impressions of a few members of the group to show how we progressed from listening to understanding:

> To listen compassionately to others is to be reminded of one's own humanity. It's like looking in a mirror and seeing oneself. To see all the fear that is inside us, and all its manifestations, like anger, is very scary. It is something we are not taught to do. In fact, we are taught to avoid it.

My experience here has given me a cradle—a place to feel held, warm and safe—so that seeing myself mirrored through others is not so scary. It is beautiful.

The conflict is not about politics. It is about human beings and about their fears.

We learned to speak from our hearts, without having fear that anyone would disturb us, and without judging and blaming.

We learned to listen with respect. We listened deeply to the others' suffering.

Sharing deeply, listening deeply, helped us to see our deepest fears and to let those fears go, flow away. Seeing the source of suffering and fear, it is now time to learn to let it go and not to drown in it. Peace begins with me. We seek peace. If we practice the love of God, we can embrace every human act and forgive.

Usually, in the Middle East, we use so much anger to express our suffering and that is why we cannot speak to or listen to each other. Here we were able to express suffering without anger and to really listen.

I was able to learn more about the suffering of my own people and the suffering of the others.

It became clear that your suffering is my suffering.

Recognizing that we all suffer, slowly seeing the nature and source of the suffering, I could see that there is also a way to end the suffering, and that there is a place, a heaven, where there is no more suffering.

Hell and heaven are in me, and in you. We have the choice to create hell for ourselves and for others, or to help each other to realize heaven. I want to choose heaven.

Both Jews and Palestinians share the same feelings of rootlessness and homelessness. We suffer deeply because of that.

Living the conflict every day, somehow it becomes routine, which is so unmindful and, in my view, dangerous. The community of Plum Village, and of course Thây and the people from all over the world, were like bells of mindfulness for me to look deeper into our mutual conflict.

I feel there is something very unique and very serious in our hands, and if we could be mindful with it, it could bring some good to this world.

It was the first opportunity for me to hear firsthand about the pain and the difficulty of both sides and to know the people in the group closely. For me, the story of the Palestinian refugees was very meaningful and made me reconsider the whole situation and the possible solutions.

I learned that I can cradle the guilt feelings in me, and the shame, to softly put them to sleep, like a mother with a fragile baby. When the guilt and shame rest like this — calm and safe in my arms — then I can listen with all my heart to painful, shocking things — to the suffering of our Palestinian brothers.

It does not matter when a peace agreement between the two people is signed, what time, what date or if we have the strength to put forth the effort needed, if we ever get to taste the fruits of the seeds we are sowing.

I learned how important practicing compassion is, and accepting the bad sides — the violence, anxiety and racism — in us Israeli-Jews, so that I can accept with love those sides when I meet them in others.

I learned that all the material I need to make peace is in me, and when I practice, touch it, and am aware of it, I do not suffer anymore.

The neutral environment, the listening, embrace the soul and enable the words and feelings, the pain, the embarrassment, the search, to come from a true place.

There is a lot of strength in the process of listening, in the permission that each member of the group is asking for, to take the time for him or herself and enable things to come up.

For me, many meaningful seeds of strength and faith in my spiritual path, in making peace, have been sown. I found support, I found partners, I found more faith in myself.

If you'd have had the chance to listen to our sharing, you would be able to understand how much this tragic conflict effects each and every one of us growing up on this land that we are all so connected to.

We learned from the very deep experiences that we shared here what we already knew; that there is no one side that is right, no one side that is a winner. In our situation, we all lose.

Our wounds will be transmitted to the next generations if we do not take care of them.

We hope that our work here has sown seeds for the continuation of the process. This work has the potential to bring transformation on a personal level, resulting in the transformation of society.

My attitude towards the Arabs, particularly the Israeli-Arabs, has changed as a result of the personal transformation gained from Buddhist meditation practice.

I have a ways to go, the one taught by the Buddha and Thây.

For the week I spent in Plum Village, I lived in paradise. I felt that plum village is paradise for two reasons. One was the location, the landscape, the atmosphere and the colors and the second reason was the fact that our enemies were friends. All the people around me were my family. I could sense the heart of love radiating from every soul and penetrating my deep, dark heart. The darkness that had been living there since my childhood, the darkness that was caused by the Jews, "our cousins." The cousins that took away my childhood, and now are aiming at my youth. In the paradise of plum village my voice was heard even during noble silence time. My heart was touched and the darkness was replaced by light.

I am ready to accept my enemies as family.

We, Palestinians and Israelis, lived with harmony, love, and compassion. It was very easy to interact positively with each other, we showed much understanding even though our house is burning and been destroyed.

The deep feelings expressed here have prepared the ground for further activities in Israel. At the moment, we are planning to share days of mindfulness together in Israel and, at Thây's invitation, to bring more groups from Israel and Palestine to Plum Village in the near future.

We are deeply grateful to Thây and the Plum Village community for their great support and guidance. We are moved by your deep caring for us and your willingness to help.

For more information about the project, you may like to browse:
www.pi.co.il/sangha/creations.html.

What the Geese Know 38

BY KARL SCHMIED

THE FOLLOWING FIVE LESSONS of the geese may make clear the foundations for building a Sangha.

By flapping its wings, each goose creates an upwind for the ones following it. Flying in a V-formation allows the flock to fly seventy-one percent further than would be possible for an individual goose.

Lesson 1: People who share a common direction and a sense of community reach their goal more quickly and easily, because they benefit from the energy of the others.

Whenever a goose swerves out of formation, it immediately becomes aware of the resistance present when one bird flies alone and quickly reenters the formation, in order to be able to use the lift caused by the preceding geese.

Lesson 2: If we are as sensible as a goose is, we will stay in formation with those wanting to go to the same place we do, and we accept their support in the same way in which we are willing to support the others.

When the lead goose becomes tired, it falls back and another goose takes the lead position.

Lesson 3: It pays to relieve one another working and to take turns in the leadership position.

The geese flying in the rear rally the ones flying up front with their calls.

Lesson 4: We should be sure of the encouragement resulting from our rallying calls.

When a goose is sick or wounded and is no longer able to fly, then two other geese leave the formation and accompany it on its way down in order to help and protect it. They stay with the goose until it can either fly again or until it dies. Then they join another formation and try to catch up to their own flock again.

Lesson 5: Sangha members should feel secure that they are not abandoned by their spiritual family. When faced with a serious illness, physical or mental problems, they can rely on the support of experienced and sympathetic Sangha friends.

A Gift for Thây

BY SISTER CHAN HOA NGHIEM

O N ONE OCCASION we had wanted to offer Thây a gift for Thanksgiving. My job was to find out what he really wanted. While others were enjoying the picnic that day, I tried to find a way to get close and ask Thây, "Dear Thây, what is it that you like the most?" Thây looked at me and smiled, "What do I like? Thây doesn't like anything the best." I felt he still hadn't answered the question, so I asked again: "But dear Thây, there must be something that you like best?" He then looked straight at me. "There is. Thây wants all his students to love each other. To love Thây means to love each other." I was so moved that I became silent. Thây only wants for us to live happily together.

APPENDIX I

Mindfulness Trainings

The Five
Mindfulness Trainings

First Mindfulness Training
Aware of the suffering caused by the destruction of life, I am committed
to cultivating compassion and learning ways to protect the lives of people,
animals, plants, and minerals. I am determined not to kill, not to let others kill, and not to condone any act of killing in the world, in my thinking,
and in my way of life.

Second Mindfulness Training
Aware of the suffering caused by exploitation, social injustice, stealing, and
oppression, I am committed to cultivating loving kindness and learning
ways to work for the well-being of people, animals, plants, and minerals. I
will practice generosity by sharing my time, energy, and material resources
with those who are in real need. I am determined not to steal and not to
possess anything that should belong to others. I will respect the property
of others, but I will prevent others from profiting from human suffering or
the suffering of other species on Earth.

Third Mindfulness Training
Aware of the suffering caused by sexual misconduct, I am committed to cultivating responsibility and learning ways to protect the safety and integrity
of individuals, couples, families, and society. I am determined not to engage
in sexual relations without love and a long-term commitment. To preserve
the happiness of myself and others, I am determined to respect my commitments and the commitments of others. I will do everything in my power
to protect children from sexual abuse and to prevent couples and families
from being broken by sexual misconduct.

Fourth Mindfulness Training

Aware of the suffering caused by unmindful speech and the inability to listen to others, I am committed to cultivating loving speech and deep listening in order to bring joy and happiness to others and relieve others of their suffering. Knowing that words can create happiness or suffering, I am determined to speak truthfully, with words that inspire self-confidence, joy, and hope. I will not spread news that I do not know to be certain and will not criticize or condemn things of which I am not sure. I will refrain from uttering words that can cause division or discord, or that can cause the family or the community to break. I am determined to make all efforts to reconcile and resolve all conflicts, however small.

Fifth Mindfulness Training

Aware of the suffering caused by unmindful consumption, I am committed to cultivating good health, both physical and mental, for myself, my family, and my society by practicing mindful eating, drinking, and consuming. I will ingest only items that preserve peace, well-being, and joy in my body, in my consciousness, and in the collective body and consciousness of my family and society. I am determined not to use alcohol or any other intoxicant or to ingest foods or other items that contain toxins, such as certain TV programs, magazines, books, films, and conversations. I am aware that to damage my body or my consciousness with these poisons is to betray my ancestors, my parents, my society, and future generations. I will work to transform violence, fear, anger, and confusion in myself and in society by practicing a diet for myself and for society. I understand that a proper diet is crucial for self-transformation and for the transformation of society.

The Fourteen
Mindfulness Trainings

1

Aware of the suffering created by fanaticism and intolerance, we are determined not to be idolatrous about or bound to any doctrine, theory, or ideology, even Buddhist ones. Buddhist teachings are guiding means to help us learn to look deeply and to develop our understanding and compassion. They are not doctrines to fight, kill, or die for.

2

Aware of the suffering created by attachment to views and wrong perceptions, we are determined to avoid being narrow-minded and bound to present views. We shall learn and practice nonattachment from views in order to be open to others' insights and experiences. We are aware that the knowledge we presently possess is not changeless, absolute truth. Truth is found in life, and we will observe life within and around us in every moment, ready to learn throughout our lives.

3

Aware of the suffering brought about when we impose our views on others, we are committed not to force others, even our children, by any means whatsoever—such as authority, threat, money, propaganda, or indoctrination—to adopt our views. We will respect the right of others to be different and to choose what to believe and how to decide. We will, however, help others renounce fanaticism and narrowness through practicing deeply and engaging in compassionate dialogue.

4

Aware that looking deeply at the nature of suffering can help us develop compassion and find ways out of suffering, we are determined not to avoid or close our eyes before suffering. We are committed to finding ways, including personal contact, images, and sounds, to be with those who suffer, so we can understand their situation deeply and help them transform their suffering into compassion, peace, and joy.

5

Aware that true happiness is rooted in peace, solidity, freedom, and compassion, and not in wealth or fame, we are determined not to take as the aim of our life fame, profit, wealth, or sensual pleasure, nor to accumulate wealth while millions are hungry and dying. We are committed to living simply and sharing our time, energy, and material resources with those in need. We will practice mindful consuming, not using alcohol, drugs, or any other products that bring toxins into our own and the collective body and consciousness.

6

Aware that anger blocks communication and creates suffering, we are determined to take care of the energy of anger when it arises and to recognize and transform the seeds of anger that lie deep in our consciousness. When anger comes up, we are determined not to do or say anything, but to practice mindful breathing or mindful walking and acknowledge, embrace, and look deeply into our anger. We will learn to look with the eyes of compassion at ourselves and at those we think are the cause of our anger.

7

Aware that life is available only in the present moment and that it is possible to live happily in the here and now, we are committed to training ourselves to live deeply each moment of daily life. We will try not to lose ourselves in dispersion or be carried away by regrets about the past, worries about the future, or craving, anger, or jealousy in the present. We will practice mindful breathing to come back to what is happening in the present moment. We are determined to learn the art of mindful living by touching the wondrous, refreshing, and healing elements that are inside and around us, and by nourishing seeds of joy, peace, love, and understanding in ourselves, thus facilitating the work of transformation and healing in our consciousness.

8

Aware that lack of communication always brings separation and suffering, we are committed to training ourselves in the practice of compassionate listening and loving speech. We will learn to listen deeply without judging or reacting and refrain from uttering words that can create discord or cause the community to break. We will make every effort to keep communications open and to reconcile and resolve all conflicts, however small.

9

Aware that words can create suffering or happiness, we are committed to learning to speak truthfully and constructively, using only words that inspire hope and confidence. We are determined not to say untruthful things for the sake of personal interest or to impress people, nor to utter words that might cause division or hatred. We will not spread news that we do not know to be certain nor criticize or condemn things of which we are not sure. We will do our best to speak out about situations of injustice, even when doing so may threaten our safety.

10

Aware that the essence and aim of a Sangha is the practice of understanding and compassion, we are determined not to use the Buddhist community for personal gain or profit or transform our community into a political instrument. A spiritual community should, however, take a clear stand against oppression and injustice and should strive to change the situation without engaging in partisan conflicts.

11

Aware that great violence and injustice have been done to our environment and society, we are committed not to live with a vocation that is harmful to humans and nature. We will do our best to select a livelihood that helps realize our ideal of understanding and compassion. Aware of global economic, political and social realities, we will behave responsibly as consumers and as citizens, not supporting companies that deprive others of their chance to live.

12

Aware that much suffering is caused by war and conflict, we are determined to cultivate nonviolence, understanding, and compassion in our daily lives, to promote peace education, mindful mediation, and reconciliation within families, communities, nations, and in the world. We are determined not to kill and not to let others kill. We will diligently practice deep looking with our Sangha to discover better ways to protect life and prevent war.

13

Aware of the suffering caused by exploitation, social injustice, stealing, and oppression, we are committed to cultivating loving kindness and learning ways to work for the well-being of people, animals, plants, and minerals. We will practice generosity by sharing our time, energy, and material resources with those who are in need. We are determined not to steal and not to possess anything that should belong to others. We will respect the property of others, but will try to prevent others from profiting from human suffering or the suffering of other beings.

14

(For lay members): Aware that sexual relations motivated by craving cannot dissipate the feeling of loneliness but will create more suffering, frustration, and isolation, we are determined not to engage in sexual relations without mutual understanding, love, and a long-term commitment. In sexual relations, we must be aware of future suffering that may be caused. We know that to preserve the happiness of ourselves and others, we must respect the rights and commitments of ourselves and others. We will do everything in our power to protect children from sexual abuse and to protect couples and families from being broken by sexual misconduct. We will treat our bodies with respect and preserve our vital energies (sexual, breath, spirit) for the realization of our bodhisattva ideal. We will be fully aware of the responsibility of bringing new lives into the world, and will meditate on the world into which we are bringing new beings.

(For monastic members): Aware that the aspiration of a monk or a nun can only be realized when he or she wholly leaves behind the bonds of worldly love, we are committed to practicing chastity and to helping others protect themselves. We are aware that loneliness and suffering cannot be alleviated by the coming together of two bodies in a sexual relationship, but by the practice of true understanding and compassion. We know that a sexual relationship will destroy our life as a monk or a nun, will prevent us from realizing our ideal of serving living beings, and will harm others. We are determined not to suppress or mistreat our body or to look upon our body as only an instrument, but to learn to handle our body with respect. We are determined to preserve vital energies (sexual, breath, spirit) for the realization of our bodhisattva ideal.

Appendix II
Contemplations

The Five Contemplations

This food is the gift of the whole universe,
the Earth, the sky, and much hard work.
May we eat in such a way as to be worthy to receive it.
May we transform our unskillful states of mind and learn
    to eat in moderation.
May we take only food that nourishes us and prevents illness.
We accept this food in order to realize the path of understanding and love.

The Two Promises

1) I vow to develop understanding in order to be able to live peacefully with people, animals, plants, and minerals.

2) I vow to develop compassion in order to protect the lives of people, animals, plants, and minerals.

The Five Remembrances

I am of the nature to grow old.
There is no way to escape growing old.

I am of the nature to have ill-health.
There is no way to escape having ill-health.

I am of the nature to die.
There is no way to escape death.

All that is dear to me and everyone I love are of the nature to change.
There is no way to escape being separated from them.

I inherit the results of my actions in body, speech, and mind.
My actions are the ground on which I stand.

Metta as Diversity Practice

Beginning with self:

May I be happy

— to learn, experience, share, and celebrate the life experiences of those who come from different backgrounds than I do

May I be free

— of any act of injury, offense, anger, stress, or indifference caused by myself or others

May I live with ease and well-being

— guided by patience, generosity, forgiveness, and understanding towards the conditioned experiences of all beings, with a heightened awareness of those who are different from me

May I be free

— to discover and experience the Buddha nature in all beings [with the openness of a newborn child towards his or her parents]

Continuing with the community with whom I most identify:

May we be happy

—to learn, experience, share, and celebrate the life experiences of those who come from different backgrounds than we do

May we be free

— from any act of injury, offense, anger, stress, or indifference caused by ourselves or others

May we live with ease and well-being

— guided by patience, generosity, forgiveness, and understanding towards the conditioned experiences of all beings, with a heightened awareness of those who are different from ourselves

May we be free
— to discover and experience the Buddha nature in all beings [with
    the openness of a newborn child towards his or her parents]

Continuing with a benefactor or dear friend:
May you be happy
— to learn, experience, share, and celebrate the life experiences of
    those who come from different backgrounds than you do
May you be free
— from any act of injury, offense, anger, stress, or indifference caused
    by yourself or others
May you live with ease and well-being
— guided by patience, generosity, forgiveness, and understanding
    towards the conditioned experiences of all beings, with a height-
    ened awareness of those who are different from yourself
May you be free
— to discover and experience the Buddha nature in all beings [with
    the openness of a newborn child towards his or her parents]

*Continuing with a neutral person with whom you may or may not share the same cultural,
ethnic, sexual, or economic background or physical abilities:*
May you be happy
—to learn, experience, share, and celebrate the life experiences of
    those who come from different backgrounds than you do
May you be free
—from any act of injury, offense, anger, stress, or indifference caused
    by yourself or others
May you live with ease and well-being
—guided by patience, generosity, forgiveness, and understanding
    towards the conditioned experiences of all beings, with a height-
    ened awareness of those who are different from yourself
May you be free
—to discover and experience the Buddha nature in all beings [with
    the openness of a newborn child towards his or her parents]

Continuing with a person with whom you have had difficult inter-cultural experiences (starting by choosing a person who has not caused you the deepest harm):

    May you and I be happy
    — to learn, experience, share, and celebrate the life experiences of
      those who come from different backgrounds than we do
    May you and I be free
    — from any act of injury, offense, anger, stress, or indifference caused
      by ourselves or others
    May you and I live with ease and well-being
    — guided by patience, generosity, forgiveness, and understanding
      towards the conditioned experiences of all beings, with a height-
      ened awareness of those who are different from ourselves
    May you and I be free
    — to discover and experience the Buddha nature in all beings [with
      the openness of a newborn child towards his or her parents]

Continuing with a community or cultural group that has been difficult (again, starting by choosing a group who has not caused you the deepest harm):

    May all of us be happy
    — to learn, experience, share, and celebrate the life experiences of
      those who come from different backgrounds than we do
    May all of us be free from the pain and suffering
    — of any act of injury, offense, anger, stress, or indifference caused
      by ourselves or others
    May all of us live with ease and well-being
    — guided by patience, generosity, forgiveness, and understanding
      towards the conditioned experiences of all beings, with a height-
      ened awareness of those who are different from ourselves
    May all of us be free
    — to discover and experience the Buddha nature in all beings [with
      the openness of a newborn child towards his or her parents]

Returning to traditional Metta practice:

May all beings be happy

May all beings be free from pain and suffering

May all beings live with ease and well-being

May all beings be free

Dedication:

May the awareness of the needs of diverse communities continue
to be recognized and to grow in all Sanghas

May all Sanghas, to the best of their abilities, take actions towards
the elimination of cultural, racial, ethnic, sexual, physical, and
economic barriers to practice

May this work on issues of diversity and oppression heal the experiences
of separation and show us all, the commonality of our nature, for
the benefit of all beings everywhere, in all directions

Orange Meditation

When you look deeply at an orange, you realize that an orange — or any fruit — is nothing less than a miracle. Try it. Take an orange and hold it in your palm. Breathe in and out slowly, and look at it as if you were seeing it for the first time.

When you look at it deeply, you will be able to see many wonderful things — the sun shining and the rain falling on the orange tree, the orange blossoms, the tiny fruit appearing on the branch, the color of the fruit changing from green to yellow, and then the full-grown orange. Now slowly begin to peel it. Smell the wonderful scent of the orange peel. Break off a section of the orange and put it into your mouth. Taste its wonderful juice.

The orange tree has taken three, four or six months to make such an orange for you. It is a miracle. Now the orange is ready and it says, "I am here for you." But if you are not present, you will not hear it. When you are not looking at the orange in the present moment, then the orange is not present either.

Being fully present while eating an orange, an ice-cream cone, or any other food is a delightful experience.

Appendix III
Practices

Tea Ceremony

Tea meditation is a time to be with the Sangha in a joyful and serene atmosphere. Just to enjoy our tea together is enough. Often in our daily lives, when we are drinking tea with a friend, we are not aware of the tea or even of our friend sitting there. Practicing tea meditation is to be truly present with our tea and our friends. We realize that we can dwell happily in the present moment in spite of our sorrows and worries. We sit together, relaxed, without having to say anything. If we like, we can also share a song, a story, a dance, or bring a musical instrument. Tea Ceremony is an opportunity for the Sangha to water the seeds of joy, understanding, and love in each one of us. The following can be used as a guideline.

This ceremony may be informal or formal. Before the ceremony, the room is prepared by the Tea Master or Mistress (Tea M.), Bell Master or Mistress (Bell M.), Incense Offerer, Buddha Offerer, Head Server, and one or two other servers. Place the cushions in a circle, with the altar in the center or at one end of the room. At each server's place, there can be a thermos for tea and one for hot water, a tray of cups for the correct number of people to be served, and a tray of cookies, each cookie on a folded napkin. In front of the Head Server (or Tea M, if there is no Head Server), there is a small Buddha plate with a flower, a cookie on a napkin, and an empty cup. The Buddha Offerer, who is often the youngest person, sits across the circle from the Tea M.

When everything is prepared and the atmosphere is serene, invite the Sangha to enter the room. The people who have prepared the room stand in two lines at the entrance to the room and welcome each person who enters, and indicate where he or she can be seated. Once all participants have been seated, the bell is invited for everyone to stand up.

The Tea M. and Incense Offerer walk mindfully to the altar. At the altar, the Tea M. accepts the incense from the Incense Offerer. The Bell M.

invites the bell three times, and then "stops" the bell for the recitation of the incense offering verse. The Bell M. invites the bell after the recitation. The Tea M. hands the incense back to the Incense Offerer who puts it in the incense holder on the altar. The Bell M. invites one sound of the bell.

The Tea M. welcomes everyone, "Welcome all, Buddhas-to-be," and with one sound of the bell, everyone bows to each other and sits down.

The Head Server pours a cup of tea, places it on the Buddha plate, and lifts the plate up. The Buddha Offerer bows, stands up, and walks mindfully toward the Head Server, bows to the Head Server, and accepts the plate. The Head Server is seated. As the Buddha Offerer accepts the plate from the Head Server, the Tea M. stands up. The Buddha Offerer walks mindfully to the Tea M., bows, and hands the plate to her. The Buddha Offerer and the Tea M. walk to the altar, and the Buddha Offerer stands with palms folded while the Tea M. places the plate on the altar. The Bell M. sounds the bell, and everyone bows. The Buddha Offerer and the Tea M. walk mindfully back to their seats.

During Tea Ceremony, participants should not stand up; all items that are needed should be passed around the circle. After the Tea M. and the Buddha Offerer sit down, the Head Server (and other servers, if there are more) bows to the tray of cookies, picks it up, and offers it to the person on the left. The person to the left bows, takes a cookie and places it in front of him or her, then bows (optional), accepts the tray, and offers a cookie to the Server, who bows and takes a cookie. The person to the left of the Server now offers the tray to the person to his left, who bows, accepts a cookie, then accepts the tray, and offers the tray to the person on the left, etc. When the tray is empty, it should return to the Server.

Once the tray of cookies is two to three seats away, the Server starts pouring the tea. When the cups are filled (be sure there are not more than seven or eight cups as the tray can become too heavy), the Server offers it to the person to the left. The same serving process follows as for the cookies.

Everyone enjoys breathing mindfully until everyone has received a cookie and a cup of tea. Then, after everyone has been served, the Head Server lifts up the cup of tea with two hands, as does everyone else. The Server recites the verse:

> This cup of tea in my two hands —
> mindfulness is held uprightly!
> My mind and body dwell
> in the very here and now.

Everyone enjoys drinking tea and eating their cookie in silence for five to ten minutes. Then the Tea M. welcomes everyone and asks the Head Server to explain how guests may signal for more tea, more cookies, or both. The Tea M. then invites people to share songs, stories, and insights. People indicate that they would like to share by bringing their two hands together in lotus bud position. Children are especially encouraged to share. The Tea M. may propose an initial introductory go-round if there are many people who do not know each other. If there is silence, people are encouraged to simply enjoy their breathing and their tea and cookie until someone offers to share.

About ten or fifteen minutes before the intended close of the ceremony, the Tea M. invites the last sharings, particularly opening the space for people who have not yet spoken. After an hour or more of sharing, the Tea M. closes the ceremony. A tray is passed around so that everyone can place their cups and napkins on the tray and assist in cleaning up.

At the end of the ceremony, there may be a bell for stretching, another for standing, another for bowing, or there may be an informal closing, including hugging meditation.

Flower-Watering

Flower-watering can be shared by a Sangha in the form of a ceremony. Arrange a fresh flower in a vase and put it in the middle of the circle. Enjoy your breathing and your concentration as you wait for someone—usually the eldest or one of the senior members—to begin the ceremony.

When someone is ready to speak, she joins her palms and the others join their palms to show that she has the right to speak. Then she stands, walks slowly to the flower, takes the vase in her hands, and returns to her seat. When she speaks, her words reflect the freshness and beauty of the flower that is in her hand. No one interrupts the person holding the flower. She is allowed as much time as she needs, and everyone else practices deep listening. When she is finished speaking, she stands up and slowly returns the vase to the center of the room.

During flower-watering, each speaker acknowledges the wholesome, wonderful qualities of the others. It is not flattery; one always speaks the truth. Watering the flower means that we sit with the other, we recognize the positive things about the other person, and we mention them. If the other person is fresh, is patient, is tolerant, has talents and skills, we can say, "You were so patient with me the other day when I was unskillful. Thank you," or, "I'm so happy when I see you gardening. You do it so well." Whatever positive qualities this person has, we recognize them and mention them.

It's not necessary to water the flowers of everyone present; participants can choose to just listen, or can water the flowers of as many or as few people as they would like, including individuals that are not present. The process continues until everyone who would like to water flowers has had the opportunity to do so.

Beginning Anew

This practice dates to the time of the Buddha, when communities of monks and nuns practiced Beginning Anew on the eve of every full moon and new moon. We begin the first part of the ceremony with flower-watering. When everyone has had the opportunity to water flowers, we move on to the second part of the ceremony, in which we express regrets for anything we have done to hurt others in the Sangha. This part of the ceremony is called "beneficial regret." It does not take more than one thoughtless phrase to hurt someone. Beginning Anew is an opportunity for us to recall some regret and undo it.

In the third part of the ceremony, we express ways in which others in the Sangha have hurt us. Loving speech is crucial. We want to heal the community, not harm it. We speak frankly, but we do not want to be destructive. We avoid blaming and arguing.

Compassionate listening is also important. We listen with the willingness to relieve the suffering of the other person, not to judge or argue with him. We listen with all our attention. Even if we hear something that is not true, we continue to listen deeply so the other person can express his pain and release the tensions within himself. If we reply to him or try to correct him, the practice will not bear fruit. We just listen. If we need to tell the other person that his perception was not correct, we can do that a few days later, privately and calmly. Then, at the next Beginning Anew session, she may be the person who rectifies the error and we will not have to say anything.

We close the ceremony with a song or by holding hands with everyone in the circle and breathing for a minute. Sometimes we end with hugging meditation. You really hug the person you are hugging, making him very real in your arms. This is not just for the sake of appearance, patting him on the back to pretend you are there. You breathe consciously and hug with all your body, spirit, and heart. If you breathe deeply like that, the energy of care, love, and mindfulness will penetrate into that person and she will be nourished and bloom like a flower.

After Beginning Anew, everyone in the community feels light and relieved, even if we have taken only preliminary steps toward healing. We have confidence that, having begun, we can continue.

The principle of the Beginning Anew Practice is that mistakes come from lack of mindfulness and concentration — mistakes come from your mind. If your mind is purified by the practice of Beginning Anew, then the mistake is gone. That is why after the practice, you feel light like a cloud and pure. This is a gatha describing Beginning Anew:

> Mistakes come from the mind.
> When the mind is transformed,
> Where will the mistakes be?
> After having practiced Beginning Anew,
> I feel pure and light like a cloud floating in the sky.

Peace Treaty and Peace Note

In order that we may live long and happily together, in order that we may continually develop and deepen our love and understanding, we, the undersigned, vow to observe and practice the following:

I, the one who is angry, agree to:

1) Refrain from saying or doing anything that might cause further damage or escalate the anger.
2) Not suppress my anger.
3) Practice breathing and taking refuge in the island of myself.
4) Calmly, within twenty-four hours, tell the one who has made me angry about my anger and suffering, either verbally or by delivering a Peace Note:

> PEACE NOTE
>
> Date:
> Time:
> Dear ——————,
> This morning (afternoon), you said (did) something that made me very angry. I suffered very much. I want you to know this. You said (did):
>
> _____
>
> Please let us both look at what you said (did) and examine the matter together in a calm and open manner this Friday evening.
> Yours, not very happy now,
>
> _____

5) Ask for an appointment for later in the week (e.g., Friday evening) to discuss this matter more thoroughly, either verbally or by Peace Note.

I, the one who has made the other angry, agree to:

1) Respect the other person's feelings, not ridicule him or her, and allow enough time for him or her to calm down.
2) Not press for an immediate discussion.
3) Confirm the other person's request for a meeting, either verbally or by note, and assure him or her that I will be there.
4) Practice breathing and taking refuge in the island of myself to see how:
   a. I have seeds of unkindness and anger as well as the habit energy to make the other person unhappy.
   b. I have mistakenly thought that making the other person suffer would relieve my own suffering.
   c. by making him or her suffer, I make myself suffer.
5) Apologize as soon as I realize my unskillfulness and lack of mindfulness, without making any attempt to justify myself and without waiting until the Friday meeting.
6) Not say: "I am not angry. It's okay. I am not suffering. There is nothing to be angry about, at least not enough to make me angry."
7) Practice breathing and looking deeply into my daily life — while sitting, lying down, standing, and walking — in order to see:
   a. the ways I myself have been unskillful at times.
   b. how I have hurt the other person because of my own habit energy.
   c. how the strong seed of anger in me is the primary cause of my anger.
   d. how the other person's suffering, which waters the seed of my anger, is the secondary cause.
   e. how the other person is only seeking relief from his or her own suffering.
   f. that as long as the other person suffers, I cannot be truly happy.

8) Apologize immediately, without waiting until the Friday evening, as soon as I realize my unskillfulness and lack of mindfulness.

9) Postpone the Friday meeting if I do not feel calm enough to meet with the other person.

We vow, with Lord Buddha as witness and the mindful presence of the Sangha, to abide by these articles and to practice wholeheartedly. We invoke the three gems for protection and to grant us clarity and confidence.

Signed, _____

the _____Day of _____

in the Year _____ in_____

Shining the Light

It's very precious to have someone show us how our practice is going. When a friend shines light on our practice we benefit greatly, because we have many wrong perceptions that can keep us in a prison of self-pride. That is why when we are offered guidance, we can make progress very quickly.

Find a friend, a sister or a brother in the practice whose way of looking at you is different from your way of looking at yourself. Then ask them with all your heart: "Please, be compassionate to me. Please shine light on me, and help me and guide me in my practice." It's important that you ask them with all your sincerity, because sometimes we are proud or angry and the other person doesn't dare tell us the truth—we have a precious jewel but we cannot use it. The person will sit down and practice looking deeply with love and with care, telling you about your strengths and your weaknesses.

Then you ask that person to suggest another five people you can ask. If you chose just one person, you might pick someone who you think would just say positive things about you. The people who you want to shine light on your practice may not be the same people who have been suggested. If you really don't want to ask a person who has been suggested, you can always discuss it. But you need at the very least six people in the Sangha to shine light on you, though you can ask sixty people if you like. The more people who shine light on your practice, the more light there will be in that darkest place of your suffering.

Listen carefully to what the people say who shine light on your practice. It doesn't matter whether you agree or disagree with them; pay attention to everything exactly as they say it. It takes time to look deeply into what they have said. Perhaps those people have seen something you haven't been able to see about yourself. If you think that maybe your brother has a wrong perception of you, you can go to him and say, "Please tell me, why do you think this about me?" Each person you ask will have some wrong perceptions, that is true. But the guidance that you receive will make your understanding of yourself more correct, and the fruit of your practice will be greater.

If you are the person who shines light on a friend's practice, use all of your wisdom and understanding. Avoid manifesting irritation or blame as you offer advice, and deliver your words with care, love, and insight. Find the good qualities, the precious things in that person, and remind them of the positive elements that are available to them.

Then you talk about their weaknesses and their negative tendencies. You do your best to look clearly into the suffering and the obstructions of that person. And if you need to, you can ask other people to help you to see that person's suffering clearly. Why can't that person be happy? Maybe they have habit energy from the past that does not allow them to enjoy the present moment. Maybe that habit energy is one of being too hasty. Perhaps they received that tendency from their grandparents. That is not their fault. You don't blame anyone—you don't take all the responsibility on yourself or put all the responsibility on the other person. We are both responsible for each other. So no blaming and no punishing, because those things are not helpful. You only need to look deeply, and that will give you compassion.

If the other person has obstructions and internal formations, you ask yourself, "How have I contributed to this?" We often think that the other person doesn't want to practice, doesn't want to transform, doesn't practice loving speech, or doesn't practice listening deeply, and we don't see our part in it. Then ask yourself, "How have I contributed to making that person freer and happier?" If you can identify your words and actions that have helped the other person, you are happy. But if you see that you have not helped them much, you promise yourself that from now on you will be more positive in helping that person.

Offering guidance in this way is a wonderful practice, benefiting not only the one who requests it, but also the ones who practice sitting down and looking deeply into the conditions and the personality of that individual. When we look after the other person, we are looking after ourselves.

Take refuge in each other. Support each other. That is a method of practice.

Second Body Practice

The practice of the second body is one way we take care of each other in the Sangha. This practice is not just for monks and nuns, but for all of us. Each member of the Sangha needs a second body. The second body doesn't need to be younger; the second body can be older. When you go to sitting meditation, you invite your second body. If your second body is sick, you must know that your second body is sick, and look for a doctor or someone to help. The second person also has his or her second body, that third person also has a second body, and so forth.

We have to be responsible for the mindful manners and the practice of our second body. If the second body's manners and mindfulness are not very good, you are responsible, and you have to remind him or her. If you feel that you cannot, then you should ask a Dharma brother or sister to help you.

When each member takes care of his or her second body, the whole Sangha is taken care of. When your second body is happy, you share that happiness. If your second body has difficulties, you need to understand these difficulties. And if alone you cannot help your second body, you need to ask for help from somebody else. You don't need to be better than your second body, you just need to help your second body.

Practicing like this, you will see a miraculous result. When you take care of your second body, your third, fourth, and fifth bodies are also taken care of. Taking care of your second body, you take care of everybody else.

The method of getting a second body is this: Everybody in turn says the name of a person they want to be their second body. At first, there are many people to choose from, but as we go along, perhaps there is only one person left, and we have to choose that person. We may feel that this person is very difficult to look after, but we should know that this is a wonderful opportunity. The person who we think would be difficult can bring us a great deal of benefit and joy in our practice. Some fruits have thorns that are hard, but when we break them open, they taste very good. There are people who on the outside are not very sweet, but if we know how to open them up, the fruit is wonderful. Don't be deceived by the outside. Don't think that the second body is difficult to look after. Bring all of your ability to look after that person and he or she will become a sweet spring of water.

The Second Body practice is a wonderful Dharma door. With sincere practice, we will have a direct experience of the benefits of the practice.

Notes

1 A "sutra" is a teaching given by the Buddha or one of his enlightened disciples.

2 The *Abhidharma* is the earliest compilation of Buddhist philosophy and psychology.

3 The Four Establishments of Mindfulness are remaining established in the observation of (1) the body in the body, (2) the feelings in the feelings, (3) the mind in the mind, and (4) the objects of mind in the objects of mind. For more on the Four Establishments of Mindfulness and a detailed analysis of the *Sutra on the Four Establishments of Mindfulness*, see Thich Nhat Hanh, *Transformation & Healing: Sutra on the Four Establishments of Mindfulness* (Berkeley, CA: Parallax Press, 1990).

4 The Eightfold Path consists of Right View, Right Thinking, Right Mindfulness, Right Speech, Right Action, Right Diligence, Right Concentration, and Right Livelihood. For more on the Eightfold Path, see Thich Nhat Hanh, *The Heart of the Buddha's Teaching* (Berkeley, CA: Parallax Press, 1998), chaps. 9–16.

5 The five cravings are the cravings for wealth, sex, fame and power, food and drink, and sleep. See Thich Nhat Hanh, *The Sutra on the Eight Realizations of Great Beings* (Berkeley, CA: Parallax Press, 1987), p. 5.

6 The *Sutra on the Five Ways to Put an End to Anger* (*Anguttara Nikaya*, Vol. III, Sutta No. 186).

7 The *Yasoja Sutra* is in the *Khuddaka Nikaya*.

8 Also called the Three Realizations and the Three Kinds of Achievements.

9 For more on the Order of Interbeing, see Thich Nhat Hanh, *Interbeing: Fourteen Guidelines for Engaged Buddhism*, Third Edition (Berkeley, CA: Parallax Press, 1998).

10 For more on the Five Mindfulness Trainings, see *For a Future to Be Possible: Commentaries on the Five Mindfulness Trainings*, Revised Edition (Berkeley, CA: Parallax Press, 1998).

11 For more on the Fourteen Mindfulness Trainings, see Thich Nhat Hanh, *Interbeing*.

12 The *Sigalovada Sutta* (*Digha Nikaya*, Sutta No. 31).

13 See Thich Nhat Hanh, *Anger: Wisdom for Cooling the Flames* (New York: Riverhead Books, 2001), p. 76.

14 See Thich Nhat Hanh, *Anger*, pp. 137–138.

15 See Thich Nhat Hanh, *Anger*, p. 193.

16 See Thich Nhat Hanh, *Touching Peace: Practicing the Art of Mindful Living* (Berkeley, CA: Parallax Press, 1992), p. 112.

17 See Thich Nhat Hanh, *Breathe! You Are Alive: Sutra on the Full Awareness of Breathing*, Revised Edition (Berkeley, CA: Parallax Press, 1996).

18 Thich Nhat Hanh, *Old Path White Clouds: Walking in the Footsteps of the Buddha* (Berkeley, CA: Parallax Press, 1991).

19 For more on mental formations, see Thich Nhat Hanh, *Transformation at the Base: Fifty Verses on the Nature of Consciousness* (Berkeley, CA: Parallax Press, 2001), chap. 30.

20 See Thich Nhat Hanh, *Teachings on Love* (Berkeley, CA: Parallax Press, 1998), p. 132.

21 For more on the Threefold Training, see Thich Nhat Hanh, *The Heart of the Buddha's Teaching*, pp. 75–76.

22 See Thich Nhat Hanh, *The Blooming of a Lotus: Guided Meditation Exercises for Healing and Transformation* (Boston, MA: Beacon Press, 1993).

23 See Thich Nhat Hanh, *Present Moment Wonderful Moment: Mindfulness Verses for Daily Living* (Berkeley, CA: Parallax Press, 1990).

24 See Thich Nhat Hanh, *Plum Village Chanting and Recitation Book* (Berkeley, CA: Parallax Press, 2000).

25 See Thich Nhat Hanh, *Mindful Movements* (Boulder, CO: Sounds True, 1998).

26 See Thich Nhat Hanh, *The Path of Emancipation: Talks from a 21-Day Mindfulness Retreat* (Berkeley, CA: Parallax Press, 2000), pp. 145–146.

27 *The Mindfulness Practice Center Guidebook: The Gift a Community Gives Itself*, Second Edition (Quechee, VT: The Mindfulness Practice Center Association, 1999).

28 See Thich Nhat Hanh, *The Blooming of a Lotus*, p. 23.

29 See Thich Nhat Hanh, *Touching Peace*, p. 113.

30 See Thich Nhat Hanh, *The Diamond That Cuts through Illusion: Commentaries on the Prajñaparamita Diamond Sutra* (Berkeley, CA: Parallax Press, 1992), p. 68.

31 See Thich Nhat Hanh, *Touching Peace*, pp. 111–112.

32 See Thich Nhat Hanh, *Touching Peace*, p. 114.

33 *Plum Village Chanting Book* (Berkeley, CA: Parallax Press, 1991), pp. 126–127. This book is out of print.

34 See Robert Wuthnow, *Sharing the Journey: Support Groups and America's New Quest for Community* (New York: First Free Press, 1996).

35 See Robert Wuthnow, *Sharing the Journey*, p.323.

36 See Thich Nhat Hanh and Daniel Berrigan, *The Raft Is Not the Shore: Conversations toward a Buddhist-Christian Awareness* (Maryknoll, NY: Orbis Books, 1975, 2001), p. 10.

37 See Thich Nhat Hanh, *The Heart of Understanding: Commentaries on the Prajñaparamita Heart Sutra* (Berkeley, CA: Parallax Press, 1988).

38 The Seven Factors of Awakening are mindfulness, investigation of phenomena, diligence, joy, ease, concentration, and letting go. For more on the Seven Factors of Awakening, see Thich Nhat Hanh, *The Heart of the Buddha's Teaching*, chap. 26.

39 For more on the fifty-one mental formations, see Thich Nhat Hanh, *Transformation at the Base*, chap. 30.

40 See Thich Nhat Hanh, *Being Peace* (Berkeley, CA: Parallax Press, 1987, 1996).

41 See Jack Lawlor, *Sangha Practice* (Berkeley, CA: Parallax Press, 2000).

42 See Barbara Casey, "A Sacred Wound," the *Mindfulness Bell* 29:8.

43 See *A Basket of Plums*, Fourth Edition (Dieulivol, France: Plum Village, 2001).

44 See Thich Nhat Hanh, *Touching Peace*, pp. 107–108.

45 See *The Mindfulness Practice Center Guidebook*, p. 9.

46 See *The Mindfulness Practice Center Guidebook*, p. 8.

47 See *The Mindfulness Practice Center Guidebook*, pp. 12–13.

48 See Jack Lawlor, *Sangha Practice*, p. 3.

49 *Majjhima Nikaya*, Sutta No. 128.

50 See Thich Nhat Hanh, *The Diamond That Cuts through Illusion*.

51 The *Upaddha Sutra* (*Samyutta Nikaya* Vol. XLV, Sutta No. 2).

52 The *Upakkilesa Sutta* (*Majjhima Nikaya*, Sutta No. 128).

53 See Thich Nhat Hanh, "Sangha," the *Mindfulness Bell* 20:1–5.

54 See Annabel Laity, "Beginning Anew," the *Mindfulness Bell* 6:11–12.

55 See Penelope Thompson and Lee Lipp, "Beginning Anew," the *Mindfulness Bell* 16:18.

56 For more on the Four Brahmaviharas, see Thich Nhat Hanh, *The Heart of the Buddha's Teaching*, chap. 22.

57 Inga Clendinnen, *Tiger's Eye* (New York: Simon & Schuster, 2001), p. 10.

58 See Merrill Collett, *At Home with Dying* (Boston, MA: Shambhala Publications, 1999).

59 See Thich Nhat Hanh, *For a Future to Be Possible*, pp. 11–12.

60 The *Culavedalla Sutta* (*Majjhima Nikaya*, Sutta No. 44).

Contributors

RICHARD BRADY, True Dharma Bridge, is a member of the Washington Mindfulness Community. He teaches high school mathematics and is a founder of the Mindfulness in Education Network.

JERRY BRAZA, True Great Response, is an ordained Dharma teacher in the lineage of Thich Nhat Hanh. He facilitates the River Sangha in Salem, Oregon and conducts retreats and workshops on mindfulness for organizations. Jerry is a Professor at Western Oregon University and author of *Moment by Moment: The Art and Practice of Mindfulness.*

JAAP BROERSE is a change manager in organizations and practices with the Sangha in Nijmegen, Holland. He has rotating tasks, which he shares with other Sangha members, in leading and assisting the Sangha activities.

JULIA BURNS is a mother, teacher, and child psychiatrist. She practices with her family in North Carolina.

TRACY COCHRAN is a contributing editor for the magazines *Publisher's Weekly*, *Tricycle*, and *Parabola*. She practices with the New York Insight Sangha of Katonah, New York and the Insight Meditation Society.

MURRAY CORKE, True Great Practice, practices with the Cambridge Sangha in England.

CALEB CUSHING, True Original Commitment, is an architect and practices with the Pot Luck Sangha in Oakland, California.

ROBERTO DEL MASTIO, Clear Inspiration of the Source, has practiced with Amici di Thây Sangha in Florence since 1990. He is now developing an "Organic Mindful Agriturismo" in the Tuscan Hills, and is excited to see what will happen.

DAVID DIMMACK, True Mirror (Chân Kinh), has assisted with young people's programs since 1991. He practices with the Open Hearth Sanghas in Ambler and Mt. Airy, Pennsylvania.

ERNESTINE ENOMOTO, True Mindfulness of Peace, practices with the Honolulu Mindfulness Community in Hawai'i. She leads monthly Days of Mindfulness where Sangha members enjoy walks along the beach, songs of joy, and natural beauty around them.

LYN FINE, True Goodness (Chân Thien), received Lamp Transmission from Thich Nhat Hanh at Plum Village in 1994. A cofounder and member of the Community of Mindfulness/NY Metro from 1989 until 2000, she now lives in Berkeley, California. Lyn leads retreats in the USA and Israel, which include mindfulness meditation, compassionate listening and nonviolent communication, and Beginning Anew practice, and offers individual and Sangha practice support for those inspired by the teachings of Thich Nhat Hanh.

JOANNE FRIDAY, True Gift of Joy, is one of the founding members of the Clear Heart Sangha in Matunuck, Rhode Island.

JAMES G. is a member of the Phoenix, Arizona Sangha. He was released from prison over a year ago. The following August he attended Thây's retreat in San Diego, which in Jim's words was "a dream come true." He is interested in networking with others to bring the Dharma into prisons.

PATRICIA HUNT-PERRY, True Precious Continent (Chân Bao Chau), practices with Budding Flower Sangha on the old farm where she was born in the mid-Hudson Valley. She works with people who are in grief and teaches graduate and undergraduate courses on death and dying at a college in New Jersey.

CHARLES KING, Fearless Compassion of the Heart, was born and raised in Virginia with a White Anglo-Saxon Protestant heritage. He has practiced with the Mindfulness, Diversity, and Social Change Sangha in Oakland, California since 1998. He enjoys the practice of compassion and deep listening as a clinical psychologist in Berkeley.

BROTHER CHÂN PHAP LAI, True Coming of the Dharma, is from Yorkshire, England. He ordained in 2002 and now lives in the Upper Hamlet. As the Sangha's first British monk, he looks forward to adding an English flavor to the Plum Village stir-fry culture.

SISTER ANNABEL LAITY, True Virtue, is the Abbess of Green Mountain Dharma Center in Hartland Four Corners, Vermont. She is also the senior editor of the *Mindfulness Bell*.

JACK LAWLOR, True Direction, has been practicing consistently in organized Sanghas since 1975. He has served as President of the Buddhist Council of the Midwest, an association of over forty Buddhist temples and centers. He has also served on the National Board of Directors of the Buddhist Peace Fellowship. Jack was ordained by Thich Nhat Hanh as a Dharma teacher in 1992, and, in addition to facilitating Lakeside Buddha Sangha in the Chicago area, has led numerous retreats and Days of Mindfulness in the American Midwest and the northern Rocky Mountain states. He has been married for twenty-eight years and has two adult children.

LAURIE LAWLOR, True Opening, writes fiction and nonfiction for children and young adults. She visits many schools as a speaker and writing workshop facilitator. Ordained as a Dharma teacher by Thich Nhat Hanh in 2001, she is a founding member of Lakeside Buddha Sangha in the Chicago area.

DAVID LAWRENCE, Great Treasure Store of the Heart, is a cofounder of Snowflower Sangha in Madison, Wisconsin. He has helped organize regional retreats in the Midwest for the past ten years.

NGUYEN DUY VINH (Chân Ngô) is a Dharma teacher and practices in Canada with the Pagoda Sangha in Ottawa, Ontario and with Maple Village in Québec.

SISTER CHÂN CHAU NGHIEM, True Adornment with Jewels, grew up in Chicago and Nairobi, Kenya and ordained in 1999. She is of African American and European American heritage. She now lives in Deer Park and is very interested in sharing mindfulness with young people.

SISTER CHÂN HOA NGHIEM, True Adornment with Flowers, was ordained in 1991 in Plum Village. She received the Dharma Lamp Transmission in 1998 and currently lives in Plum Village where she is a mentor to many younger monastic sisters.

SISTER NHO NGHIEM, True Adornment with Refinement, is 16. She ordained in February 2002 in the Sugar Palm Tree Family in Plum Village. Born in the U.S., she grew up in California and is of Vietnamese origin. She enjoys writing and inspiring other teenagers to practice mindfulness.

SUSAN O'LEARY, Deep Confidence of the Heart, is a teacher and writer. She practices with Snowflower Sangha in Madison, Wisconsin.

IAN PRATTIS, True Body of Understanding, practices coast to coast in Canada as part of the Sangha outreach of Ottawa's Pine Gate Sangha.

MITCHELL RATNER, True Mirror of Wisdom, practices with the Washington (D.C.) Mindfulness Community and the Still Water Mindfulness Practice Center in Takoma Park, Maryland.

KARL AND HELGA RIEDL, True Communion and True Loving Kindness, are both Dharma teachers and recently moved to the newly-established Intersein Zentrum in Germany.

AMOGHAVAJRA KARL SCHMIED, True Dharma Eye, is a Dharmacharya, teacher of the Community of Mindful Living, Bavaria, and one of the three teachers of Haus Maitreya (Center of Interbeing) in Hohenau.

ELLEN STUEBE, Silent Smile of the Heart, practices Zen and mindfulness in Australia. She is a freelance writer on subjects of health, well-being, and the environment. She is currently working on a Zen radio feature exploring peace.

MICHELE TEDESCO, Beautiful Nature of the Heart, and her family practice with the Breathing Heart Sangha in Atlanta and Athens, Georgia.

EMMY VAN DEN BERG develops policy on different subjects in a small town and practices with the Sangha in Nijmegen, Holland. She has rotating tasks, which she shares with other Sangha members, in leading and assisting the Sangha activities.

JAQUELIEN VAN GALEN, Mindful Direction of the Heart, is a teacher and practices with the Sangha in Nijmegen, Holland. She has rotating tasks, which she shares with other Sangha members, in leading and assisting the Sangha activities.

LARRY WARD, True Great Sound, is a Dharma Teacher and a businessman. He lives at and is cofounder of Clear View Practice Center and Still Water Sangha in Santa Barbara, California.

LARRY YANG, LCSW , trains psychotherapists at San Francisco General Hospital's outpatient psychotherapy clinic as part of his role as clinical supervisor and coordinator of diversity and multicultural services. Being a gay man of color who is training in the Theravadin Buddhist tradition, he is on the Diversity Council of Spirit Rock Meditation Center and is part of their Community Dharma Leaders and Dedicated Practitioners Programs.